Delivering IT and E-Business Value

Delivering IT and E-Business Value

Leslie Willcocks

Valerie Graeser

BUTTERWORTH
HEINEMANN

OXFORD AUCKLAND BOSTON JOHANNESBURG MELBOURNE NEW DELHI

Butterworth-Heinemann
Linacre House, Jordan Hill, Oxford OX2 8DP
225 Wildwood Avenue, Woburn, MA 01801-2041
A division of Reed Educational and Professional Publishing Ltd

A member of the Reed Elsevier plc group

First published 2001

British Library Cataloguing in Publication Data

A catalogue record for this book is available from the British Library

ISBN 0 7506 47442

Composition by Genesis Typesetting, Rochester
Printed and bound in Great Britain

Contents

3 Project planning for risk, prioritization and benefits 43

4 Project management and post-implementation evaluation 87

5 Developing a balanced business scorecard for IT 123

Butterworth-Heinemann/
Computer Weekly
Professional Series

There are few professions which require as much continuous updating as that of the IT executive. Not only does the hardware and software scene change relentlessly, but also ideas about the actual management of the IT function are being continuously modified, updated and changed. Thus keeping abreast of what is going on is really a major task.

The Butterworth-Heinemann/*Computer Weekly* Professional Series has been created to assist IT executives to keep up-to-date with the management ideas and issues of which they need to be aware.

Aims and objectives

One of the key objectives of the series is to reduce the time it takes for leading edge management ideas to move from academic and consulting environments into the hands of the IT practitioner. Thus, this series employs appropriate technology to speed up the publishing process. Where appropriate some books are supported by CD-ROM or by additional information or templates located on the publisher's Web site (http://www.bh.com/samples).

This series provides IT professionals with an opportunity to build up a bookcase of easily accessible but detailed information on the important issues that they need to be aware of to successfully perform their jobs as they move into the new millennium.

Would you like to be part of this series?

Aspiring or already established authors are invited to get in touch with me if they would like to be published in this series:

Dr Dan Remenyi, Series Editor
(Remenyi@compuserve.com)

Series titles published

IT investment – Making a business case
The effective measurement and management of IT – Costs and benefits
(second edition)
Stop IT project failures through risk management
Understanding the Internet
Prince version 2: A practical handbook
Considering computer contracting?
David Taylor's Inside Track
A hacker's guide to project management
Corporate politics for IT managers: how to get streetwise
Subnet design for efficient networks
Information warfare

Forthcoming

Reinventing the IT department
Delivering IT strategies
e-Business strategies for virtual organizations
How to become a successful IT consultant
How to manage the IT help desk (second edition)
The project manager's toolkit
Network security
E-business
Implementing ERP
IT management

About the authors

Leslie Willcocks has an international reputation for his work on outsourcing, e-business, evaluation and information management. He is Andersen Professor of Information Management and E-business at Warwick Business School, UK, Associate Fellow at Templeton College, Oxford University, holds Visiting Chairs at Erasmus Universiteit, Rotterdam and University of Melbourne, and is co-editor of the *Journal of Information Technology*. He is co-author of 18 books including *Investing in Information Systems* (TB Press, 1996), *Beyond the IT Productivity Paradox* (Wiley, 1999), *Global IT Outsourcing* (Wiley, 2001) *Moving To E-business* (Random House, 2000) and *Building the E-business Infrastructure* (Business Intelligence, 2001). He has published over 130 refereed papers in journals such as *Harvard Business Review, Sloan Management Review, MIS Quarterly and Communications of the ACM*. He is retained as adviser by several major corporations and government institutions, and is a regular keynote speaker at international academic and practitioner conferences.

Valerie Graeser is General Manager in San Diego of Enterprise Transformation Services, a business engineering consulting firm. She is also a Research Affiliate at the Oxford Institute of Information Management at Templeton College, Oxford University and holds an MBA from the University of California at Los Angeles and a BSc in Computer Science from Duke University. She is the co-author of *Developing the IT Scorecard* (Business Intelligence, 1998), as well as a number of journal and conference articles on technology evaluation. Her practitioner work includes 13 years in systems development and IT management across a number of industries, including with

Exxon and with the infrastructure software company Peregrine Systems, and five years as a project manager for American Management Systems, working for a range of clients. Her research work is in the areas of evaluation of systems and project management.

Acknowledgements

We owe a large debt to many colleagues who have supported this work. We would like to thank all at Templeton College, Oxford University, for making it a great place to work and for their kindness over many years. In particular, we would like to thank several people with whom we we have worked closely, and who have influenced what is written here. David Feeny's contribution is most obvious in Chapters 3 and 9, but is much more profound than that. Chris Sauer and Robert Plant have influenced our thinking and contributed to the research for Chapters 7 and 8, while Mary Lacity's work on IT outsourcing helped enormously with Chapter 6.

We would like to thank all the executives at the case study organizations described in this book, and the many other executives, market commentators, students and consultants who have contributed to our understanding of evaluation of IT and e-business over the years. Hopefully, their patience, understanding and insight is reflected at least a little in the contents of this book. Given the surveys, the interviews, the classes and the seminars, we are talking here of many hundreds of people, not all of whom, obviously, can be mentioned by name. Of the more direct contributions, in many cases anonymity was requested, but where this was not the case, then the respondent is gratefully noted in the text. Enormous thanks are also due to Business Intelligence for supporting some of the original research carried out for this book, and for its more recent support for a study with Chris Sauer on building e-business infrastructure, that has influenced some of the thinking in Chapter 9 of the present book.

Acknowledgements

1 | Introduction: trends and challenges in IT evaluation

1.1 Introduction

> The issue is how do you justify more money on IT when you are trying to manage all costs down. You may have to accept that IT goes the other way. It's understanding that need – and how you justify it – that is the key.
>
> Leslie Holt,
> IT Director, Membership, Automobile Association

> People measure what they can and the givens, for example systems availability, not what they need. It's difficult but it's about measuring business impact, and information achievement, not just technology achievement.
>
> Robert White, Lucidus

> There are mosquito bites and snake bites. Good managers can tell the difference.
>
> J. Titsworth, Vice-president, Xerox

The last decade has witnessed enormous increases in information technology (IT) investments around the world, with information-based technologies penetrating ever more deeply into the core of organizational functioning. In fact, the IT industry has grown through infancy to lumbering, ungainly adolescence in a mere five decades. In the process of examining the problems resulting from this rapid growth, we will see how the industry is not mature, and how it will grow at increasing speeds for at least a decade to come – creating real challenges for the understanding and measurement of IT and e-business costs, risks, benefits and value.

In 1995, according to research company IDC, the worldwide IT market was US$530 billion. This covered packaged software, data communications equipment, services, and single and multi-user systems. On a wider definition of IT – to include voice telecommunications, special purpose computer equipment (e.g. automatic teller machines, mail sorting systems) and customer expenditure on their own information systems personnel – a market size of US$1 trillion could easily be defended. IDC expected the overall IT market to grow at 10% annually in the 1996–2000 period, an estimate that has turned out to be on the cautious side, not least given the rising cost of fixing the Year 2000 problem, estimated by some to have been as high as US$300 billion for corporate America alone. When one adds in the rising annual cost of moving to e-business, estimated by some, for 2000, as globally exceeding US$400 billion, then it is likely that, by 2001, annual IT expenditure worldwide exceeded US$1.6 trillion.

Total expenditures on IT in the UK were predicted to rise from £31.72 billion in 1996 to £40.94 billion in the year 2000. *Services* and *networking* grew significantly in this period, reinforcing the widely touted shift toward a network-centric era (see Chapter 7). Interestingly, spend on staff has been predicted to decline, perhaps indicating a consolidation in the industry.

It is interesting to note that, even in these figures, it is difficult to determine if knock-on costs, such as user training and maintenance, have been included. Moreover, by 1998 even these estimates had been superseded. Thus a Kew Associates/ *Computer Weekly* survey saw 1998 spend as £44.4 billion, up 5%

from 1997, a substantial part of the growth being driven by Year 2000 work. As a prelude to later chapters, note that of this aggregate 1998 expenditure, £3.9 billion was estimated for Year 2000, £1.47 billion for Economic and Monetary Union (EMU) conversion and £1.58 billion on the Internet – each registering between 45 and 70% increases for each year from 1997 to 2001. In fact, with these influences, annual UK IT expenditure was over £60 billion by 2001.

With the ever-expanding IT and e-business horizon comes a host of problems and issues. Many organizations are spending large sums of money on IT simply to keep up with IT market developments and their competitors. Senior managers in many organizations are not fully informed about the detailed reasons for continuous, and rising spend, nor do they understand the breadth of the spend – how far IT is pervasive in contemporary organizations. Many IT departments also fail to comprehend the full extent of IT expenditure – there are many hidden and knock-on costs, and increasingly IT costs appear in non-IT budgets. At the same time, there are many areas where IT expenditure is almost obligatory – fixing the Year 2000 problem, European Monetary Union conversion, maintaining/enhancing legacy systems and e-business infrastructure investments being four obvious ones. Our own work on components of the typical IT budget found in 80 organizations in 1999–2000 produces the picture shown in Figure 1.1.

There seems little let-up in the onward march of IT costs. According to a 1998 Compass report, IT rocketed from a typical 2–3% of total costs in the 1980s to 7–10% in 1998. By 2001 we found some leading financial service firms devoting more than 20% of their expenditure to IT. In the USA, government statistics in 2000 showed IT making up over 40% of capital investments by US businesses.

Not surprisingly, the first steps toward effective evaluation of IT have often been based on pure cost rationalization. However,

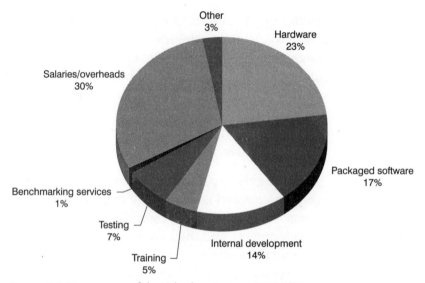

Figure 1.1 Components of the IT budget (source: OXIIM/BI)

the view that sees IT as a necessary support cost to be minimized is a very incomplete one. If IT spend is an investment, the next piece of the puzzle is the suggestion that benefits are derived from that investment. In practice, our many surveys across the 1992–2001 period indicate that organizations strongly acknowledge that a measurable relationship must exist between IT spend and business performance, but much depends on timing and focus of the spend, and how well investments are evaluated. More on this later.

A high-level problem confronting both business and IT managers today relates directly to their ability to manage the portfolio of IT assets used by the organization. The IT revolution has seen a number of investment phases, from an early systems-centric era, then the PC-centric era, through the present network-centric era and on to a future content-centric era (see Chapter 7). Given these waves of IT investments, each building on top of its predecessor, how do managers

responsible for the IT portfolio control the plethora of assets –
that vary in cost analysis and even more so in timing, size
and type of benefits yielded? We will see that a 'lifecycle'
approach to evaluation can provide the necessary focus (see
Chapter 2).

This chapter will first review the variety of challenges and
weaknesses in IT evaluation practice today. This will lead on to
Chapter 2, which will provide an overview of ways to address
these evaluation challenges. Subsequent chapters take the
reader around the lifecycle. Thus Chapter 3 looks at setting up
risk analysis, prioritization, feasibility and benefits evaluation.
Chapter 4 examines development, implemenation and post-
implementation evaluation, while Chapter 5 brings these
strands together in putting forward how to develop a balanced
business scorecard for IT. Later chapters deal with key issues
across the lifecycle. These include the key role of evaluation in
managing IT outsourcing (Chapter 6); whether moves to
e-business require new evaluation approaches (Chapters 7 and
8); and finally (Chapter 9) how to deal with the evaluation issues
surrounding infrastructure, quality, benchmarking, cost of
ownership, and mergers and acquisitions.

1.2 The IT evaluation challenges model

The IT evaluation challenges model shown in Figure 1.2 shows
the two sides of the evaluation equation as 'costs and risks' and
'benefits and value'. If costs and risks represent the downside of
IT investment, then benefits and value represent the upside. All
must be considered in a detailed, balanced fashion through
appropriate evaluation criteria, mechanisms and processes, in
order to delineate the *net* benefit from any specific IT investment. Our extensive research from 1990–2001 has regularly
identified significant generic weaknesses in IT evaluation
practices.

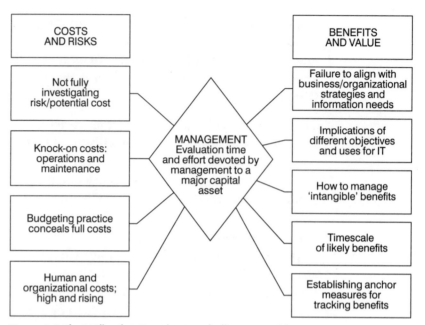

Figure 1.2 The Willcocks' IT evaluation challenges model

Cost and risk issues

(1) **Not fully investigating risk/potential cost**. Risk is a component of IT investments and project undertakings that is often ignored. Chapter 3 will examine the full range of risk issues in detail. Risk can rest on project size or relationship to other projects, and can be inherent in the particular project portfolio mix of a company. However, external and internal contexts and history also need to be analysed. Left unexamined and under-managed, risks, especially in combination, can lead to disastrous results for IT investments and their host organizations. The cost of trying to address the impact of risks likely to affect a project is referred to as 'potential cost' in Figure 1.2. In sum, this contribution to IT evaluation is the reminder to analyse risk and the methods by which to manage/

mitigate that risk. Chapter 3 will provide examples of a number of projects where risks were under-analysed and consequently destroyed the project.

(2) **Knock-on costs: operations and maintenance**. In the course of investment analysis, reviewed costs are confined frequently to the hard, identifiable costs of the project, while additional knock-on costs are understated and/or not explicitly associated with the project. These types of costs are often ignored because they are considered overhead, and not direct costs of IT investments. Consequently, the organizational costs increase without an appropriate perspective on the categorization of those costs. Across a system's lifetime, such knock-on costs can be 250% (or more) than the original IT investment. The 'cost of ownership' of various technology platforms is an issue that has moved to the forefront of media and IT professional concern (see Chapter 9).

(3) **Budgeting practices conceal full costs**. In a related manner, when the IT department has the mandate to manage a budget, the isolation of that budget from the rest of organizational spend can contribute to the failure to identify IT-related costs in other parts of the organization. In several organizations that we researched IT expenditure in non-IT budgets was between 28–40% of the total IT spend. Chapter 5 describes the operational barrier that results with the separation of the budgeting process from strategy planning. If the budgeting process happens in a vacuum without the complementary strategy planning, the budget will fail to reflect strategic needs/goals. While this separation is observed frequently between the IT organization budget and the overall organizational strategy, this problem is not unique to the IT organization.

(4) **Human and organizational costs: high and rising.** The growing infiltration of technology into the organization and the varied uses of that technology, defined at the point of use

rather than at the point of production, contribute to the need for additional knowledge workers in organizations. The relationship between such human/organizational costs and IT spend, on the other hand, is difficult to establish and blurs further the issue of derived benefits. As one insurance company example: in one project human and organizational costs were found to exceed the technical costs by 300%, but only one-fifth of those were included in the feasibility evaluation. These costs in IT-enabled change typically include retraining, redundancy, managerial time and effort, downtime, new salary levels and lost productivity. Moreover, workers are available in relatively scarce quantities and are bid for accordingly. The cost of recruiting an employee into the organization is high enough and the attrition rate significant enough to rate a 'resource' focus somewhere in whatever evaluation regimes are pursued.

Benefits and values: concerns

(1) **Failure to align with business/organizational strategies and information needs**. Case study research and a plethora of literature suggest that IT spend can and has contributed value to business performance in many instances, yet in order for the benefits to be worthwhile, they must be related to the goals of the organization, not merely goals for the sake of technology. Our recent survey shows that organizations view the strategic match of an IT investment to the business as the most significant investment evaluation criteria, yet those same organizations note the difficulty in attaining such alignment (Chapter 3 will deal with methods for achieving alignment). Even more serious has been the perennial widespread failure to link business strategy with information (as opposed to technology) requirements – a gulf often made worse by information overloads generated by e-business.

(2) **Implications of different uses and objectives for IT.** Again, as technology pervades the organization, and workers adopt technologies for previously unidentified uses, the benefits and value of the technology are spread throughout the organization. Often, technology has unpredicted effects on the organization's ability to function and produce. Also it may be difficult to isolate the particular effect of technology. Moreover, in order to understand those benefits, some sort of measurement or evaluation regime must exist. Our 1999 OXIIM/BI survey cited a number of benefits to such evaluation practices, including increasing strategic alignment between IT strategy and overall business strategy, organizational learning and the transformation of measurement into a management process. Evaluation regimes require the flexibility to recognize such unpredicted and difficult-to-identify results and include them in any follow-up benefits management. The cost/contribution model, discussed in Chapter 2, addresses this requirement.

(3) **How to manage intangible benefits.** Organizations are beginning to shift towards business-oriented measures of technology use because it is recognized that technology spend can produce less-than-tangible benefits. Moving from the industrial-based financial measures of productivity and benefit, however, is proving a difficult task for organizations. In our recent survey, respondents cited the ability to identify and manage intangible benefits as a significant issue in various stages of IT evaluation. The intangible nature of many benefits should lead to the concept that 'measurement is not just a number'. In other words, evaluation or measurement does not have to boil down to a concrete number. Instead, if the appropriate stakeholders in an organization understand the terms of an IT investment and agree on the types of benefits to be derived in descriptive terms, then the investment can be pursued in the knowledge that benefits elicitation – and the commitment to achieve

those benefits – will depend on the interaction among, and actions of, salient stakeholders.

(4) **Timescale of likely benefits**. Correspondingly, any number of benefits, both tangible and intangible, are affected by the timescale upon which the benefit in question is recognizable. In other words, a lag could exist between the IT investment/ spend and the ultimate delivery and recognition of the benefit. How best to convince management that the time lag does not defeat the purpose of the investment in the first place? Some have suggested that time lags between implementation of IT investments in the 1980s and the achievement and recognition of benefits in the early 1990s might explain the seeming IT productivity paradox (see below). Others have been pursuing research to determine if such a time lag really exists and if so, how it can be quantified. One of the complaints frequently made about more traditional forms of IT feasibility investment has been that they result in hurdle rates too high, and payback periods too short, for many types of IT applications to meet. One observable consequence in several researched cases has been for project champions to overstate benefits and understate costs in order to make a business case acceptable. This issue is pursued in Chapter 3.

(5) **Establishing anchor measures for tracking benefits**. The benefits to be derived from technology spend are evolving as quickly as the technology itself. Consequently, the measures of those benefits must also evolve. Many widely used measures may not actually represent suitable baselines against which to measure progress. For example, input measures such as IT costs as a percentage of revenue or IT costs compared to an industry average are not as useful as output measures related to the business drivers and key business processes of the organization. Moreover, organizations must recognize that evaluation is not merely a one-off exercise but an enduring undertaking that can contribute

significantly to the management process. Unfortunately, organizations tend to have average-rated evaluation practices; moreover, such average-rated evaluation practices have a clear relationship to average-rated IT performance. Genbank's scorecard (see Chapter 5) recognizes the need to allow for the establishment of measurement patterns. In other words, measurements will gradually attain desired levels and indications, rather than occurring the day after they are implemented.

All of these issues contribute to the need for the implementation and holistic management of IT evaluation. In addition, the issues also point to IT spend and usage being treated as an investment and asset rather than merely as an expense to be minimized. Unfortunately, partly because of how we structure budgets and financial statements, all too often a management is not sufficiently aware of the size and historic cost of building the IT asset held. A lack of business management attention occurs. This leads to IT not being evaluated, managed and exploited as the major capital asset it invariably is. Suggestions for addressing the themes proposed by the Figure 1.2 model will be made throughout this book. As the research will show, evaluation is a necessary *management* undertaking in an organization. Historically, however, significant evaluation initiatives and improvements only seem to occur in a *sustained* way under five circumstances:

(1) a new senior executive wants to 'get a handle' on what is going on with IT spend;

(2) senior executives are somehow exposed to an evaluation tool that seems to address their particular concerns;

(3) the organization is experiencing some sort of crisis and institutes evaluation mechanisms to try to understand the problems;

(4) the IT function comes under strong pressure to justify its costs; or

(5) the organization is considering outsourcing some portion of its IT and needs an effective evaluation regime to understand where it is and where it wants to go.

One goal of this book will be to convince the reader that evaluation is a valuable management tool and, consequently, should not be merely the result of one of the circumstances listed above. However, it is necessary that IT evaluation problem areas are identified as comprehensively as possible before we examine potential solutions. The evaluation challenges model illuminates many of the issues facing evaluation; the following discussion of the IT paradox will serve to elaborate on those, and additional challenges.

1.3 Is there an IT productivity paradox?

Alongside the seemingly inexorable rise of IT/e-business investments in the last 15 years, there has been considerable uncertainty and concern about the productivity impact of IT being experienced in work organizations. This concern has been reinforced by several high-profile studies at the levels of both the national economy and industrial sector suggesting in fact that if there has been an IT pay off, it has been minimal and hardly justifies the vast financial outlays incurred. A key, overarching point needs to be made immediately. It is clear from our reviews of the many research studies conducted at national, sectoral and organization-specific levels that the failure to identify IT benefits and productivity says as much about the deficiencies in assessment methods and measurement, and the rigour with which they are applied, as about mismanagement of the development and use of information-based technologies.

Interestingly, the IT productivity paradox is rarely related in the literature to manufacturing sectors for which, in fact, there are a number of studies from the early 1980s which show rising IT expenditure correlating with sectoral and firm-specific productivity rises. The high-profile studies raising concern also tend to base their work mainly on statistics gathered in the US context. Their major focus, in fact, tends to be limited to the service sector in the USA. Recently, a number of studies have questioned the data on which such studies were based, suggesting that the data is sufficiently flawed to make simple conclusions misleading.

Still others argue that the productivity payoff may have been delayed but, by the mid-1990s, recession and global competition had forced companies finally to use the technologies they put in place over the last decade, with the corresponding productivity leaps from 1996–2001, particularly in the USA. This explanation fits quite well with the fact that the research periods of many of the studies uncovering lack of IT productivity were restricted to the early 1980s or before. In any case, one can also point out that productivity figures always failed to measure the cost avoidance and savings on opportunity costs that IT can help to achieve.

Others also argue that the real payoffs occur when IT development and use is linked with the business process re-engineering (BPR) efforts that came on-stream in the 1990s. However, recent UK evidence by the authors develops this debate by finding that few organizations were actually getting 'breakthrough' results through IT-enabled BPR. Organizations were 'aiming low and hitting low' and generally not going for the radical, high-risk re-engineering approaches advocated by many commentators. Moreover, there was no strong correlation between size of IT expenditure in re-engineering projects, and resulting productivity impacts. In BPR, as elsewhere (see below), it is the management of IT, and what it is used for, rather than the size of IT spend that counts.

In relation to this, Bakos and Jager in *Computerworld* (September 1994) provide an interesting further insight. They argue that computers were not boosting productivity, but the *fault lies not with the technology but with its management and how computer use is overseen*. Along with Quinn and Baily in a 1994 study of IT productivity, they question the reliability of the productivity studies, and posit a new productivity paradox: 'how can computers be so productive?'[1].

In the face of such disputation, Brynjolfsson in his 1993 article in *Communications of the ACM*, makes salutary reading[2]. He suggests four explanations for the seeming IT productivity paradox, and these have relevance today.

(1) **Measurement errors**. In practice, the measurement problems appear particularly acute in the service sector and with white collar worker productivity – the main areas investigated by those pointing to a minimal productivity impact from IT use in the 1980s and early 1990s.

(2) **Time lags due to learning and adjustment**. Benefits from IT can take several years to show through in significant financial terms, a point made by others when arguing for newer ways of evaluating IT performance at the organizational level. On our evidence, Brynjolfsson is perhaps somewhat over-optimistic about the ability of managers to account rationally for such lags and include them in their IT evaluation system.

(3) **Redistribution**. IT may be beneficial to individual firms, but may be unproductive from the standpoint of the industry or the economy as a whole. IT rearranges the share of the pie, with the bigger share going to those investing heavily in IT or perhaps focusing their investment more wisely, without making the pie bigger.

(4) **IT is not really productive at the firm level**. Brynjolfsson posits that despite the neoclassical view of the firm as a

profit maximizer, it may well be that decision-makers are, for whatever reason, often not acting in the interests of the firm: 'instead they are increasing their slack, building inefficient systems, or simply using outdated criteria for decision-making'. The implication of Brynjolfsson's argument is that political interests and/or poor evaluation practice may contribute to failure to make real, observable gains from IT investments. Although Brynjolffson discounts these possibilities, recent IT evaluation literature suggests more evidence showing poor evaluation practice than Brynjolfsson has been willing to credit (see also Chapter 3). In the e-world many of the perennial issues of IT not being productive, or not being evaluated properly, would seem to be being replayed, with similar results (see Chapter 7).

1.4 Organizational variations in IT performance

It is on this point that the real debate on the apparent IT productivity paradox should hinge. Studies at the aggregate levels of the economy or industrial sector conceal important questions and data about variations in business experiences at the organizational and intra-organizational levels. In 1999, in *Beyond The IT Productivity Paradox* (edited by Leslie Willcocks and Stephanie Lester) Brynjolfsson and Hitt published a study of 367 large US firms generating $1.8 trillion in 1991 output. For 1987–1991 they found 'IS spending making a substantial and statistically significant contribution to firm output'[3]. They concluded that the IT productivity paradox, if it ever existed, had disappeared by 1991 for their sample firms, which together represented a large share of total US output. Although they used models similar to those of previous researchers, Brynjolfsson and Hitt attributed their different findings mainly to the larger and more recent data set they used. Even so, they pointed to further analysis being needed of the factors which differentiate firms with high returns to IT from low performers.

In practice, organizations seem to vary greatly in their ability to harness IT for organizational purposes. In a 1983 study, Cron and Sobol pointed to what has since been called the 'amplifier' effect of IT[4]. Its use reinforces existing management approaches, dividing firms into very high or very low performers. This analysis has been supported by later work that also found no correlation between the size of IT spend and firms' return on investment. Subsequently, a 1994 analysis (by Strassmann in *Computerworld*) of the information productivity of 782 US companies found that the top 10 spent a smaller percentage (1.3% compared to 3% for the bottom 100) of their revenue on IT, increased their IT budget more slowly (4.3% in 1993–1994 – the comparator was the bottom 110 averaging 10.2%), thus leaving a greater amount of finance available for non-IT spending[5].

The calculation of information productivity in Strassmann's study does make a rather large assumption, namely that management productivity is synonymous with information productivity because management is so highly dependent on information. This is probably not sustainable. Notwithstanding this, not only did the the top performers seem to spend less proportionately on their IT; they also tended to keep certain new investments as high as business conditions permitted while holding back on infrastructure growth. Thus, on average, hardware investments were only 15% of the IT budget while new development took more than 50%, with 41% of systems-development spending incurred on client/server investment. Clearly, the implication of this analysis is that top performers spend relatively less money on IT, but focus their spending on areas where the spend will make more difference in terms of business value. An important aspect of their ability to do this must lie with their evaluation techniques and processes.

Gus van Nievelt and Leslie Willcocks, in their 1998 report *Benchmarking Organizational and IT Performance*, add to this picture[6]. Analysing database information on over 300 organizations, van Nievelt found empirically that IT as a coordinating, communicating and leveraging technology was capable of enhancing customer satisfaction, flattening organizational pyramids and supporting knowledge workers in the management arena. At the same time, many organizations did not direct their IT expenditure into appropriate areas at the right time, partly because of inability to carry out an evaluation of where they were with their IT expenditure and IT performance relative to business needs in a particular competitive and market context. Van Nievelt's work shows the paradox as faulty. His statistical analysis of data at the business unit level provides strong evidence for a significant, positive, but multi-faceted IT effect on productivity. However, timing and placement of IT expenditure emerge as all important. Willcocks and Plant in their spring 2001 *Sloan Management Review* paper 'Pathways to E-Business Leadership' found similar results for IT usage in e-business initiatives[7].

The work reported here shows how complex it is to identify IT impacts and effects, and points to the need to examine a range of correlated factors before rushing to judgement. It also serves to highlight how macro-economic studies of IT productivity can mislead, and how micro-economic studies of how individual organizations and markets behave are altogether more helpful. At the same time, it becomes clear that IT and e-business events must become continually correlated to business performance in ways frequently not represented in existing assessment practice.

1.5 Key learning points

- Cost cutting/control appears to be the first step in rationalizing IT spend; however, mere cost controls cannot hope to provide the management required to achieve the plethora of benefits available from IT spend.
- 'Measurement' does not necessarily equate to assigning a number to something; measurement can be a mutually agreed

understanding (on behalf of management, IS staff and user group) of a technology spend goal/benefit.

– 'Costs' and 'benefits' are traditionally compared to one another in an attempt to evaluate an investment; the same principles hold true for IT investments, but a number of other nuances complicate the equation as represented in an IT evaluation challenges model.

– The debate about the existence of an IT productivity paradox – the continuation of IT spend without matching benefits – adds caution to unthinking IT investment. On the other hand, the paradox discussion prompts more careful analysis and a basis for considering more informed answers to IT and e-business evaluation challenges.

2 | **Answering the challenges: lifecycle evaluation and more**

> Our organization suffers from, first, a questionable level of understanding about IT in business management, and second, the perception that IT is just a cost – not an opportunity.
>
> IT Director, retail organization

> We have found the most difficult question to answer is to measure the effectiveness and the long-term return on IT investment.
>
> IT Director, health sector

So far, we have examined the issues giving rise to a need for evaluation, and some of the difficulties in implementing evaluation schemes. The two contributions here will be to introduce the lifecycle evaluation framework, and also a simple but powerful cost/contribution model that can be used to categorize, then manage IT investments. This chapter provides the background for later chapters, which offer more in-depth methods, tools and routes out of the evaluation challenges presented by IT and e-business.

2.1 Towards lifecycle evaluation

At the heart of one way forward for organizations is the notion of an IT evaluation and management cycle. A simplified dia-

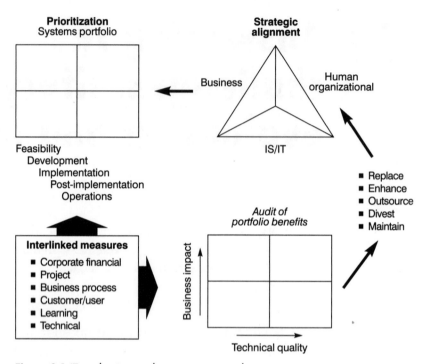

Figure 2.1 IT evaluation and management cycle

grammatic representation of this is provided in Figure 2.1. Research by the authors in 1994, 1996, 1999 and 2000 found that few organizations actually operated evaluation and management practice in an integrated manner across systems' lifecycles. For example, our 1999 survey reported that only 32% of the responding organizations practised evaluation throughout the entire lifecycle of the investment. The evaluation cycle attempts to bring together a rich and diverse set of ideas, methods and practices that are to be found in the evaluation literature to date.

Such an approach consists of several interrelated activities:

(1) Identifying net benefits through strategic alignment and prioritization.

(2) Identifying types of generic benefit and matching these to assessment techniques.

(3) Developing a family of measures based on financial, service, delivery, learning and technical criteria; ensuring that risk is assessed in the feasibility phase and throughout the rest of the lifecycle.

(4) Linking these measures to particular measures needed for development, implementation and post-implementation phases.

(5) Ensuring each set of measures runs from the strategic to the operational level.

(6) Establishing responsibility for tracking these measures and regularly reviewing results.

(7) Regularly reviewing the existing portfolio and relating this to business direction and performance objectives.

A key element in making the evaluation cycle dynamic and effective is the involvement of motivated, salient stakeholders in processes that operationalize the evaluation criteria and techniques. Our previous research points to the need to operationalize these practices across a lifecycle of six interrelated phases: alignment, prioritization, feasibility, development and implementation, post-implementation and operations. Some detail of previous findings on evaluation at these different phases now follows. The framework will then be used as a template to analyse a case study.

Alignment

In an earlier review of front-end evaluation (*Beyond the IT Productivity Paradox*, 1999) Willcocks and Lester pointed out how lack of alignment between business, information systems and human resource/organizational strategies inevitably compromised the value of all subsequent IT evaluation effort, to the point of rendering it of marginal utility and, in some cases, even counter-productive[1]. In this respect, they reflected the concerns of many authors on the subject. At the same time, the importance of recognizing evaluation as a process imbued with inherent political characteristics and ramifications was emphasized, reflecting a common finding amongst empirical studies. Many tools have been advanced to enable the evaluation and achievement of alignment. Amongst the more well known are McFarlan and McKenney's strategic grid, Porter and Millar's value chain analysis, and Earl's multiple methodology. The concept of strategic alignment in light of several of these models will be discussed in Chapter 3.

Prioritization

The notion of a systems' portfolio implies that IT investment can have a variety of objectives. The practical problem becomes one of prioritization – of resource allocation amongst the many objectives and projects that are put forward. Several classificatory schemes for achieving this appear in the extant literature (see Chapter 3 for details). Others have suggested classificatory schemes that match business objectives with types of IT project. Thus, on one schema, projects could be divided into six types:

(1) efficiency;

(2) effectiveness;

(3) must-do;

(4) infrastructure;

(5) competitive edge; and

(6) research and development.

The type of project could then be matched to one of the more appropriate evaluation methods available, a critical factor being the degree of tangibility of the costs and benefits being assessed. The portfolio and classification approaches to prioritization will be visited in Chapter 3.

Feasibility

After alignment and prioritization, the feasibility of each IT investment then needs to be examined. All the research studies show that the main weakness here has been the over-reliance on and/or misuse of traditional, finance-based cost-benefit analysis. The contingency approach outlined above helps to deal with this, but such approaches need to be allied with the active involvement of a wider group of stakeholders than those being identified in the current research studies. Following this, Figure 2.1 suggests that evaluation needs to be conducted in a linked manner across feasibility, systems' development and into systems' implementation and operational use. A key issue here is the establishment at the feasibility stage of interlinked, anchor measures. Feasibility evaluation and its many and varying approaches are reviewed in Chapter 3. Although initially an issue during feasibility evaluation, risk assessment and subsequent management is an issue that requires attention throughout the lifecycle.

Development and implementation

The evaluation cycle posits the development of a series of interlinked measures that reflect various aspects of IT/e-business performance, and that are applied across a system's lifetime. These are tied to processes and people responsible for monitoring performance, improving the evaluation system and also helping to 'flush out' and manage the benefits from the investment. Figure 2.1 suggests, in line with prevailing practitioner thinking by 2001, that evaluation cannot be based solely, or even mainly, on technical efficiency criteria. For other criteria there may be debate on how they are to be measured, and this will depend on the specific organizational circumstances.

Kaplan and Norton, in their work on the balanced business scorecard, have been highly useful for popularizing the need for a number of perspectives on evaluation of business performance. Chapter 5 will review the scorecard concept in light of its potential usefulness within an IT department and more specifically, as an IT evaluation tool. To add to that picture, most recent research suggests the need for six sets of measures. These would cover:

(1) the corporate financial perspective (e.g. profit per employee);

(2) the systems project (e.g. time, quality and cost);

(3) the business process (e.g. purchase invoices per employee);

(4) the customer/user perspective (e.g. on-time delivery rate);

(5) an innovation/learning perspective (e.g. rate of cost reduction for IT services); and

(6) a technical perspective (e.g. development efficiency and capacity utilization).

Each set of measures would run from strategic to operational levels, each measure being broken down into increasing detail as it is applied to actual organizational performance. For each set of measures the business objectives for IT would be set. Each objective would then be broken down into more detailed measurable components, with a financial value assigned where practicable.

Responsibility for tracking these measures, together with regular reviews that relate performance to objectives and targets are highly important elements in delivering benefits from the various IT investments. It should be noted that such measures are seen as helping to inform stakeholder judgements, and not as a substitute for such judgements in the evaluation process.

Post-implementation

One phase of review that is taken all too often as routine is that of post-implementation. Research suggests that this is one of the most neglected, yet most important areas as far as IT evaluation is concerned. Again, our recent survey reported that post-implementation evaluation was the least practised of any evaluation approaches in the lifecycle (at 50% of the responding organizations). An advantage of the above schema, in practice, is that post-implementation evaluation arises naturally out of implementation assessment on an on-going basis, with an already existing set of evaluators in place. This avoids the ritualistic, separated review that usually takes place in the name of post-implementation assessment.

On-going operations

There remains the matter of assessing the on-going systems portfolio on a regular basis. Notoriously, when it comes to evaluating the existing IT investment, organizations are not good at drop decisions. There may be several ramifications. The IT inheritance of 'legacy systems' can deter investment in new systems – for example, it can be all too difficult to take on new work when IT staff are awash in a rising tide of maintenance arising from the existing investment. Existing IT-related activity can also devour the majority of the financial resources available for IT investment. All too often such failures derive from not having in place, or not operationalizing, a robust assessment approach that enables timely decisions on systems and service divestment, outsourcing, replacement, enhancement, and/or maintenance. As Figure 2.1 shows, such decisions need to be based on at least two criteria (the technical quality of the system/service and its business contribution), as well as being related back to the overall strategic direction and objectives of the organization.

A further element in the assessment of the on-going systems portfolio is the relevance of external comparators. External benchmarking firms (e.g. RDC and Compass) have already been operating for several years, and offer a range of services that can be drawn upon, but mainly for technical aspects of IT performance. However, there is a growing demand for extending external benchmarking services more widely to include business and other performance measures. Benchmarking as such will be dealt with in detail in Chapters 4 and 9. There are a growing number of providers of diagnostic benchmarking methodologies that help to locate and reposition IT contribution relative to actual and required business performance. It is worth remarking that external IT benchmarking, like all measures, can serve a range of purposes within an organization, and, like all measurement systems, are open to political as well as objective uses.

Evaluating IT sourcing options

Evaluation of on-going operations will point to the need to replace, enhance, divest or maintain particular systems. This leads into the final point. An increasingly important part of assessing the existing and any future IT/e-business investment is the degree to which the external IT services market can provide better business, technical and economic options for an organization. As mentioned, the possibility of outsourcing tends to drive an organization to review, improve and perhaps implement an evaluation regime. According to Lacity and Willcocks, by 2001 73% of organizations outsourced some aspect of their IT services[2]. Of all those who outsourced, the average percentage of IT budget outsourced was over 28% and is set to average between 30–35% by 2004. However, despite this rapid growth, in practice few organizations seemed to be taking a strategic approach to IT-sourcing decisions, although many have been deriving economic and other benefits from incremental, selective, low-risk, as opposed to high-risk, 'total' approaches to outsourcing. Figure 2.1 shows how IT-sourcing decisions need to link not only with evaluation of existing operations but also with issues of strategic alignment.

Evaluation of IT-sourcing options, together with assessment of on-going vendor performance in any outsourced part of the IT service, needs to be integrally imbedded into the systems lifecycle approach detailed above. Not least because an external vendor bid, if carefully analysed against one's own detailed in-house assessment of IT performance, can be a highly informative form of benchmarking. Even where an organization does not outsource IT, our case evidence is that it is good practice to assess in-house performance against what a potential vendor bid might be, even if, as is increasingly the case, this means paying a vendor for the assessment. Benchmarking IT performance against external comparators can also be highly useful in providing insight into not only in-house IT performance, but also the efficacy of internal evaluation criteria, processes and the availability or otherwise of detailed, appropriate assessment information.

IT evaluation as a process

The lifecycle evaluation framework must evolve as a *process* within the organization. This means recognizing evaluation as:

- a social and political process (in other words, the process of evaluation engenders social, political and cultural factors in its undertaking);

- a joint and collaborative process (IT evaluation cannot be conducted effectively without the buy-in and collaboration of a number of different parties, including senior management, IT staff, user management and user staff);

- a teaching/learning process (the process of IT evaluation can improve future IT investment proposals as well as on-going projects);

- a continuous, recursive and highly divergent process (the 'continuous' factor in lifecycle evaluation gets at the heart of that process, in other words for IT evaluation to be a highly useful management tool, it must be undertaken in a linked manner across all phases of the lifecycle);

- an evolving process (IT evaluation is part science and part art – the process of evaluation will require some level of flexibility and adaptability on behalf of the evaluators and the organization itself); and

- a process with unpredictable outcomes (although the lifecycle approach to IT specifies that benefits are tracked throughout the lifecycle, the mere process of evaluation may identify unforeseen benefits – the evaluation process should leave room for such discoveries).

Some organizations practise evaluation regimes across the entire lifecycle, whereas many others are only starting to implement such regimes. As we will see in a number of cases throughout this book, the resulting approaches are many and varied; but the central roots of success lie in seeing IT evaluation as a process, rather than merely as a set of metrics to apply, and as an integral component in how the organization is managed.

2.2 Evaluation: additional perspectives and enhancements

Cost/contribution model and IT value

Increasingly, organizations are trying to tie IT spend to resulting business performance – a concept that can be referred to generically as 'the value proposition' from IT. In other words, what value is the organization deriving from the IT/e-business

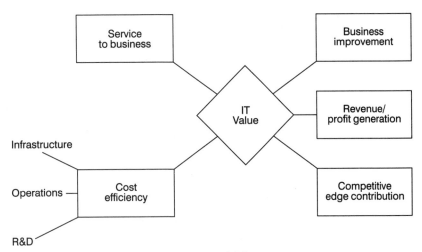

Figure 2.2 Willcocks' cost/contribution model for IT investments

investment? In 1999 we found 32% of organizations claiming to actively measure the impact of IT spend on business performance. This trend is encouraging in its message despite the fact that the 'how to's' in defining the derived value are still unclear. A perspective on the concept of value in the light of IT investments is integral to the purposes of this book.

The cost/contribution model in Figure 2.2 provides a starting point for examining those components of an IT/e-business investment that provide value.

The basic concept illustrated by the model is the idea that IT value derives from service provided to the business, cost controls/efficiency, business improvements, direct revenue/ profit generation and competitive edge contribution. Each of these components has an evaluation-related issue which requires in-depth examination.

(1) **Service to the business**. An IT department provides service to the business through speed (of response, repair, etc), quality (of product and service delivered), and support (i.e.

helping the business accomplish its tasks using IT). Consequently, this component of value requires metrics that quantify, for example speed, quality and support.

(2) **Cost**. An IT department adds value to the business through 'cost' by controlling the costs of infrastructure, operations, and research and development (R&D) activities. Operational costs are relatively easy to control because of the long history associated with them. Infrastructure and R&D, on the other hand, both suffer from the 'evaluation problem' of relatively intangible benefits. As the benefits are difficult to describe directly, providing a strong business reason is presented for the investment, then the main focus of the IT organization will be to control associated costs. Infrastructure issues are covered in Chapter 9.

(3) **Business improvement**. The basic proposition to the IT department is: 'can the business be improved with IT and if so how?' Where business processes are being improved, metrics for the required improvements need to be devised and the IT contribution assessed. Examples are provided in Chapter 5.

(4) **Direct revenue/profit generation**. This component of IT value derives from the possibility that the organizational IT department has developed some set of products and/or services to the extent that they can be sold externally, thus bringing in a profit to the organization. The bottom line in this case is obviously money in the bank, yet this financial gain, and other performance measures, need to be included in whatever evaluation regime is selected by the organization.

(5) **Competitive edge contribution**. Many IT investments must be made simply to keep up with industry. Some also need to be made as a competitive response. Some organizations, on the other hand, have successfully implemented technology that provides a competitive advantage to the organization.

One 'classic' case that is often quoted is the American Airlines SABRE reservation system. Today, by comparison, British Airways also considers its own yield management system as a major source of competitive advantage. Measurement of this type of contribution to organizational value will require different approaches. Again, remember that 'measurement' does not necessarily mean a bottom line number, but can be a set of outcomes agreed upon by the appropriate stakeholders. In the work cited in Chapter 1, van Nievelt found that relative (external) customer satisfaction is a particularly powerful, although neglected, measure of competitive edge contribution.

These contributions to IT value add yet another dimension and a focus to the lifecycle evaluation approach. A final word of caution about the cost/contribution model before moving on to other evaluation enhancers: information-based technologies do not contribute business value in themselves but do so only in combination with other factors such as the use of human resources, organizational structure and marketing strategy. This must be reflected in the evaluation regime and measures adopted, too.

The value proposition: external and internal customers

These 'value propositions' highlight a number of up-and-coming issues/enhancements to IT usage and evaluation. In 1999 we found that 61% of respondents measured customer perceptions of IT service. Later survey findings paired with additional research into e-business reflect further developments in the customer service focus. Although understanding of IT is still not widespread, customers are becoming more knowledgeable and demanding as expectations about the benefits from IT rise. Therefore, customer service measures become critical.

In their book *Creating Value* (1996), Mathur and Kenyon explore the customer service focus[3]. Competitor-focused as opposed to customer-focused business strategies all share a potential problem: they may deliver competitively priced products that customers no longer wish to buy. The problem can be formulated another way: these strategies fail to detect and respond to shifts in customer preferences. The marketing concept, on the other hand, traditionally puts the customer centre stage. Marketing recognizes the simple fact that sales revenues represent the aggregate result of numerous customer decisions to purchase, repurchase or not to purchase. From the market-oriented perspective, competitive advantage exists when customers prefer a business's products or services over competitive alternatives. In other words, market-driven organizations aim to gain and sustain a competitive advantage by keeping both close to the customer and ahead of the competition. In the words of Mathur and Kenyon, what competes is what a customer can choose instead. This perspective forces managers to focus on understanding the purchase decision process, specifically what causes customers in their market to purchase a specific product or service for the first time (i.e. new customer acquisition) and what causes them subsequently to repurchase that same item (i.e. customer retention or loyalty) or to switch?

It is useful to distinguish between the concepts of 'quality' and 'customer satisfaction':

– the **quality** concept is product (and producer) oriented; and

– the **satisfaction** concept is customer (and market) oriented.

Mathur and Kenyon's thinking can be applied to the IT arena in at least two ways. Firstly, it is clear that focusing on the customer relates directly to the development of sustainable competitive strategy. The IT evaluation question here is: 'how does IT contribute and leverage the customer proposition in the external marketplace?' Secondly, the thinking can also be applied to internal, specifically IT, customers. Thus in his article 'Hang on to what you've got' (*Computer Weekly*, January 1998), Taylor tied this need to satisfy the customer together with competitive pressures. He argued that, in the light of increased global competition, organizations must do what they can to retain customers. From an IT perspective, this applies to the IT department's supply of services and products to its organization. Instead of focusing on mere service levels, the IT department should look for what it can do to help 'customers' (i.e. the rest of the business) to be more successful. Given such a mandate, the organization should think carefully through its measurement strategy to ensure that whatever evaluation framework is adopted is getting at the heart of organizational needs/strategy and customer requirements.

Having detailed some fundamental ways of taking an holistic and time-based approach to IT and e-business evaluation, let us look at the application of the lifecycle approach to a real organization as a diagnostic tool during a consultancy engagement of one of the authors.

2.3 An in-depth case study: applying lifecycle evaluation at Insuror

Evaluation practice was investigated in the business and systems contexts provided by a newly formed business division of Insuror, a major insurance company. To provide a triangulation of perspectives, eight managers drawn from the senior team, business change and systems department, and line management were interviewed. The managers were also chosen as those people most involved with and knowledgeable about information systems and their evaluation within the company. Semi-structured questionnaires, interviews and access to documentation provided the data required for the case study.

Business context

Insuror is a large insurance company with headquarters in the UK. In 1995, it held £4,833 million in insurance premiums and employed over 17,000 people. In 1994, the company was organized along product lines. Consequently, a customer would be required to deal with different divisions for different products. During 1995, the company was reorganized from geographic regions into customer type, for example from 'UK region' to 'motor insurance' and 'personal insurance'. The case concentrates on one UK division we will here call Corporate Alliances (CA).

CA sold primarily housing, health, legal and emergency insurance, worth about £650 million. The majority of its business was with five large financial institutions, building societies and banks. These customers in turn sold CA's products to end-customers, most typically their own employees. CA worked in a highly competitive market where profits were difficult to achieve. In early 1996, CA was challenged by the decision of a major customer to provide its own insurance. To increase revenues, throughout 1995–1996, CA looked to expand into Europe, but ran the danger of intruding the customer base of Insuror's Europe-based business division. Another set of problems in CA was poor processing of end-customer claims, resulting in fraud, exaggerated claims and excess payments. Reducing the cost of operations became a critical necessity and an IT-based re-engineering project had been started more than a year before.

Information technology/systems context

By 1995, CA had a functional organizational design, including underwriting, marketing, account managers, core and support services. There were two departments in the support service unit: business technology and service delivery. The business technology department had a £15 million budget and directly employed 180 people, mainly systems developers. In late 1995, another 300 staff were being devolved from the business units to better integrate applications development. These included network support and IT operations staff, but increasingly, these business units and the group IT division were opting for outsourcing. In February 1996, the network activity was outsourced to IBM, and the Group-run mainframe operation was about to be outsourced, the effect anticipated as a reduction of 150 in staff numbers. Upon initial figures, the perception amongst senior management was that outsourcing the mainframe would save £46 million over five years.

At the time of the initial interviews, the business technology department was developing five major projects:

(1) a business re-engineering of core processes, including claims processing;

(2) a system to replace the insurance policy administration system on the mainframe;

(3) a system to apply imaging technology to scan policies, forms and letters;

(4) a system to implement telephony; and

(5) a client/server system for claims processing.

The service delivery department ran seven regional data centres throughout the UK. It employed 800 staff, primarily dealing with operations support and data entry for policies and claims. CA had no plans to outsource these data centres.

According to senior IT managers, the major challenges facing the IT staff were: managing user expectations, prioritizing work and managing large-scale projects. Much of this was a balancing act – high IT spending would annoy senior management and business sponsors of systems, while spending too little on IT would cut services and functionality and increase user dissatisfaction. Some sense of the pressures, how different stakeholders might perceive an IT productivity paradox, and how this might be related to the lack of commonly held evaluation practices, was conveyed by the business technology manager:

Between 1992 and 1995, we saw a dramatic headcount rise and a £10 million budget rising to £15 million. A lot of people do not understand why this amount of spend occurs and how it compares with other companies. For example, they do not understand that it takes four person years just to handle the systems changes to the date year 2000. In fact the business decisions explain the spend. For example, a decision to diversify means new systems. Moreover, in practice, there are no mechanisms in place to reduce this spend by synergies across the group and standardizing and identifying commonalities across the company.

Evaluation practices

The Managing Director of CA had previously headed Insuror's Group Management Services. Several senior managers had come from IT-related functions. This meant that there was a strong belief in the importance of IT amongst the senior management team. However, in the 1980s and early 1990s, in the old company from which CA had split off, IT had had low credibility amongst line managers. In some cases, system failures had resulted directly in financial losses. Part of the problems stemmed from omissions in evaluation practice, with little attempt to tie investments to business needs and measure and demonstrate business impacts. By the early 1990s, there was a disciplined, centralized evaluation procedure, but this created a very bureaucratic way of raising a request for IT. This created tensions between IT and business staff, together with accusations of IT being unresponsive. The IT function was reorganized into customer-facing teams. While this approach improved customer service, it also meant that, by 1995, an increasing number of requests escaped central prioritization. As we will see, this fractured an integrated lifecycle approach at a vital point, and respondents readily admitted this.

Alignment

By 1995, senior managers evaluated primarily in terms of financial benefit either directly through productivity improvements or indirectly through ability to win clients – a critical issue in the 1995–1996 period. However, respondents indicated ways in which alignment of IT expenditure with business strategy did not always occur. One senior manager stated:

> With the strategic projects we go through a proper lifecycle of measuring what the benefit was when . . . implemented, and do a customer satisfaction survey. But that is only really for the top three or four projects. For a lot of the other work, we are not doing that kind of activity . . . there are satisfaction surveys but not so much of a business benefit analysis . . . it's being given a test before it's adopted – is it important to the business – but it's not really being given a cost benefit analysis.

Prioritization

Much of the problem seemed to stem from weaknesses in prioritization processes and in the type of criteria used:

> What we tend not to do is prioritize the low level requests properly . . . when they are doing useful IT rather than strategic IT, because of our desire to get close to the users and deliver what they want, we tend to deliver everything they ask for and there is a long list of the things we can do . . . People can actually ask for new IT relatively easily and that . . . may actually be wasting money.

From feasibility to on-going operations

The ways in which IT productivity – in terms of business, as opposed to user, benefit – can escape through weaknesses in evaluation practices are indicated by the following comment from a senior manager:

> The things that come through with five person days, two person days, ten person days we call 'business normal'. We would expect to get a lot of those things because once you've put in a system, it's like a living system. But I think it covers about 40% of our budget spend . . . if we could get the executives responsible for different areas to understand their net costs and if we could put down an invoice and say this is what we have delivered and it costs, say £100,000, and the benefit is £250,000 and may be closer to £500,000, they will look at that and feel good about it. But then we also need to follow through and say well now, deliver the £250,000 worth of benefit.

What the IT manager is recommending here fits well with the notion of an evaluation approach integrated across a system's lifecycle, with a range of measures, not just technical criteria being applied. It should also be realized that, as with other organizations, IT resource in terms of people is both expensive and limited. IT resource use in CA for the type of work detailed by the IT project manger creates an opportunity cost for more strategic work with much higher business impact, thus affecting the IT productivity equation potentially quite radically.

Benchmarking and outsourcing

Two other evaluation areas at CA can be compared against our proposal for evaluating across the system's lifecycle. These areas are benchmarking and outsourcing. Respondents generally agreed that CA systems in the health and creditor areas were at the leading edge in Europe. However, in the household area there was definite feedback from clients that CA systems were not up to the level of competitors. However, respondents indicated that CA did not possess enough good benchmarking information to make detailed assessments against competitors. One IT manager stated:

> In the past, we've tried to gain more information about our competitors through visits and attending seminars, but some more formal benchmarking we believe is now appropriate.

On IT outsourcing, the most recent decision to outsource IBM mainframes on a five-year contract was actually made at corporate level. The mainframes in fact took in work from a number of business divisions. The business division did not drive the decisions, although it related them to its own strategic plans. However, subsequently, there was some concern at CA, as a senior manager explained:

> Having been on the receiving end, we are looking at it in terms of cost management and how we make sure we get all the benefits . . . there is a cost in having to manage that . . . at CA, we may not save a lot of money by the deal . . . we've got to live with the decision and minimize impact on the business and maximize any benefit . . . this creates new tasks – monitoring the vendor performance and user satisfaction for example.

Summary

In terms of the system's lifecycle approach detailed in this chapter, this case history highlights a number of strong evaluation practices and a number of weaknesses. These practices also relate to IT productivity issues in a number of interesting ways. A history of indifferent evaluation practice and, in business terms, uncertain IT productivity had been challenged by restructuring, a highly competitive business environment and new senior management personnel. By 1996, evaluation practice was strong on identifying some strategic projects. However, respondents indicated that a difficulty lay with the lack of precision within the business strategy itself. In March 1996, senior management had embarked upon a review of both business and IS strategy with a view to achieving more precise alignment.

Feasibility and prioritization procedures seemed weak for what in fact covered some 40% of total IT expenditure. Respondents also indicated that they were actively looking at ways in which interlinked measures could be set up across development and implementation of systems so that IT business benefits could be assessed more easily. Another concern was with improvements in the process of evaluation, so business managers would be more responsible for evaluating and managing benefits.

External benchmarking was also on the new agenda. The original outsourcing evaluation was out of the hands of CA managers, but it became clear that there were a number of concerns about how productive the results would be for CA itself. One way forward seemed to be put in place close monitoring of vendor performance, while one manager intimated that if this monitoring indicated low value for the CA Division, the option to withdraw from the outsourcing agreement needed to be considered.

Case learning points

Evaluation practices influenced IT productivity in a number of ways:

(1) from the 1980s, stakeholder perceptions of the value of IT could be seen to have been influenced by how IT evaluation was conducted, and the ability, or otherwise, of evaluation procedures to demonstrate business value;

(2) the CA Division was beginning to align IT expenditure with strategic business necessities and this would, in the assess-

ment of senior IT managers, enhance the productivity in business terms;

(3) weaknesses in feasibility evaluation and prioritization were channelling substantial IT expenditure into less productive areas;

(4) weaknesses in interlinked measures and assignment of responsibility for monitoring development and implementation meant that benefits from the IT expenditure were less significant than they could have been;

(5) more detailed benchmarking might also have induced a clearer focus on where to make IT expenditure and what level of IT productivity should be attainable ((4) and (5) were acknowledged by senior IT managers, who subsequently actively attempted to change evaluation practices in these areas); and

(6) the non-involvement in the original IT outsourcing evaluation, in our analysis, tied CA to a less than productive arrangement, while incurring subsequent management and monitoring time and effort, deflecting IT skills and capabilities better used elsewhere.

It would seem that so far as the IT productivity paradox exists in such organizations, it is best explained by the practical considerations detailed above. Moreover, as the case history helps to illustrate, improvements in evaluation practice can have a significant role to play in the resolution of IT productivity issues.

2.4 Key learning points

- IT/e-business investment should be viewed increasingly as a 'value producing' proposition related to the strategic goals of an organization. The IT investment alone does not provide the value, rather it is the application of the IT to the business.

- More organizations are developing a business focus to the process of IT and e-business evaluation, rather than a solely financial focus.

- The old adage 'what gets measured gets managed' touches on the need for evaluation regimes in the IT world as a basis for on-going management. Consequently, 'measurement' can be seen as a form of management and should be thought of in such an holistic manner as opposed to some additional, and bureaucratic, task that does not obviously contribute to firm performance.

- A comprehensive solution to the need for IT/e-business evaluation can be found in lifecycle evaluation, that is the measurement of the IT investment from its initial feasibility through to its on-going maintenance, and included in that measurement, well-defined expectations of the benefits, both tangible and intangible, to be expected from the investment. Iterative lifecycle evaluation provides the fundamental basis for continuous assessment and improvement.

2.5 Practical action guidelines

- Inculcate a 'measurement as management' philosophy across the organization.

- Implement an evaluation regime across the entire lifecycle of all technology investments. Apply the lifecycle evaluation concept and the six types of measures.

- Ensure that every technology investment undertaken is driven by a defined business need.

- Utilize the cost/contribution model to categorize IT/e-business investments and build suitable metrics regimes.

- Spend time on measuring customer satisfaction with IT service provision. It builds credibility and business confidence in the relevance and importance of IT evaluation.

3 Project planning for risk, prioritization and benefits

3.1 Introduction

> Risk in computer-based projects are surprisingly under-managed.
>
> Willcocks and Griffiths[1]

> We've minimized risk because we are sharing the risk (between the client and the vendor) . . .
>
> Assistant Executive Officer, California Franchise Tax Board

> What we tend to find with IT projects is that they may not produce a positive NPV. And what I'm trying to get people to do more and more is recognize that some projects are enablers and not every project you do is going to pay back. So just recognize that some of it is invested in the infrastructure of the business.
>
> Financial Controller, Major Retail Company

> Focus has been less on only cost and more and more emphasis on 'what should we be doing to move our business ahead' . . . managers of the larger projects begin to

speak about the IT investment now more in terms of return versus simple cost minimization.

Information Technology Manager,
Hewlett Packard Test and Measurement Organization

In this chapter, we will identify approaches for justifying and planning IT projects. Remenyi has capably and effectively covered risk assessment in his book *Stop IT Project Failures Through Risk Assessment* (in this same Butterworth-Heinemann series), but a brief discussion of risk from a complementary perspective is relevant at this juncture. Despite their importance to all phases of an IT/e-business project, and especially in the initial assessment, risk assessment and management are often overlooked throughout those phases because:

(1) the client/users care less about development productivity than about the ultimate product's fit-for-purpose;

(2) additional time is required for measurement in a schedule that is already tight;

(3) there is lack of knowledge of effective measurement approaches;

(4) of adherence to a traditional lifecycle design methodology which does not specify adequate measurement;

(5) there is lack of organizational learning from previous projects; and/or

(6) the IT organization already has approval for the project; now the focus is on delivery of an end product.

Risk is to be understood as exposure to the possibility of a loss or an undesirable project outcome as a consequence of uncertainty. The failure to consider risk has been the downfall of many IT investments. We will now review specific examples and consider possible risk-mitigating techniques.

3.2 Why IT-based projects fail

Research and experience alike continually cite a failure to measure risk. For instance, the OTR Group found that only 30% of companies surveyed in 1992 applied any risk analysis in the IT-investment and project-management processes. Depressingly, in two later surveys, Willcocks found that 'little formal risk analysis was identified amongst respondent companies, except that in financial calculation, e.g. discount rates'[1]. In addition, in 1998 Willcocks and Lester found that in some organizations up to 40% of the IT projects realized no net benefits, however measured.

On a daily basis, the trade press reflects examples of failed projects. The following examples of outright project failure provide a basis for the consideration of risk and its contribution to on-going project assessment.

– The London Stock Exchange's TAURUS (Transfer and Auto-mated Registration of Uncertified Stock) project was con-ceived in the early 1980s as the next automation step toward a paperless dealing and contractual system for shares. The main impetus for TAURUS came in 1987 with a crisis in settlements stemming from back office, mainly paper-based, support systems failing to keep track of the massive number of share dealings and related transactions. Many of the international banks were keen to automate as much as possible and as quickly as possible. Other parties, such as registrars who would be put out of business if share certificates were abandoned, fought against any further expansion of technology. Consequently, the Stock Exchange had to balance its international reputation while maintaining the support and confidence of all City interests.

The Siscott Committee was appointed by the Bank of England to provide some sort of compromise solution. Unfortunately, with each compromise, expectations, systems design and complexity of the desired solution increased exponentially. Additionally, the Department of Trade and Industry began to impose restrictions to protect investors. In the confusion, the main project focus was lost and the decision between a massively centralized computer system or an integrated network of databases remained undecided.

Eventually, a project team was appointed and given the go-ahead to purchase for the core system a £1 million software package from Vista Concepts in New Jersey. Work commenced on customization of the system, despite the lack of a central design for the system and the absence of a planned operating architecture. The project grew out of control very quickly and ultimately was declared an outright failure.

The outcome of the TAURUS project is perhaps the most familiar large-scale IT project failure in the UK. A multitude of sins comprises the list of errors on the project:

(1) up front, the project lacked clear objectives;

(2) the size and complexity of the project were unaccounted for in terms of appropriate controls;

(3) communication channels across many aspects of the project were poor at best;

(4) project procedures were not followed;

(5) quality control was limited by the lack of accountability on the project;

(6) sourcing decisions were made with no rhyme or reason;

(7) vested parties were not in agreement on the 'solution';

(8) no central design for the system existed;

(9) no operating architecture had been planned; and

(10) the appointed committees failed to reach any compromises and/or engender the support of appropriate parties.

– The Governor of California pulled the plug on the US$100 million plus State Automated Child System (SACSS) in response to repeated project slippages and the rampant dissatisfaction voiced by counties already live on the system (note that the SACSS implementation plan called for a phased roll out to the counties originally spread over 12 to 18 months). This failure fell in line behind several other large IT project failures for the State of California including a Department of Motor Vehicles (DMV) US$50 million debacle. A number of issues can be cited regarding the failure of SACSS:

(1) the system was intended to be transferred from one implemented in a state with a much smaller caseload. Consequently, the original application was not built for a caseload with the size of California's; the resulting 'enhancements' resulted in a nearly entirely redesigned application;

(2) the system was intended to run as 58 individual county systems all connected through a central hub database which permitted communications between counties; the resulting inability to engender agreement across counties for functionality severely crippled the developer's ability to deliver;

(3) the application was not sized correctly for the hardware to be used;

(4) the timescale of the project created a situation where the application to be delivered was relatively out of date when rolled out to the initial counties;

(5) project complexity confused many issues;

(6) project management suffered due to multiple vendors and continual staff changes at the State level; and

(7) the system was mandated by the federal government without acknowledgment of the complexity required to satisfy the generic requirements.

TAURUS and SACSS were big projects, often using new technology while lacking big project disciplines. Large e-business projects run similar risks – no new rules here. Moreover, by definition, e-business projects also involve considerable re-engineering and organizational change risks. How should risk be addressed? What repeatable and consistent approaches can be applied to the assessment, management and mitigation of risk in any sort of IT undertaking? In answer, we will review several perspectives on the many dimensions of risk, then suggest a set of prevalent risk factors for consideration and on-going evaluation.

The portfolio dimensions of risk

McFarlan's portfolio approach to project management[2] suggests that projects fail due to lack of attention to three dimensions:

(1) individual project risk;

(2) aggregate risk of portfolio of projects; and

(3) the recognition that different types of projects require different types of management.

For example, a simple support application with relatively straightforward specifications and a goal of increasing efficiency would require only simple task management, whereas a high-risk strategic application would require more management directed at risk mitigation. Moreover, the risk inherent in projects is influenced by project size, experience with the technology and project structure. All of the caselets provided demonstrate this failure to assess project risk. Additionally, from McFarlan's proposals, it seems obvious that risk assessment on one project is complicated by an organization's need to manage many such projects at once.

The domains of risk relative to IT investments

Lyytinen and Hirschheim[3], supplemented by Ward and Griffiths[4], describe the domains of potential failure as:

- **technical** – the domain of IT staff, who are responsible for the technical quality of the system and its use of technology (this is usually the easiest and cheapest problem to overcome);

- **data** – describes the data design, processing integrity and data-management practices under the control of IT combined with the user procedures and data quality control handled by the user (this is clearly a shared responsibility);

- **user** – the primary responsibility for using the system must lie with user management;

- **organizational** – describes the possibility that, while a system may satisfy a specific functional need, it fails to suit the overall organization in its operations and interrelationships; and

- **business environment** – the possibility that a system may become inappropriate due to change in market requirements and related changes in business strategy.

The domains of failure, then, can span the breadth of the organization and depend on external influences as well.

The sources of risk

Willcocks and Griffiths[5] present a complementary perspective on why an IT project might fail. Their research reflects five broad categories contributing to such failures. We'll explain these five categories in light of the failed project examples provided earlier.

(1) **Lack of strategic framework**. The California SACSS project illustrates a lack of strategic framework. It failed to convince the 58 counties' users of the benefits of SACSS. The resulting in-fighting about system functionality prevented a cohesive system. In addition, perhaps because the original concept for the SACSS was a federally mandated requirement, a strategic focus owned by the state never developed.

(2) **Lack of organizational adaptation to complement technological change**. Again, the SACSS project was intended for implementation in 58 counties, all of which previously conducted business in 58 different ways. Efforts to educate users in the context of their existing systems failed to convince users to adopt the new application.

(3) **IT supplier problems and general immaturity of the supply side**. The TAURUS project was based on a piece of vendor-supplied packaged software that required so much customization that £14 million in additional funds was required to rewrite the software; even so, the effort was never completed.

(4) **Poor management of change**. The projects mentioned paid little attention to the management of change. Project management was questioned in its effectiveness on all projects, and users were either not effectively involved in development processes or were not well informed about upcoming changes. Project management focused on the delivery of the physical and/or tangible product with little attention to (indeed no assigned responsibility for) the more

subtle and less tangible aspects of organizational change required by the overall business need/metric for which the systems were being built.

(5) **Too much faith in the technical fix.** The TAURUS initiative illustrates the keen desire to implement customized automation technology regardless of the lack of an appropriate central design. It was thought that automation was the 'be-all' solution without regard to the ramifications of such an approach.

While the 'technological' focus of an IT project is obvious, it is perhaps less obvious and often forgotten, that an IT project should not be an end in itself. Instead it should be a means to support a more comprehensive business project and related business metric. Although technology plays a part in the reasons provided for project failure thus far, the more significant factors (and those less easy to repair) appear to be organizationally and human-related. Willcocks and Griffiths reference a survey of abandoned projects which were halted due to organizational factors (e.g. a loss of management commitment) and/or political and interpersonal conflicts, rather than technical issues. Thus, the number of project risk factors to be evaluated on a continual basis throughout the life of a project expand from merely technological factors to include organizational and human dimensions.

Ultimately, Willcocks and Griffiths summarize succinctly the required attention to risk: 'underlying all the issues so far identified is the degree to which risk factors and level in large-scale IT projects are explicitly recognized, then managed'.

Much of what has been discussed here relates to analysis that precedes a project undertaking. In looking at project management and development issues, these analyses must be thought of as an on-going review process. Risk cannot be assessed only once with the expectation that such assessment will be satisfactorily for the life of a project. With a 'project lifecycle' concept in mind, consider the following successful examples of risk mitigation.

3.3 Successful risk mitigation: some examples

The following caselets examine organizations that consciously adopted some tailored form of risk mitigation. The common significant factor of success in each case was the simple fact that risk was recognized and planned for.

– BP Exploration's global IT organization, XIT, has been measuring financial information since its creation in 1989. In 1993, XIT outsourced all of its IT supply services. In the same year, XIT introduced the balanced business scorecard as a means to assist in the transformation of the remaining IT function from a traditional IT group to an internal consultancy focused on adding value to the business units. The balanced business scorecard went through a number of iterations before it reached its current form. In its metamorphosis, XIT recognized the need for risk assessment and management. Consequently, it has added a risk matrix to the performance management process. The matrix maps risk probability against risk manageability and is used to map identified risks according to these two dimensions. In doing so, BP XIT makes explicit risk elements and provides a vehicle to communicate to the organization the significance of those risks.

– As will be demonstrated by the case study at the end of Chapter 4, the CAPS/PASS projects for the California Franchise Tax Board created an environment of shared risk between vendor and client. AMS bore the burden of development costs while creating a new saleable product; FTB donated a great deal of staff time and knowledge to the development of a flexible solution within the constraints of defined benefit streams, perfected as the project proceeded. Project team members worked hard to identify risks before they became impediments. The balancing of benefit, cost and quality created a keen focus on project goals: both client and vendor concentrated on making investments which added measurable value to the organization.

3.4 Risk assessment: emerging success factors

From the discussion above and the examples of successful risk mitigation, we can identify a number of dimensions that contribute to the ability to assess and mitigate risk in the design, development, implementation and post-implementation phases of a system's lifecycle. These factors provide the setting for an examination of various project measurement methods in Chapter 4.

User involvement

The user's involvement in a project is inherent to a project's success. Such involvement is required to provide information about the business setting in which a new IT project is to be implemented. The user explains the business processes that are being automated perhaps and/or the innovative opportunity technology can provide to accomplish a task not yet surmountable. Regardless of their need to be involved, history shows that user involvement in projects is relatively negligible. Some traditional lifecycle development methodologies specify that the users are involved in the 'functional specification process' then effectively disappear until acceptance testing. How should users be involved in the design and development process in an effective and cooperative manner? More importantly, how can users provide measurements of progress and success in the design/development process?

Commitment from management, key staff and IT professionals

In order to see a project through to its end, a number of parties are required to participate. The levels of participation may vary, but the vested interest on behalf of management, key user staff and IT professionals is a necessity. These parties can contribute to the successful process of on-going measurement during design, development and implementation.

Flexibility

There is much debate about flexibility in the continual updating of functional specifications, program design and program code. Again, more traditional lifecycle models specify that functional specifications should be shut down at a certain point based on a project description that is probably outdated by the time the project actually begins. Confusion in the design and development process reigns because of the constant specification discussions. Perhaps, however, some level of flexibility built into the process would ease the tension and make the design and development processes more effective.

Strategic alignment

Strategic alignment is required for an IT department as a whole and as part of the investment process. 'One-time' alignment is not enough. Again, because of the rapidly changing horizon for both technology and business, strategic alignment could disappear before an approved project has been completed. Consequently, on-going strategic alignment assessment must be performed. Increasingly, especially with moves to e-business, an IT project should really be supporting a more comprehensive business project, and that business project should provide business metrics with which the IT project can align. Thus, the business project as a whole must continue to answer the strategic needs of the organization in order for the subsumed IT projects to do the same.

Time constraints

There is an increasing body of evidence suggesting that large-scale, long-time IT projects are particularly susceptible to failure. The SACSS project in California, examined in the beginning of the chapter, is a case in point. On the other hand, the time dimension can provide an effective measurement stick to monitor design and development. Organizations are more often imposing time caps on IT projects for the sake of driving requirements through quickly without losing out on available opportunities.

Project size

As demonstrated by the SACSS project, the overwhelming size of a project, as a single factor, can significantly impair the ability to deliver. In those instances the recommended response is to break the project down into smaller pieces in order to develop a reasonable delivery schedule.

Scope control

Many projects suffer from 'scope creep', that is the inimitable addition of functionality at later stages in the project outside the formal planning process and outside of allegedly 'nailed down' specifications. In Chapter 4, it will become obvious that traditional methodologies specifying a limited time for specification development might not serve the best purpose. For now, scope control should be considered a hazard of ineffective working relationships between users and IT staff.

Contingency planning

In the quick-moving world of technology and IT project delivery, project plans and budgets are usually stripped to the bone. Research has demonstrated time and again, however, that contingency planning and padded estimates could do wonders to establish appropriate expectations on behalf of both users and IT staff, as well as to create a more effective working environment.

Feedback from the measurement process

Finally, assuming that all of these project/risk variables should be taken into account when planning any kind of management/ measurement system, it is important to remember that the measurement process should provide feedback into the organizational learning loop, which can continually improve the organization's ability to perform and analyse risk. In other words, risk assessment and measurement must feed into a system of risk management in order for risks to actually be pre-empted and dealt with.

3.5 Project planning issues

Now that we have established a case for on-going risk analysis, we will examine the other dimensions of project planning. The following caselets provide detail about managers in large, complex organizations, and their approaches to feasibility assessment, planning and prioritization, and benefits management.

– The Chief Information Officer (CIO) of Genstar Container Corp (GE subsidiary) always takes the 'business approach' in the assessment of IT investment. The IT organization has undergone a dramatic transformation since the beginning of 1997 and the assignment of Jonathan Fornaci as CIO. Since 1997, Genstar has overhauled all of its technology base and moved to an Internet/Java-based set of applications to support the customer. The first step in getting to the 'new' vision was to subsume the technology under the business case. In the eyes of Genstar, that business case must have the singular goal of attaining closeness to the customer via the exploitation of IT. Interestingly enough, the CIO explains that the business case analysis is built solely on 'hard costs'; intangibles are not included.

– A large financial services organization based in the UK is moving toward an era in which all IT investments need to be about commercial ventures rather than about technology. This new perspective has contributed to making a number of key IT investment decisions, for example the decision to outsource voice and data network support and development. The IT organization determined that, while the company could easily build its own voice and data networks, it would incur an opportunity cost by doing so.

– As the multinational pharmaceuticals firm Glaxo Wellcome entered 1998, it was undergoing significant cost rationalization in the face of patents which expired in mid-1997 and declining market share, both of which resulted in a less cash-rich environment. The centralized IT department was experiencing the results of this new cost-consciousness, as the International IT Manager, explained:

> In the good old days of Glaxo before the merger (with Wellcome) when we were growing at 20% odd per annum because of one particular product no one cared too much about putting a decent cost benefit analysis together, we didn't care too much about the internal rate of return or payback. Certainly, measuring the benefits was something that was never spoken about. A lot has changed and now any case for expenditure will be carefully scrutinized. We will look at how quickly it's paying back to the business. We will be looking for a very solid business case. And we will be looking for evidence that someone somewhere is trying to put into place a process at the end to measure benefits.

Budgeting and project prioritization were also affected into 2000: 'The organization is finding difficulty with determining an effective overall budget given the piecemeal approach of project development. Hard-nosed prioritization is becoming a necessity.'

In these cases, it can be seen that, until comparatively recently, most assessment and planning has been predominantly financially based. Research evidence up to 2001 continues to indicate that although organizations understand the need for comprehensive evaluation conceptually, they have been a long time in recognizing that a financially based investment case does not provide the complete story about IT investment. Amongst other things, managers struggle with the types and identification of less tangible benefits.

Our most recent research suggests that 70% of organizations practise some sort of feasibility assessment, yet a significant portion of those organizations rank 'difficulty in identifying benefits, particularly intangible benefits' along with 'difficulty in assigning costs to benefits' as the most notable obstacles in feasibility assessment. Moreover, organizations identified 'strategic match with the business' and 'satisfaction of customer needs' as the most critical criteria affecting the investment decision, followed closely by 'return on investment' and 'traditional cost benefit analysis'. It would appear that these criteria reflect a subtle shift in evaluation practices toward less tangible benefits, with supporting financial analysis.

Whereas organizations once hoped to cut costs by automating, now organizations have discovered completely new ways of doing business that expand both the need for IT investment and the profitability of the business. The successive adoption of the new technologies, including Internet-based technologies, has complicated the process of analysing new IT investments because:

(1) resulting paybacks/benefits cannot be measured solely in terms of money spent or saved;

(2) resulting benefits filter throughout the organization, sometimes in surprising and unpredictable ways; and

(3) the overall role of IT has changed from being supportive to also being of strategic importance; moreover, the benefits derived from IT investments have evolved from time and cost savings to the provision of additional competitive advantage, cooperative advantage, diversification and new marketing opportunities.

Regardless of these complications, measurement processes that begin with a feasibility assessment can assist more effectively in the task of identifying costs, investments, intangible benefits and consequently, measuring those same effects throughout the life of the project. Overall planning and prioritization of IT projects can provide a bird's-eye view of the whole picture and how various projects relate to one another and to other initiatives and operations within the organization.

3.6 Planning and prioritization approaches

The practices exhibited in the following Hewlett Packard case are typical of the better practitioners of planning and prioritization. Even so, it is fairly clear that there is plenty of opportunity for improvement.

– In 1998 the IT department of the Test and Measurement Organization (TMO) within Hewlett Packard had relatively rudimentary project assessment processes in place. According to Steve Hussey, TMO Information Technology Manager:

I would characterize our assessment here as being pretty much on the front end of the learning curve. Most are not very sophisticated. The reason I say that is because on large investments, assessments tend to be more robust, and there's always a financial component. Increasingly, there is a business strategy, business impact component . . . and on the end of the spectrum, for smaller projects, there is often little return analysis in the traditional sense at all, because those projects may move very quickly, and there's not a lot of analytical framework around them. However, almost all projects go through a fairly disciplined project lifecycle process.

He does note that the decision process differs, depending on the part of the investment portfolio under consideration. For instance:

At the highest level, overall infrastructure strategies are supported by the senior level executives in the business; the infrastructure investment is usually not based on a return to the business in the more traditional sense . . . There's a different set of investments that I would term project or solution based, and those decisions are usually based completely on business needs . . . Those are all business based, they are not based on an IT strategy by themselves, they are based on what we need to do in the business. In these cases, the IT investment levels are really part of the overall business program. Those IT investments tend to be measured much more on a return basis.

The planning process derives significance from the fact that it is the way into identifying application needs and allocation of resources. Some combination of top-down and bottom-up planning is required in order to:

(1) identify and understand organizational strategy;

(2) understand IT capability and applicability; and

(3) develop a plan, albeit a flexible one, for future IT undertakings.

Let us turn to investigating possible best practice in this area.

Application portfolio analysis

As far back as 1981, McFarlan recommended that organizations should analyse their technology/systems investments by assessing risks across the portfolio of applications in the organization[6]. As addressed earlier in the risk assessment discussion, he suggested three 'serious deficiencies' in IT management practice:

(1) the failure to assess individual project risk;

(2) the failure to assess aggregate risk across the application portfolio; and

(3) the failure to recognize that different types of projects require different types of management attention.

Since McFarlan's recommendations, a number of ways of categorizing IT application have arisen, including those suggested by Willcocks[7], Farbey, Land and Targett[8], and Ward and Griffiths[9] (see Figure 3.1 for a summary of these classification schemes). As will be examined later in the chapter, each application type gives rise to variations in benefits. This suggests that different types of applications require different evaluation and management approaches.

The use of a classification process to identify the application portfolio can assist the organization in the planning and prioritization process, and, as McFarlan suggests, it can help assess technology risks in a more comprehensive manner.

Willcocks	Effectiveness	System required in order for organization to function appropriately
	Architecture	System/platform undertaken to provide infrastructure
	Must do	System required to satisfy a minimum market or legal requirement
	Efficiency	System required in order to improve performance of organization
	Competitive edge	System undertaken in order to achieve a competitive leap
	R&D	System pursued in order to be prepared for future
Farbey, Land and Targett	Mandatory changes	System undertaken in order to follow competitor's lead out of necessity, to follow technological necessity, or to adhere to legal requirements
	Automation	System designed to replace existing methods in order to reduce costs
	Direct value added	System that not only reduces cost, but adds value, perhaps by performing something not previously handled
	MIS and DSS	System that provides planning, control or decision-making information
	Infrastructure	System that provides general capability as foundations
	Interorganizational	System shared across at least two organizations (e.g. EDI)
	Strategic	System used to gain competitive advantage
	Business transformation	System that transforms business into profitable organization
Ward and Griffiths	Support	System that is valuable, but not critical to success
	Key operational	System upon which organization currently depends for success
	Strategic	System which is critical to sustaining future business strategy
	High potential (R&D)	System which may be important to achieving future success

Figure 3.1 Classifications of IT applications

Planning and prioritization: a business-led approach

Planning and prioritization in its simplest iteration can be thought of as aligning, at a very early stage, business direction and need with IT investment. A complementary way of looking at the issue is the business-led approach suggested by Feeny in Willcocks, Sauer and associates in *Moving To E-business* (2001)[10]. This examines IT investments in light of the concept that IT expenditure alone does not lead to business benefits. Feeny points out that only the adoption of new business ideas associated with IT investment can lead to significant business benefits: 'If there is no new business idea associated with IT investment, the most that can be expected is that some existing business idea will operate a little more efficiently, as old existing technology is replaced by new.' The analysis he pursues to arrive at this key point encapsulates and reformulates a

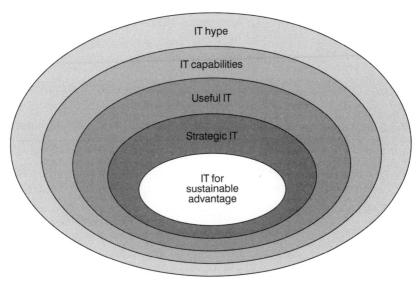

Figure 3.2 Five IT domains

combination of the planning and prioritization approaches already discussed.

Developing David Feeny's work, we suggest that five IT domains exist, and by referring to each domain executives can assess their organizational goals for IT. Figure 3.2 represents the five domains.

(1) **IT hype.** This domain goes beyond the actuality toward a focus on potential capabilities and outcomes. The information highway, predicted to transform the existence of every individual, is a good example of where the IT rhetoric goes beyond what actually can be provided reliably.

(2) **IT capability.** Within IT hype lies the every-increasing domain of IT capability, comprising products and services available today for organizations to exploit. Within this domain, the counterpart to the information highway is the Internet: it does exist and is used by organizations. Clearly,

other technology strands are more mature than the Internet; the sum total of this domain represents a vast tool-kit of technology.

(3) **Useful IT**. No organization uses everything available in the IT capability tool-kit; consequently, this domain consists of all the investments that provide at least a minimum acceptable rate of return to the organization.

(4) **Strategic IT**. This domain comprises the subset of potential investments which can make a substantial rather than marginal contribution to organizational achievement.

(5) **IT for sustainable competitive advantage**. Scale (gaining a dominant market position in a broad or a niche market), brand and business alliances are significant factors for high-profile Internet exponents such as Dell, Amazon and Cisco Systems, Yahoo and AOL. However, sustainable advantage also comes from generic lead time, and more importantly building asymmetry and pre-emption barriers.

These IT domains allow the further examination of organizational goals for IT. Feeny defines organizational exploitation of IT to be successful navigation through the domains, such that organizational resources become consistently focused on 'strategic IT' rather than merely on 'useful IT'. Consequently, the next issue to be addressed is the manner in which an organization navigates through the domains. Feeny outlines the following three approaches.

(1) In an **IT-led** approach, senior management look to the IT function to assess professionally the domains and to propose an agenda for IT investment. Most organizations have operated in this manner at some point in the lifetime of technology. The difficulty with this approach lies in the inherent lack of application purpose for IT. In other words, technology's application is defined at the point of use, not at

the point of manufacture. Consequently, the relevance of technology is a function of the user's imagination, not that of the product designer. The desire on behalf of the IT professionals to learn and understand new technology, and to attempt to apply it in a useful manner for the organization, results in 'IT capability' or at best 'useful IT' rather than 'strategic IT'.

(2) In a **user-led** approach, the natural response to the lack of application purpose is for the users to develop and argue the investment cases for technology usage. Unfortunately, this approach also commonly results in merely 'useful IT' for a number of reasons. Firstly, only a number of users take up the challenge, and who that do tend to be IT enthusiasts (and so subject to the same issues as the IT professionals in making recommendations). Secondly, the users are operating within a bounded domain of responsibility. Consequently, their proposals may represent potential improvements to non-critical portions of the business.

(3) The **business-led** approach is represented by Figure 3.3[11]. The navigation process is reversed from outside in to inside out. The business-led approach works on the assumption that anything is possible, envisions the ideal business initiative, then checks to see if the necessary IT is available. The second aspect of this business-led approach is that the IT investment evaluation flows naturally from the navigation process. Most organizations still operate investment appraisal processes that demand cost benefit analyses of the proposed IT expenditure. The business-led approach requires that the adoption of new business ideas (rather than the IT expenditure) leads to business benefits and consequently to 'strategic IT', as a step towards 'IT for sustainable competitive advantage'.

Feeny's approach provides a categorization of IT in the form of domains, a target domain for effective IT expenditure and a

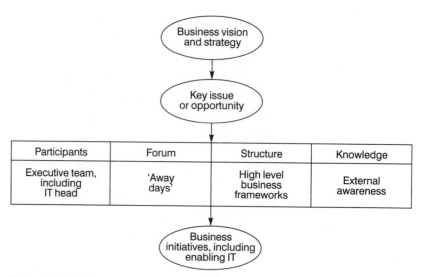

Figure 3.3 The business-led approach (source: Feeny, 2000)

navigational tool through the domains. The usefulness of the approach derives from its prescriptive direction.

3.7 Feasibility assessment

Whether or not organizations pursue risk assessment and project prioritization, most are pursuing some forms of feasibility assessment. Feasibility assessment is best defined as 'evaluating the financial and non-financial acceptability of a project against defined organizational requirements, and assessing the priorities between proposed projects. Acceptability may be in terms of cost, benefit, value, socio-technical considerations . . .'[12].

Of course, feasibility assessment is only one step in the process of directing attention to IT spend as investment. The following will examine a number of significant feasibility assessment approaches found in the organizations. The approaches will be described together with an investigation of their benefits and limitations.

Return on investment

Return on investment was the feasibility evaluation tool most often mentioned, and is also known as the 'accounting rate of return'. It depends on the ability to evaluate the money to be spent on the IT investment, and the quantification, in monetary terms, of a return associated with that investment. In other words, simple return on investment is the ratio of average annual net income of a project divided by the internal investment in the project. A refined version of return on investment is the evaluation of current value of estimated future cash flows on the assumption that future benefits are subject to some discount factor. The internal investment should include both implementation costs and operating costs. To apply return on investment to the feasibility investment, one would compare a rate of return against an established 'hurdle' rate to decide whether to proceed with a project. Although the technique permits decision-makers to compare estimated returns on alternative investments, it suffers from a number of weaknesses:

(1) unfortunately, the financial figures resulting from this sort of analysis are just that: financial in nature and accommodating only hard costs;

(2) 'good' investment possibilities may be withheld because benefits are difficult to assess in attributable cash flow terms;

(3) consequently, a project analysed under this approach may not provide a favourable return on investment and fail to be approved, even though other intangible benefits, such as increased competitive advantage, may be apparent.

Cost benefit analysis

An example of cost benefit analysis is as follows.

- In the late 1990s, the IT investment decisions of the Royal & SunAlliance UK Life and Pensions involved the right people with the right experience. All potential investments were reviewed by the Life Board Finance Committee. Each potential investment required an IT sponsor who needed to make a case for IT expenditure based on cost benefit analysis accompanied by a business rationale. Standard criteria included payback in two years and a fit with the strategic plan. For infrastructure investments, the organization asked the question: 'What will happen if we don't do it?'

A sound cost benefit analysis includes the use of discounted cash flow to account for the time value of money, the use of life cost analysis to identify and include the spectrum of relevant costs at each stage of the lifecycle, the use of net present value to aggregate benefits and costs over time, and the use of corporate opportunity cost of capital as the appropriate discount rate in discounted cash flow calculations. By way of explaining the process of cost benefit analysis, consider the following five steps.

(1) Define the scope of the project – all costs and benefits should be evaluated. In practical terms, this is not always possible and it is important that any assumptions and limitations are clearly defined and agreed up front.

(2) Evaluate costs and benefits – while direct costs are usually relatively straightforward to quantify, benefits and indirect costs are often problematic. Potential benefits can be identified by using a checklist and sometimes can be estimated only crudely.

(3) Define the life of the project – this definition is required because the further into the future the cost/benefit analysis reaches, the more uncertain predictions will become.

Furthermore, benefits will continue to accrue over the life of the project, so that the longer it continues, the more likely a favourable return on investment will appear. A risk in this definition is the failure to account for on-going, post-implementation costs such as those for maintenance.

(4) Discount the values – most cost benefit analyses attempt to take into account the time value of money by discounting anticipated income and expenditure. The corporate opportunity cost of capital has been widely considered to be an acceptable approach.

(5) Conduct sensitivity analysis – examine the consequences of possible over- and under-estimates in costs, benefits and discounting rates.

Cost benefit analysis is widely used. It is important to caution, however, that while benefits are considered in the assessment, the benefits identified tend to be traditional in nature and avoid some of the softer benefits associated with new technology.

Critical success factors

An example of the use of critical success factors is as follows.

– A major multinational retailer regularly uses critical success factors in its quarterly evaluation of IT performance. The Senior Manager of IT Services, explains:

> We have what we call our critical success factors, performance measures of the organization. We monitor those on a quarterly meeting of our senior management team with the Managing Director. We discuss the results, formulate actions plans. What you've got is a planning process where we have a business plan for the year which includes our objectives, our strategies for improvement and our performance measures. We then regularly review those and adapt the plans. So you get

the effect of achieving your objectives at what you set out at, and you get performance improvements year on year. And that's what we use as a process.

The use of critical success factors is a well-known 'strategic' approach to evaluating information systems. Executives express their opinions as to which factors are critical to the success of the business, then rank those factors according to significance. Following this exercise, the organization and the executives can use these critical success factors to evaluate the role that IT in general, or a specific application, can play in supporting the executive in the pursuit of critical issues. The method is significant in light of its focus on those issues deemed important by the respondents; in other words, those issues which will be revisited if trade-offs in IT decisions are required.

Return on management

Return on management, developed by Strassmann[13], is a measure of performance based on the added value to an organization provided by management. Strassmann assumes that, in the modern organization, information costs *are* the costs of managing the enterprise. In this sense, information costs are equated with management. If return on management is calculated before and then after IT is applied to an organization, then the IT contribution to the business (so difficult to measure using more traditional measures) can be assessed. Return on management is calculated in several stages:

(1) total value added is established from the organization's financial results as the difference between net revenues and payments to external suppliers;

(2) contribution of capital is then separate from that of labour;

(3) operating costs are then deducted from labour value added to leave 'management value added'; and

(4) finally, ROM is calculated as the management value added divided by the costs of management.

While return on management presents an interesting perspective on the softer costs associated with IT, one must question the validity of the underlying assumption that 'information costs are management costs'. Moreover, the before and after approach may indicate that this method is better suited to the evaluation of existing systems than initial feasibility assessment.

Net present value

An example of the use of net present value is as follows.

– A large UK-based retailer we researched used net present value to evaluate IT investments. Although the organization used fundamentally financial measures of investments, including net present value, it was beginning to understand that hard financials were not the only effective measure of a sound IT investment. The Corporate Financial Director explained:

> What we will do for each project is record the P&L [profit and loss] impact of the current year, the P&L impact of the next year, the cash flow impact of the current year, the level of capital expenditure, net present value, IRR [internal rate of return], payback ... it's actually a combination of them all ... everything is (evaluated) on a 5-year basis and we use cost of capital of 13.25. That's the consistent (investment evaluation process) across all projects. What we tend to find with IT projects is that they may not produce a positive net present value. So that, on cost of capital, they may actually look as though they are losing us money. And what I'm trying to get people to do more and more is to recognize that some projects are enablers and not every project you do is going to pay back. So just recognize that some of it is invested in the infrastructure of the business.

Net present value can be considered to be an effective approach to investment appraisal in so far as it allows for benefits to accrue slowly and provides a clear structure which can help in overcoming the political and hyped claims sometimes attached to IT projects. On the other hand, a number of problems arise with the use of net present value. In the first place, its use does not encourage the consideration of project alternatives, instead it tends to encourage the concept that the alternative under consideration is the 'right' way. Additionally, net present value is complicated by the need to select an appropriate discount rate. Finance theory indicates that the cost of capital adjusted for risk is the appropriate discount factor, but an adjustment to accommodate risk is very subjective in nature.

Net present value can be adapted in the following three ways to circumvent the problem with intangible benefits:

(1) alternative estimates of intangible benefits (i.e. associating a tangible cost) can be entered into the net present value model to explore the project's sensitivity to the delivery of intangibles;

(2) expected values can be used in the net present value model – expected values are obtained by multiplying the probability of an intangible benefit by its estimated value; or

(3) net present value can be calculated only for cash flows of the tangible benefits and costs – if it is positive, accept the project; if it is negative, calculate the values required from the intangible benefits to bring it to zero, then assess the probability of achieving these values for intangibles.

Information economics

The Parker et al.[14] information economics model for linking business performance to IT is primarily an investment feasibility model. In this model, demonstrated in Figure 3.4, 'value' is

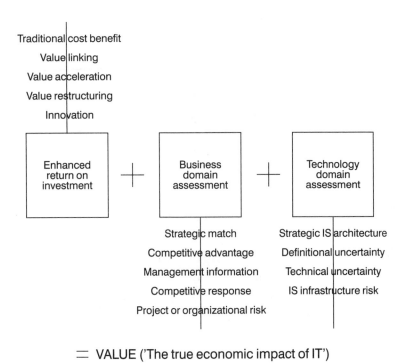

Traditional cost benefit
Value linking
Value acceleration
Value restructuring
Innovation

Enhanced return on investment

Business domain assessment

Technology domain assessment

Strategic match
Competitive advantage
Management information
Competitive response
Project or organizational risk

Strategic IS architecture
Definitional uncertainty
Technical uncertainty
IS infrastructure risk

= VALUE ('The true economic impact of IT')

Figure 3.4

identified by the combination of an enhanced return on assessment analysis, a business domain assessment and a technology domain assessment. The components of these various assessments are touched upon as follows.

> value = enhanced return on investment
> + business domain assessment
> + technology domain assessment

Enhanced return on investment includes:

– value linking – assesses IT costs which create additional benefits to other departments through ripple or knock-on effects;

- value acceleration – assesses additional benefits in the form of reduced timescales for operations;

- value restructuring – used to measure the benefit of restructuring jobs, a department, or personnel usage as a result of IT introduction, and is particularly helpful when the relationship to performance is obscure or not established as in R&D departments and personnel departments; and

- innovation value – considers the value of gaining and sustaining competitive advantage, whilst calculating the risks or cost of being a pioneer and of the project failing.

Business domain assessment comprises staff and business units that utilize IT. Value is based on improved business performance. Thus, the concept of value has to be expanded within the business domain:

- strategic match – assessing the degree to which the proposed project corresponds to established corporate goals;

- competitive advantage – assessing the degree to which the proposed project provides an advantage in the marketplace;

- management information support – assessing the contribution towards management information requirements on core activities;

- competitive response – assessing the degree of corporate risk associated with not undertaking the project; and

- project or organizational risk – assessing the degree of risk based on project variables such as project size, project complexity and degree of organizational structure.

Technology domain assessment reviews the technological risks associated with undertaking a project:

- strategic IS architecture – measuring the degree to which the proposed project fits into the overall information systems direction;

- IS infrastructure risk – measures the degree to which the entire IS organization needs and is prepared to support the project;

- definitional uncertainty – assesses the degree to which the requirements/specifications of the project are known; and

- technical uncertainty – evaluates a project's dependence on new or untried technologies.

The model dictates a number of components in the analysis of an investment decision. The combination of the enhanced return on investment, business domain assessment and technology domain assessment provides a comprehensive look at the IT investment across business needs and technological abilities. It is manifestly a model capturing some necessary complexity, and factors commonly neglected. Consequently, however, it can be difficult to implement. The learning point from two respondent organizations – a retailer and an insurance company – which have utilized information economics is that its primary purpose should be to encourage debate across the managerial layers and functions and provide heightened understanding of the risks, costs and benefits associated with different IT investments. In this respect, building any scoring system around the framework works, as long as the process of evaluation is regarded as more important than its quantified result which necessarily is a mix of subjective judgements.

Balanced scorecards

The balanced business scorecard (examined in greater detail in Chapter 5) provides a well-rounded approach to evaluation by taking into account not only financial measures but also measures related to customer satisfaction, internal organizational processes, and organizational learning and growth. For now, let it suffice to say that the use of the comprehensive set of scorecard measures applied to investment feasibility could identify otherwise ignored costs and benefits. GenBank, for example, found the scorecard useful to the initial feasibility assessment process as a reminder of the types of costs and benefits that should be considered (see Chapter 5 for the detailed case study).

3.8 Benefits management: feasibility stage

Benefit management should be pursued across the life of any IT/e-business project. It is in the feasibility stage, however, that benefits are initially identified, making feasibility crucial to the success of the entire project and application portfolio. Benefit identification and quantification are, based on the findings of our research, two very difficult tasks at the heart of the evaluation dilemma. More specifically, it is probably the range of 'intangible benefits' that complicate all discussions of benefits. Intangibles include improved customer service, development of systems architecture, high job satisfaction, higher product quality, improved external/internal communications and management information, gaining competitive advantage, cost avoidance, avoiding competitive disadvantage and improved supplier relationships. Although the literature is rich with benefit measurement/identification concepts, we will focus here on two benefit management approaches that have proved particularly useful and that translate easily into the e-enabled world.

The benefits management process: Ward and Griffiths (1996)

Earlier in this chapter, Ward and Griffiths' application portfolio classification was identified: support systems, key operational

Strategic	High potential
Business innovation and change Business process restructuring	(R&D projects)
Business effectiveness Process rationalization and integration	Business efficiency Process elimination and cost reduction
Key operational	Support

Figure 3.5 Generic sources of benefit for different IT applications

systems, strategic systems and high potential systems. This classification system can be used not only to examine the application portfolio, but also to identify the classes of benefits that might be available. Figure 3.5 provides a summary.

Ward and Griffiths reiterate what we have confirmed so far, namely that 'there is no point in any sophisticated system of investment evaluation and priority setting unless the "system" is examined in terms of whether or not it delivers the business improvements required'[15]. The matrix shown in Figure 3.5 provides a rough idea of the types of benefits that might be identified and quantified. Effectively, an organization should quantify benefits as much as possible at the outset then, over the life of the project, continue to measure the project's ability to deliver those benefits. Ward and Griffiths suggest five interactive stages in benefits management. This is represented by Figure 3.6.

The stages pertinent to planning and prioritization and investment evaluation are as follows.

(1) **Identification and structuring of benefits**. This is the first stage of assessing the reasons for embarking on application development. The process of identifying target benefits

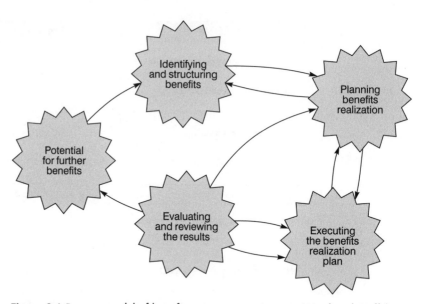

Figure 3.6 Process model of benefits management (source: Ward and Griffiths, 1996)

should be an iterative one, based on on-going discussions about system objectives and the business performance improvements to be delivered by the system. Each identified benefit should be expressed in terms that can be measured, even if the measures are subjective ones such as surveys of opinion.

(2) **Planning benefits realization**. This is the process of understanding the organizational factors that will affect the organization's ability to achieve the benefits. It is basically a process of obtaining ownership and buy-in from the appropriate parties. If an organization cannot create a plan for a particular benefit, the benefit should be dropped.

The other benefits management stages (executing the benefits realization plan, evaluating and reviewing the results, and identifying the potential for further benefits) will be examined in Chapter 4. While Ward and Griffiths' benefit management approach obviously crosses the line of feasibility investment into project management and post-implementation assessment, it is important to note it here along with feasibility assessment because, as mentioned, the initial identification and quantification of benefits is critical to success.

Benefits management examples

While these frameworks seem theoretical, all have been utilized to advantage in operating organizations in both the private and public sectors. Case study organizations revealed a variety of approaches to, and understanding of, benefits management. The potential usefulness of the frameworks can be read into the following scenarios.

– A large-scale UK-based retail organization was struggling to institute benefits comprehension throughout its organization. After following a mainly financial focus in evaluation for many years, the company attempted to refocus business performance measurement as it relates to IT. During feasibility assessment, the IT organization was attempting to classify benefits in a more standard manner, and to instill an understanding of benefits across the organization. In the late 1990s it identified four benefit categories: hard costs, enablers, migration ('have to's') and intangibles/non-financials. The IT group established a Systems Investment Group in a fresh attempt to provide emphasis on the investment evaluation process. This group of cross-functional senior managers was made responsible for understanding IT costs, identifying business needs and their link to the business strategy, and selecting the appropriate investments to satisfy those needs. This group was to be a conduit for benefits comprehension for IT investments within the organization.

– In recent years, Sainsbury PLC's attention to the planning and IT investment assessment process has been marked by the attitude that IT is an investment rather than a cost. Sainsbury, the second largest food retailer in the UK, has discovered the difficulty associated with identifying and measuring benefits related to the implementation and use of technology. As a senior manager noted:

> That's a big profit return, but you'll never measure it . . . For the 20 years up to about 1995 Sainsbury's had a fantastically successful formula that was highly repeatable. So the business plan was to repeat it as often as you could and profits grew by 20% compound per year for 20 years. And it was a fantastically successful business. What then happened was the opportunities to replicate that reduced and the competition caught up with what we were doing. And suddenly the businesses had to have a business plan of a more detailed nature to become a business plan that's truly trying to deal with the competitive edges rather than the competitive body. So we've not been in this position before. We are now, and it will be interesting to see how, as people go through this planning process, they make it happen in their processes . . . (and operations).

– In the late 1990s, Unipart, one of Europe's largest independent automotive parts companies, was using cash flow, payback, 'real benefits' in investment evaluation. Project proposals passed through UGC/IT then GEC, basically a group operating committee. The IT department had also developed a new measure of 'proportion of customer IT spend used on strategic spend' to drive good behaviour. According to Peter Ryding, Managing Director of Unipart Information Technology:

> For a business application, we use cash flow and payback (for investment evaluation) . . . virtually all IT project investments have to be signed off by customers signing on to a real business benefit that it obtained.

Ultimately payback is the word we tend to use more than anything else. Sometimes we go through where the financials don't add up, but we believe it's customer service and as a very customer service oriented business we are prepared to take the hit on that.

3.9 Summary

Risk assessment, planning and prioritization, feasibility evaluation and benefits management are key components of the lifecycle evaluation methodology, and, in fact, should be considered/revisited in all phases of that lifecycle. Feasibility evaluation is practised in some form by most organizations, although the evaluation emphasis tends to be financial in nature. The concept of benefits management, that of reviewing the delivery of benefits from an IT investment on an on-going basis, is a relatively new addition to the mix and, when applied effectively, provides a path through the financial bias of feasibility evaluation. Risk assessment, on the other hand, is often overlooked in the evaluation process, in spite of the overwhelming evidence that all IT investments have some level of associated risk that requires assessment and management.

Each of these evaluation components (risk assessment, planning and prioritization, feasibility evaluation and benefits management) have a number of techniques or approaches – no one technique in any category will satisfy all situations faced by an organization undertaking an IT investment. Consequently, care must be taken to match the technique best-suited to delivering the business objectives of a particular investment. In other words, potential investments should be reviewed in light of agreed organizational strategy. Moreover, at some point, investments should be reviewed collectively to identify synergies or discontinuities. As we saw in the case of Glaxo Wellcome, its piecemeal review of projects precluded a strategic view of the portfolio as well as obscuring its ability to control costs.

3.10 Key learning points

- The examination of failed projects presented in this chapter demonstrates the critical need to assess and manage risk. Chapter 4 details how measurement can assist in the process of keeping IT investments on track across the development, implementation and on-going phases of the system lifecycle.

- Risk assessment should take place on all projects/technology investments, as all will have some degree of associated risk. Risk assessment should ultimately provide part of the foundation for project management and measurement.

- Risk assessment requires the identification of risks, the estimation of impact of the risk and the on-going management of the risk.

- Risk identification, the process of proactively seeking out risks and their sources, and risk estimation must be the prelude to risk management. Risk identification can only diagnose and highlight risks, but this activity must lead to a risk management system which ensures that action is taken to mitigate those risks across the system's lifecycle.

- Risk management plans require resources. Resourcing will depend upon decisions about the trade-offs between how much risk aversion is required and how much risk can be accepted. Responsibility for risk aversion actions and the authority to take action are also determined in the resourcing phase.

- Models of risk assessment and diagnosis reveal a number of significant project variables to be managed from the perspective of risk mitigation, including:

  (1) the need for user involvement;

  (2) the level of commitment from management and key staff;

(3) a need for flexibility;

(4) on-going assessment of IT project alignment with strategy;

(5) a need to impose time constraints;

(6) attention to project size;

(7) the need for scope control;

(8) the inclusion of contingency planning; and

(9) the need for a feedback process from the measurement loop.

- Integrated project planning provides the focus for IT usage.

- With regards to planning and prioritization, the investment characteristics of IT highlight three factors to be included in the prioritization process:

(1) what is most important to do for the organization (benefits);

(2) what realistically can be accomplished (resources); and

(3) what is likely to succeed (risks).

In all likelihood, the constraint on IT investment will be available resources. Attention to this constraint will contribute to the concept of value maximization.

- The conduct of IT planning and investment feasibility is greatly influenced by management style and organizational culture. It is important to diagnose these with a view to assessing their appropriateness in terms of likelihood of supporting suitable IT evaluation methods.

- Users should participate in the feasibility assessment in order to assist in the identification of the benefits to the business of various alternatives, and to prevent the pursuit of technology merely for the sake of technology.

- Feasibility assessment should be carried out within the framework of lifecycle evaluation and is, in fact, a basis for on-going evaluation.

- In spite of the difficulty in identifying and quantifying intangible business benefits, they must be examined as well as those that are tangible.

- Benefit identification methods should be matched to the objectives of the specific IT application. Inappropriate methods often overlook vital benefits.

3.11 Practical action guidelines

- View IT expenditures as investments.

- Proactively seek out risks and their sources, then manage those risks throughout the life of the investment.

- Aim to maximize the value delivered out of an IT investment from the resources available.

- Engage in strategic alignment between IT investments and business objectives.

- Prioritize resulting IT investments, also according to objectives.

- Include total IT costs in the budgeting process, including hardware, software, corporate support, data access, training and user costs.

- Match feasibility assessment and lifecycle evaluation techniques to prospective benefit types.

- Integrate the evaluation process across IT lifetime.

- Establish metrics at the strategic level, the business process/ operations level, and the customer perspective level.

- Engage in organizational learning and establish metrics which enhance the pursuit of this capability.

4 Project management and post-implementation evaluation

4.1 Introduction

The business case should be an enduring theme throughout the project. Reviewing it regularly is a way to keep the project on track. It also helps you to deal with proposed changes in the requirements. It provides a basis for balancing the business benefit of a change against the cost of making it, and the opportunity cost of whatever you may have to leave out to make way for it.

Max Dobres, Cambridge Technology Partners

Business does not stay static and neither does technology . . . so if you are going to use technology to change the way people do business, then you need some kind of model to give you flexibility to match dynamic business problems with dynamic technology solutions.

Carlos Zamarippa,
California Franchise Tax Board CAPS Project Manager

The lifecycle evaluation model introduced in Chapter 2 suggests that successful attainment of technology investment benefits

requires on-going evaluation across the lifecycle of the investment. This chapter provides recommended evaluation approaches for the next steps in the IT project's lifecycle: project
management (including the development and implementation
phases in traditional lifecycle methodology) and post-implementation. Section 4.2 'Development and project management',
reviews several overall approaches to project management, then
extract and examine the related measures against a backdrop of
the project risk variables identified in Chapter 3. The post-
implementation evaluation frameworks examined include
benchmarking, service level agreements and benefits management. The chapter concludes with an indepth case study which
outlines benefits funding and a lifecycle approach to
measurement.

4.2 Development and project management

The following cases represent a wide variety of approaches to IT
evaluation during the process of a project. Section 4.3 then
identifies formalized approaches to evaluation during the
project management process.

– In 1997, Jonathan Fornaci, Genstar's new CIO, introduced a
  broad-scale conversion of existing systems to the Internet. All
  design was 'JAD/RAD' based, meaning joint application
  design (between users and technologists) proceeded according to rapid application delivery. Users were brought in at key
  points during the design and development process in order to
  ensure on-going cohesiveness with specifications and business needs. The project was rolled out in nine months. By
  2001, the target for project delivery in Genstar and many other
  leading organizations was down to five months or less.

– In a major insurance company IT requires that all projects
  have a sponsor to control and ensure success. The timescale of

each project is fixed, but the functionality to be delivered is flexible within that timescale. Project management reporting has been introduced on an on-going basis; monthly reporting occurs at management level to monitor projects and particularly to review benefits management. The reporting process includes information about milestones, project issues and key performance indicators. It is hoped that this monthly reporting process, which spans all projects underway, will force management to look at the entire portfolio of projects in order to optimize resource utilization. In addition, the company hopes to gain insight to additional project opportunities, unforeseen at the outset, by continual project monitoring.

– In a major manufacturing company, each IT project had a development manager as well as a project sponsor from the user area. Regardless of this user accountability which had been in place for a number of years, delivery was considered a challenge: the users reinforced a corporate culture of 'we don't get what we want'. After struggling with this user/IT gap, the company instituted a 'trial pilot rollout' step in their major development and delivery processes. After user acceptance but prior to 'go live', the company introduced the system into a pilot phase which was geared to test the implementation process, but *not* to do additional system testing. The pilot reviewed both the implementation rollout process and the training to ensure that it addressed user needs.

4.3 Need for design, development and implementation measurement

Once an IT/e-business project has been approved, many organizations fail to pursue any on-going measurement of the predicted benefits/goals as the project progresses through development and implementation. Primary reasons for this omission include:

(1) lack of appropriate organizational resources to pursue project measurement practices;

(2) a focused concern for the end product to the exclusion of the development productivity, on behalf of the users; and/or

(3) lack of appropriate measurement tools.

In addition, in some cases, the design process was perceived as hopelessly complicated by users (who did not know, or kept changing, what they wanted) and technologists (who did not understand the users' needs – further diminishing the likelihood of effective measurement). Our research for this book indicates that only 67% of organizations practise on-going project management evaluation, and, of those, even fewer than two-thirds use the evaluation process to determine if a given project is still a worthwhile undertaking. Moreover, those same organizations identified the following significant problems with the evaluation process:

– changes in scope over the life of a project created obstacles to the determination of whether the project was satisfying user needs;

– the evaluation process suffered from a lack of buy-in on behalf of both management and the users; it was seen as an additional cost and a delay in delivery;

– the knowledge base to conduct an effective evaluation did not exist and/or was required for services elsewhere; and

– benefits were difficult to define (even if they had been tacitly identified in the feasibility evaluation).

An alternative, more positive perspective is that measurement during design, development and implementation potentially adds a significant and useful layer of management to the entire project process. Depending on the measurement approach selected, an IT organization and its clients can:

– identify significant project risks and plan for containment;

– ensure that an on-going project continues to meet organizational strategic needs or is modified in order to meet such needs; and

– identify previously unknown opportunities arising from the current project in order to harness more effectively the technology for business use.

4.4 Project development, management and implementation methodologies

In order to provide a basis for IT assessment, several popular project management and development methodologies will be reviewed and assessed according to the project risk variables introduced in Chapter 3. These project risk variables can all be considered specific dimensions of risk to be taken into account in the evaluation of a project. As a reminder, these variables include:

– user involvement;

– commitment on behalf of management, key staff and users;

– flexibility;

– strategic alignment;

– time constraints;

– project size;

– scope control;

– contingency planning; and

– measurement process feedback.

The methodologies assessed here are not measurement pro-grammes themselves. Instead, they are approaches to the development cycle that can provide realistic frameworks for on-going measurement. Additionally, as will be noted, each of these methodologies may be more appropriate to particular types of applications across the varied IT portfolio.

Traditional lifecycle development methodologies

The method

What are termed 'traditional lifecycle development' method-ologies are the family of methodologies covering six standard phases in a project, namely:

(1) functional specification – the 'business' description of the application-to-be; usually co-authored by the users and the IT staff;

(2) technical design – the technical description of the business function (it is at this stage that the number of program modules required are identified and 'pseudocode' is created by module); generated by IT staff;

(3) development – computer programming of application mod-ules (sometimes includes individual program test); gen-erated by IT staff;

(4) systems' testing – testing of completed application modules independently and in series; conducted by IT staff;

(5) acceptance testing – functional testing of application; con-ducted by the user staff (who have mysteriously dis-appeared since the functional specification phase); and

(6) implementation – delivery of the application into produc-tion; generally the responsibility of IT staff with some involvement on behalf of the users.

This methodological approach to application development and delivery worked adequately with previous generations of code. Popular theory says that the lion's share of project time should be spent on the first two phases (functional specification and technical design) in order to minimize problems on the back end. Note that this 'theory' was dependent on the concept that functional specifications could be set in stone at some point in time, never to be modified again. However, new technology and the arrival of e-business, as well as advances in human and organizational factors, have highlighted a number of problems with the concept of 'frozen' specifications specifically and with the development cycle in general. Traditional development methodologies are most appropriately applied to key operational systems and support systems because such systems are usually replacements for a manual process and, thus, are simpler to implement and more straightforward than strategic IT undertakings. In such automation/operationalization, functional specifications have more of a chance of being considered 'finalized' at some stage in the process without requiring on-going scope modification.

Appropriate measures

The on-going measures used during a project following a traditional lifecycle development methodology include relatively simple 'hard' measures, such as:

- percent completed relative to total project time;

- budget spent versus available funds;

- function points;

- design match to specification (this can occur during the design phase as well as during acceptance testing); and

- system test results compared to design specification.

To be more specific, the typical project management metrics would include a resource plan comprising both timescales and human resources, an explanation of the critical path tasks and major milestones, and task allocations. This type of project plan would be used to monitor the phases of the project and the adherence to budget and schedule.

As a result of the organizational arrangements in a traditional lifecycle approach to development, specifically a notable separation between the IT staff and the users, applicable measures seem to take place in somewhat of a vacuum. The measurement processes do not provide much of an opportunity for users and IT staff to engage in on-going conversations that might otherwise improve the quality of the application. Moreover, these rather simple measures do not provide a platform for any type of benefits management.

Assessment

With regard to the project risk variables, a number of weaknesses need to be highlighted in traditional development methodologies. First and foremost, *user involvement* in the process is limited and not necessarily cooperative. Later methodologies will highlight a more extensive give-and-take process. In much the same way that user involvement is limited, so is *flexibility*. In the case of these methodologies, following the plan is almost more important than a continual focus on best value for money spent. *Risk assessment, strategic alignment* and *measurement process feedback* are almost non-existent. On the other hand, given the stated desire to freeze functional specifications, *scope control* was at least a desired goal. *Commitment* from key IT staff probably exists, but traditional methodologies did not specify a user sponsor, unlike more recent approaches considered below.

Development benchmarking

The methods

A number of firms offer benchmarking services for data centre operations. More recently, the same types of firms (e.g. Compass) have begun to offer benchmarking services on project development. In the late 1990s, Safeway PLC (UK) began benchmarking on-going projects for productivity, quality and efficiency in order to provide timely feedback into the project process. As of 2001, however, not much in the way of concrete results exists from project benchmarking. Moreover, benchmarking may not be effective for measuring systems' development. The process of development benchmarking consists of collecting project-related data such as staffing consumed, time elapsed, number of programs in what stages, budget spent and program defects identified and repaired. This data is then used to make a number of comparisons among data categories collected. Assuming that an external agent is performing the benchmarking, this data would then be compared to similar data from other organizations and a relative performance indicator created. If conducted internally, performance would need to be compared against previous organizational experience that had been codified into suitable benchmarks.

The measures

Development benchmarks provide feedback on quality, productivity and efficiency. The specific types of measurements calculated in respondent organizations included errors per lines of code as a quality measure, and/or function points or lines of code produced per person per time increment as a measure of productivity. Our research reflects some limitations with these measures.

Assessment

Benchmarking provides inherently relative measures – it provides the organization with feedback about its position relative to some other set of organizations. Given that aspect, benchmarking cannot possibly provide any feedback on strategic alignment or risk assessment. Depending on the nature of the measures calculated, however, some relative data about *time constraints*, *project size*, *management and staff commitment* and *measurement process feedback* may be available.

A number of sources express concern about the usefulness of development benchmarking. In 1996 a Wentworth report on assessing IS performance noted (at p. 6) that:

> IS directors' satisfaction with development benchmarking services is notably worse than their satisfaction with operations benchmarking. One reason is that development productivity is often less important to users than fitness for purpose and speed of delivery.

More recently, the Head of IT Planning and Performance at a major bank commented: 'Benchmarking the development side is inherently more difficult (than benchmarking a data centre) and leads to far more debate than gives true comparison.' Likewise, the IT Managing Director of a large British manufacturer/ distributor said:

> We are currently undergoing an application development benchmarking exercise. I'm not convinced that it's really going to move the needle in our understanding of what we should be doing differently.

Managers additionally complained that the time required to collect benchmarking data, along with the historical rather than future-looking nature of the benchmarking data, diminishes its usefulness.

Prototyping

The method

Prototyping is an approach to development whereby a 'quick and dirty solution' is developed on a very small scale then implemented on the same scale to evaluate benefits, usefulness and user/customer response. Prototyping can be explained in terms of the 'time box' philosophy used by Ford from the mid-1990s into its Internet projects. Projects pursued under the time box approach have the following attributes:

- fixed time period – an end date that cannot slip;

- 60–120 days in development and review;

- system definition;

- mixed team of users and IT staff; and

- user reviews of implementation.

Safeway PLC, the retailer, has used prototyping for a number of its newer systems into 2001. The additional benefit of prototyping is the possibility of identifying additional, unforeseen opportunities when the prototype is reviewed, thus allowing the organization to finetune the product before larger scale rollout. The recently merged Norwich Union, although not pursuing a prototyping approach per se, has gone about adopting a culture which specifies very short project times in order to keep up with the changing insurance marketplace. Prototyping is an appropriate approach to 'high-potential' projects for which benefits are either not identified or only outlined.

The measures

Measurement at a high level in prototyping could be as simple as reviewing the project against the 'time box'. Was the targeted end date met? Did the users find the prototype useful? Is the prototype the basis for a more structured system definition?

More pertinent to the focus of value, however, the 'measurements' evolving from a prototype would involve the types and degrees of benefits identified as a result of the prototype's implementation and use. The concept of prototyping suggests that a number of individuals will be involved in the somewhat informal evaluation process: the developers of the prototype, the internal users and perhaps the customer base will contribute to the review of the prototype results. Safeway has used prototyping on a number of undertakings.

– Safeway has accomplished much of its new project identification and delivery via prototyping in the 1997–2001 period. Mike Winch, former IT Director, used strong relationships within the business, built over a long period of time, to convince the organization to pursue various 'technological' opportunities envisioned by the IT department not just by the business. His selling approach was a small-scale prototype to be reviewed for benefits and unforeseen opportunities. The prototype review requires a go/no-go decision to pursue the project on a broader scale. Main success criteria relate to the organization's number 1 issue: delivery of customer service.

Once a project is a 'go', Safeway follows a reasonably prescribed project management method. From 1998 the organization also implemented development benchmarking, using CSC Index as the service. This involved collecting uniform data from on-going projects with the intention of benchmarking development productivity, project quality and efficiency. This provided feedback during the project process in order to help managers run projects more effectively and for managers to receive some feedback on their management skills.

Assessment

In terms of project risk variables, prototyping effectively addresses *user involvement, flexibility, time constraints, project size containment, scope control* and *measurement process feedback*. Additionally, since the small initial implementation dictated by prototyping proves results quickly, it can be postulated that *key management and user commitment* can probably be attained. What is unclear is whether prototyping can engender *strategic alignment* and *contingency planning*.

Benefits funding

The method

The final project management/methodology to be reviewed is a relatively new approach called 'benefits funding'. In its simplest form, benefits funding requires that a vendor agrees to take on the development of an application and receive payment only after benefits begin to flow from the implemented application. The client, in turn, provides a significant amount of user expertise towards identification and development of a quality solution. When implemented properly, benefits funding provides a shared risk between the vendor and the client. Obviously, this approach does not seem well suited for use by an internal IT department. Other than that, however, its benefits are many and its critical success factors include:

– a sound vendor/client relationship (or user/IT relationship);

– the commandment to 'know the business';

– the need for quantifiable results;

– executive support;

– on-going commitment from key staff;

– its validity for high-result, high-risk projects; and

– the development of a corresponding benefit measurement system.

Rather than examining benefits funding in detail in the body of this chapter, a detailed case study is provided at the end of the chapter to illustrate its benefits and methods.

4.5 Post-implementation and on-going evaluation practices

Post-implementation review can refer to a project evaluation immediately following the implementation of a project or a longer-term review of an application project. Post-implementation review here will comprise tailored post-implementation evaluations, benchmarking, service level agreements and benefits management.

Our research shows that, if applied rigorously and acted upon, post-implementation review can provide a number of beneficial results, most notably:

– an improvement of systems' development practices;

– support for decisions to adopt, modify or discard information systems;

– assistance in evaluating and training personnel responsible for systems' development;

– ensured compliance with user objectives;

– an indication of areas for improvement in effectiveness and productivity of design; and

– demonstration of the achievement of cost savings.

Our research indicates that post-implementation evaluation practices are limited, and that where post-implementation reviews have been conducted, the involvement of the user was limited at best. The reviews tended to be conducted by the IT staff, severely limiting the possibility that any severe system flaw, in a business context, would be recognized. Finally, and most significantly, the same survey results indicate that post-implementation review paid little attention to benefits management.

Given the ever-increasing customer focus of the IT industry, it would seem that post-implementation review processes should increase in their significance. The following section considers the various post-implementation methods mentioned in light of what they encompass and how they can be applied.

Benchmarking on-going IT operations

Benchmarking was mentioned above as a relatively new approach to development evaluation. Benchmarking of implemented projects, or parts of the organization such as the data centre, is more advanced in its usage and its ability to deliver valuable results. In our research, many of the case study organizations conducted some sort of post-project benchmarking, including Hewlett Packard, Sainsbury PLC, Royal & SunAlliance and Unipart.

As with the development benchmarking described earlier in the chapter, any type of post-implementation benchmarking also includes the collection of data from internal or internal and external sources, then the generation of a number of measures and a relative basis of performance against either previous organizational experience or external organization performance.

The measures

The case study organizations provide samples of the use of benchmarking in on-going operations.

- Using an external organization, Sainsbury PLC conducted a benchmarking exercise to understand how its IT organization compared to that of its competitors. The results showed that Sainsbury IT was more informal in its approach to systems' development, and, more significantly, that Sainsbury managers were less committed to delivery of benefits associated with systems. As a result, Sainsbury is pursuing mechanisms to engender best practices in the organization and to establish ownership of benefits.

- Unipart IT has been benchmarking its network and mainframe areas for some time. In spite of reasonably good reports resulting from the benchmarking exercise, one senior IT manager 'has not been convinced by the results'. His concerns ranged from the ability of a benchmarking exercise to compare apples to apples (in terms of data centre comparisons) to the customer concerns that are not addressed by benchmarking. More specifically, the mainframe benchmarking may have nothing to do with what the customer wants and how to deliver to the customer in a cost-effective way.

- Hewlett Packard's Test and Measurement Organization, headquartered in Santa Clara, California, has participated in high-level benchmarking of cost and network performance. A senior IT manager explains the advantages and disadvantages:

  What we've tended to do at the enterprise level is to work with some of the external benchmarking groups and consortia, which are usually working with infrastructure areas. So for example, benchmarking often covers some of the key attributes of the client environment, and some high-level cost/performance information. We do this on a regular basis. We also benchmark the cost and performance of our networks on a regular basis. Any of the businesses have the option of playing a part in those benchmarking activities as they see fit. So you have different businesses and IT functions around HP occasionally doing that. It's not very widespread because most really good benchmarking is very expensive; it takes a lot of tough work, effort and thought to get some value out of it. So it happens, but it is not widespread.

Assessment

While benchmarking has the ability to provide useful feedback that can assist an organization in finetuning processes, a number of issues should be considered. Firstly, as one senior IT manager responded: 'benchmarking traditionally looks backwards'. Although benchmarking still provides goals for improvement, the relative comparisons made, particularly using an external benchmarker, are based on data that could be as much as one year old. Moreover, the historical bent of benchmarking data prevents it from being of much use in the on-going management of benefits or in identifying sources of competitive advantage.

Lacity and Hirschheim[1] point out that when the IT strategy and the business strategy are misaligned, benchmarking can be used very manipulatively and politically to give a 'good report card'. Furthermore, benchmarking statistics can be misleading if they are not provided in the appropriate context. A senior manager at an international bank explained that the internal data centre operation announced a 28% increase in performance which belied the industry average performance improvement of 27% based on benchmarking analysis. In other words, the data centre's relative improvement was really a watered-down 1%, demonstrating that benchmarking can be used to misdirect, although not necessarily deliberately.

Nevertheless, benchmarking can provide some of the benefits mentioned. If used in combination with other techniques, it can provide the basis for a service focus in the IT organization (see also Chapter 9).

Service levels: agreements and measures

Service level agreements represent a managed approach to service delivery. According to service expert Jenny Dugmore[2], good service level agreements:

- provide a description of issues critical to the customer;

- are short and sweet;

- are worded in the customer's terminology;

- include only targets that can be measured against objectively; and

- define both the customer's and supplier's responsibilities.

Service level agreements were used originally to focus on specific problems and those that were limited in scope. More recently, they have been used in conjunction with other service-focused tools (e.g. customer surveys) to provide:

- improved understanding of what types of service are required by the customer(s);

- proof of service quality (concrete evidence that an IT organization is serving its customer);

- staff motivation in the form of attainable yet challenging goals (these must be clearly stated and understood by the organization as a whole);

- service reporting (a mechanism for broadcasting service delivery performance);

- a means for learning from failure to meet targets; and

- cultural changes in the organization – providing the basis for a transition to a service-oriented culture.

Some idea of the usefulness to organizations of service level reporting is conveyed by the IT Director of an insurance company:

> What we have found more success with is a series of discrete reports, customer satisfaction reports, service level reports, project reporting. Those are the things that have made a difference and had a resonance. They have had a real resonance with the managers in the jobs.

An IT organization must, if possible, lay the foundations by beginning to report service levels (e.g. mainframe availability, server availability and response time to user calls for help) before the implementation of formal service level agreements. This early adoption provides a basis for comparison and clearer results once the service level agreements are implemented. Next, the IT organization must work with the clients/users to establish the compromises that constitute effective service level agreements. Finally, piloting an agreement is a good mechanism for finetuning and offering exposure to organizational issues.

The measures

Again, the case study organizations provide examples of the use and implementation of service level agreeements.

– BP Exploration outsourced the bulk of its computing services from 1993. By 2001, service level agreements with the multiple suppliers continued to be the contractual basis for defining and agreeing upon service performance and quality targets. BP XIT appointed partner relationship managers to manage the interaction with the suppliers and to develop processes around the service level agreements enabling the outsourced suppliers to assure BPX of the appropriate quality of service. The suppliers provide monthly and quarterly reporting on the adherence to the main service levels, such as 'up time for servers > 98%' and maintaining 'error rate < 1 in 750'. In addition, the suppliers administer customer satisfaction surveys soliciting feedback on the 'service lines' they manage: e-mail services, help desk, desktop support, printing, plotting, file servers, telecom systems, video-conferencing, etc.

– GenBank has used a plethora of service level agreements for a number of years. At one stage, the IT organization was managing 57 high level agreements, which had any number of related line items. Its scorecard effort, described in Chapter 5, helped to rationalize the use of service level agreements by focusing on what the customer really wanted from the IT organization and by prioritizing the agreements.

As the GenBank case reveals, it is possible to become over-focused on the implementation of service level agreements. However, they can contribute to a service-focused organization as long as they are well thought out and measurable in terms of the service aspects with which a customer is concerned.

Benefits management

Benefits management is usually considered an investment feasibility device, despite use of the word 'management' which seems to suggest a more comprehensive process. Ward and Griffiths[3] explain that 'there is no point in any sophisticated system of investment evaluation and priority setting, unless the "system" is examined in terms of whether or not it delivers the business improvements required'. Effectively, an organization should quantify benefits as much as possible at the outset, then continue to measure the project's ability to deliver those benefits. Chapter 3 introduced the five-stage Ward and Griffiths benefits management model and covered the two stages relevant to investment feasibility. The remaining three stages are now explained as follows.

- **Executing benefits realization plan**. This phase occurs during development and involves monitoring the progress of benefits delivery against the activities and deliverables of the plan.

- **Evaluating and reviewing the results**. This phase and the following are the most applicable for post-implementation and on-going evaluation. It should take place as a formal review with the dual purposes of maximizing the benefits of a particular project and providing experience for future projects.

- **Potential for further benefits**. In the 'final' phase, the organization should identify if any unexpected benefits have been achieved. Such identification only becomes apparent after the system has been running for some time and any associated business changes have been made.

The measures

The types of benefits yielded by a project are usually a combination of hard (generally financial) and soft (intangible) benefits. An organization can focus more effectively on the appropriate benefits by considering the type of project undertaken. Strategic systems usually deliver business innovation and change benefits and/or business process restructuring. Key operational systems provide business effectiveness and process rationalization benefits. Support systems deliver business efficiency and process elimination/cost reduction. The in-depth case study in Section 4.6 demonstrates the benefits management process related to strategic systems. Additionally, the following case illustrates an alternative approach to the management of benefits.

- B&Q, the DIY Retailer, was keen to align its IT department and projects more closely to business needs. The IT and Logistics Director spent a great deal of time building effective relationships within the business in order to ensure this alignment. Even more importantly, he established account manager roles within the system's function charged with owning the relationship with each function in the business. To reinforce the alignment in project development, B&Q then implemented a new business project management process as part of which all projects have one clearly defined business sponsor, responsible for ensuring that benefits are delivered over the course of the project, and one project manager, from either business or systems.

Assessment

Given today's environment with the search for value and performance delivered by IT, it would seem that benefits management processes should provide a fundamental project objective. The following case study demonstrates how the focus on 'benefit streams' combined with a performance-based contract provided a sound, on-going measurement system and an effective partnership between client and vendor.

4.6 In-depth case study: California's Franchise Tax Board

Background: pressures for change

California's Franchise Tax Board (FTB), the state tax agency (hereafter referred to as the agency and/or FTB), processes over US$30 billion in annual tax revenues. At its most simplified level, the agency's mission is to bring in revenue for the state while providing numerous taxpayer services. Figure 4.1 provides a high-level picture of both the structure and responsibilities of the agency.

The mass of returns processed and the amount of money involved dictated a significant level of automation for the agency. However, developments within the tax agency in the

The agency	Business functions	Types of tax returns
<ul><li>an independent board</li><li>4,500 employees</li><li>17 California districts</li><li>multi-state offices in<ul><li>Houston</li><li>Chicago</li><li>New York</li><li>Long Island</li></ul></li></ul>	<ul><li>tax return filing</li><li>revenue/collections processing</li><li>tax policy support</li><li>legislative services</li><li>audits</li><li>administrative services</li><li>technology division</li></ul>	<ul><li>personal income tax (approx. US$15 million annually)</li><li>banking and corporation (approx. US$2 million annually)</li><li>partnerships</li></ul>

Figure 4.1 The California Franchise Tax Board

early 1990s as well as external factors had begun to erode the agency's ability to manage its business. The agency had identified an increasing 'tax gap' between revenues owed the state and revenues collected. Additionally, the agency's ability to close the tax gap was hindered significantly by deteriorating technology support systems. Technologically, the agency's substantial requirements in automation exceeded in terms of scope and timeframe the ability of the staff to meet those needs – project cycles were too long to be manageable, limited technological know-how within the organization constrained efforts to implement improvements and automation was fragmented across the agency. As a result of these issues, the agency constructed an organization-wide 'strategic systems plan' in 1992 intended to provide a long-term (five- to ten-year horizon) blueprint for the organization's technological needs relative to business needs, such as improved collections processing and target audit identification.

Although the strategic systems plan predicted that ten years would be required to modernize strategic IT systems, the agency was anxious to progress with its plans. Unfortunately, in light of the several recent IT disasters for other Californian public sector agencies publicized both within the state and nationally (including a failed large-scale IT project at the Department of Motor Vehicles), there were significant barriers to funding additional large-scale, high-risk IT ventures. Consequently, the Californian legislature was sceptical of providing additional funding for IT-based projects for the FTB and other Californian agencies where risk was perceived to be significant. FTB was caught by a perceived IT paradox: why should the legislature commit to providing additional funding for unproven IT projects?

A careful examination of the traditional low-cost procurement process used by the state of California demonstrated that this existing procurement process merely reinforced the problems the agency was trying to overcome. Specifically:

– the detailed technical requirements included in a 'request for procurement' obscured the relationship between the value of the technology and the related business problem;

– the overly long request for procurement cycle combined with the rapid rate of technology advance and related protracted contract negotiation meant that the required technical solution was outdated even before a vendor was selected and design undertaken;

– requests for procurement were put together by the agency staff and consequently hindered by whatever technological limitations existed within the staff;

– whenever an RFP was signed into a contract, the participating vendor focused on providing the explicit technical requirements in the original request for procurements at low cost with little or no emphasis placed on reviewing the solution for value and appropriateness to the organization.

Ultimately, providing the best solution to the business problem got lost in the details. Clearly, the request for procurement process would not, in the current environment, convince the legislature to spend money on high-risk 'technology' projects.

Developing an approach: performance-based procurement

To convince the legislature to provide funding for its IT needs, the agency required a solution which addressed the afore-mentioned problems. The FTB attended the state of California IT project conference in 1993, which was also attended by Californian oversight agencies, other service agencies and private executives. The agencies met to discuss problems with traditional procurement processes and related projects. The participants agreed that small purchases, commodity purchases and large complex procurements each required distinctive procurement solutions. The FTB volunteered to lead a two-year experiment in search of a procurement solution for large complex projects. The FTB agreed that the procurement solution needed to embrace the following principles:

– strategic partnering;

– business-driven solutions;

– 'best-value' evaluation; and

– performance-based payments.

Agency leadership subsequently determined that a 'perform-ance-based procurement' concept might be the answer to the problem. To use this process, the soliciting agency documented a business problem requiring a well-defined, strategic perform-ance improvement (e.g. order of magnitude improvement in collections and audit models designed to close the tax gap), then requested the assistance of a vendor not only in provid-ing the technical solution, but, first and foremost, in determin-ing a comprehensive business solution. According to this process, interested vendors invested time up-front to learn the agency's business in order to craft a solution with assistance and expertise provided by the client. To satisfy the ultimate goal of performance improvement, vendor and client alike had to focus on a value-based solution that made appropriate trade-offs of risk and reward, rather than focusing merely on low cost.

Although the performance-based procurement process provided a path to a 'best-value' business solution, the agency still required a funding mechanism that reinforced the desired performance improvement goals, and, more importantly, convinced the Californian legislature to provide project approval.

Benefits funding: a measurement mechanism

The underlying mechanism agreed upon for effective application of the performance-based procurement process was 'benefits funding'. In simple terms, 'benefits funding' translates to a vendor willingly taking on the up-front marketing and development costs of a technological solution, then receiving payment from pre-defined 'benefits' streams, identified in the original contract and refined over the course of the project (as opposed to the client paying the vendor out of appropriate funds set aside for the purpose of a project). By the use of this mechanism, the vendor must agree to shoulder a significant amount of the financial risk related to the assumption of a project. Consequently, such funding arrangements focus the client and vendor on the successful delivery of the solution in a timely fashion – the client for the purpose of improving business processes quickly and the vendor in order to get paid. Thus, through reduced financial risk to the state and improved chance of project success, benefits funding provided the lever required by the agency to induce the Californian legislature and other related control agencies to approve projects that might otherwise go unfunded.

Since the aim of the performance-based procurement is a 'best-value' solution, the resulting development of the solution will not necessarily be merely technological in nature. Instead, the client and vendor will review the entire business process in question and search for not just technological improvements but also for a comprehensive business solution, distillable into measurable business benefits. It is in this manner that performance-based procurement and benefits funding manage to align the business processes with the technology, making IT the servant of the business.

It is important to reinforce that performance-based procurement in combination with the benefits funding 'measurement' process defines success according to measured results. It would seem that such measured results should be key factors in all projects. In reality, however, many projects fail because of indecisive measurement schemes, usually based on technology results rather than business results.

The road to the Pass-Thru-Entity (PTE) Automated Screening and Support project 1995–1997

Vendor selection: 1993

Perhaps without realizing it, the agency and the state of California had pursued a process that made the business needs the driver of the IT development and implementation. That direction in and of itself dictated particular requirements for a vendor.

The agency decided to qualify interested parties prior to engaging in specific projects. In mid-1993, the agency solicited the marketplace to research the interest in the performance-based procurement/benefits funding process. Based on their solicitations and related discussions, six vendors were selected as appropriate candidates for undertaking performance-based procurement projects with the agency. Each vendor was asked to sign a 'quality partnering agreement' specifying the intention to undertake with the agency a partnering process based on trust, open communication and teamwork. Only these selected vendors would be allowed to bid on strategic projects outlined in the agency's strategic systems plan under the auspices of the performance-based procurement process (note, however, that in the interim the process was changed such that a vendor can be added during the bid process). One of these vendors was American Management Systems (AMS), the vendor later selected to undertake the Pass-Thru-Entity Automated Screening and Support (PASS) project (as well as several other FTB projects).

The PASS project

For the PASS project, the performance-based procurement process required that the agency prepare a business problem statement with a defined business scope in the form of a solicitation for conceptual proposal. Strategic technology directions of the agency were outlined, but specific technical requirements were not. This period of solution definition required a commitment on behalf of the client to provide 'open books' to AMS to describe the state of computing within the organization, future needs and plans, and the business problem at hand. AMS then took the responsibility for learning the client business, researching an appropriate technical solution and ultimately presenting a comprehensive solution, which detailed any necessary process re-engineering, organizational change and the specific technology solution. During the identification of a technological solution to the business problem, agency and vendor would work together to identify the benefits resulting from the implementation of functionality delivered by the project. The benefits identified must be measurable indicators of improved performance.

The second contract undertaken between the agency and AMS dealt with another major issue identified in the FTB 1992 technology plan: auditing effectiveness and efficiency. The PASS developed around the simple business problem that pass-thru entities had, for some time, remained fairly inauditable and contributed little in the way of revenue to the agency. According to a senior manager, pass-thru entities are:

... business entities like partnerships and Subchapter S corporations where the tax liability or (more commonly) the tax benefit is not realized by the PTE itself; instead, the liabilities or benefits are passed through to the individuals, partners, shareholders, partnerships, and so on that own the PTE.

The PASS project focused on information access related to audit data, the development of a more effective PTE pre-audit process, audit modelling and an auditor's desktop.

The contract

The contract resulting from a performance-based procurement/ benefits funding procurement documents anticipated benefit streams, the projected annual amount of benefit improvement (expressed in dollars), and a proposed formula for benefit measurement. Such a contract would specify that the vendor would be paid from the benefit stream improvements identified and related to the implementation of the business solution. Payment schedules would be included as would contingencies for higher- or lower-than-expected benefits. In any case, as long as the benefits were realized in some degree, the vendor would be paid up to a contracted cap amount, the differentiating factor being time.

The PASS contract identified four potential benefit streams:

(1) effective assessment of bank and corporation audits with an estimated increase in resulting revenue of US$10 million annually;

(2) efficient bank and corporation audit process (fewer hours spent) with an estimated increase in related audit revenues of US$12 million annually;

(3) pass-thru audit assessment with a projected annual benefit of US$8 million; and

(4) pass-thru filing enforcement with a projected annual benefit of US$10 million.

The PASS contract, signed in March 1995, specified a fixed price for AMS of US$22.2 million with five-year benefits in excess of several hundred million dollars. The PASS contract specifications with regard to anticipated benefit streams were much the same as those identified in CAPS. As before, once the contract commenced, baseline measurements of the benefit streams were established to provide a basis for later measurement. Similar to the CAPS project, the contract provided an effective negotiation basis for the project. According to Charlie DeMore, AMS financial analyst, the contract 'was written with certain flexibilities' such that 'as partners, we (AMS and the agency) can deal quickly and effectively with unforeseen problems before they become overwhelming'.

Project organization

Once a performance-based procurement/benefits funding contract was signed, a project could begin. Project roles and organization differed very little from traditional projects; the significant difference being the addition of a 'benefits funding' specialist responsible for determining the benefits to be had from the business solution and adjusting the benefit measurements as the project progressed. These roles and the related project structure will now be examined in more detail.

The assembled PASS project team included 35 AMS analysts, programmers and managers, as well as 35 FTB employees, made up of a combination of business analysts and systems staff. Both agency and vendor continued to focus on the desired benefits to tailor the solution. According to Charlie DeMore, in dealing with project issue disagreements, it was 'really in both parties' interest for the benefit streams to be both significant and measurable/verifiable'.

Within the project staff, a team comprising a vendor financial analyst (Charlie DeMore) and a client financial analyst (Eilene Wilson) took responsibility for developing more fully the benefit stream formulas over the course of the project. Charlie DeMore explained the process:

> ... ultimately (benefits) evolved and as they were more carefully scrutinized, concrete measurement algorithms were developed to identify actual incremental revenue. That's where Eilene and I came in, looking at what actually could be reported and extracted and seen with hard numbers that come in on accounting reports that would document the types of benefits that the project needed to produce.

Comparison formulae were created and enhanced resulting in a benefits 'cookbook'. Appropriate parties used this cookbook to review benefit streams at appropriate intervals during and after the project in order to identify enhanced revenue streams.

Over the course of the project, AMS staff and FTB staff worked closely together to develop a comprehensive business solution for the pass-thru auditing identification problem. Although the CAPS project had provided some degree of technological base for the PASS project, the agency users/analysts still depended on AMS staff for significant IS expertise. Eilene Wilson explained: 'I think we were able to build a system that (FTB or AMS) would not have been able to build individually'. In her eyes, AMS provided the resources which 'made a difference to the success of the system'.

The PASS project was implemented in several stages between mid-1995 and mid-1997. Benefits are measured quarterly and the predictions of US$40 million annually in improved revenues to the agency as a result of the project are currently on target. As of 31 December 1997, the project had generated a total of US$56.5 million in additional revenues.

Emerging results

Given the implementation of two projects, the client and the agency agree on a set of results out of the performance-based procurement/benefits funding process, which resolved many of the problems encountered in the traditional request for procurement. These results are represented in Figure 4.2.

Case study summary

Chapter 2 cited the Willcocks and Lester proposition for a lifecycle measurement approach combined with an emphasis on a cultural change in evaluation from 'control through numbers' to a focus on quality improvement as a way out for organizations experiencing a seeming IT paradox. The performance-based procurement/benefits funding process adopted by the FTB and carried out with the vendor AMS, provides support for that suggestion. Performance-based procurement creates a solution-driven approach to resolving a business problem, thus aligning the possible technical solutions with the business strategy. Benefits funding provides the mechanism which drives both parties in the same direction – the client because of the desire for a comprehensive effective business solution in return for time spent developing a solution and the vendor in order to obtain payment from resulting benefit streams.

Case learning points

– One critical factor determining the success of the AMS/FTB deal was the *preferred contractor relationship* formed by the agency and AMS (or 'partnering' quality): both client and vendor were induced by the same goal to produce a result. The two parties played an equally significant role in reaching

Traditional request for procurement problem addressed	Action	Comment
(1) Restrictive, detailed technical solution that hampers quality solution.	Engaging in on-going identification of solutions to problems aimed at creating 'valuable' business-driven solution.	The contract flexibility and the alignment with business strategy creates an environment of mutually beneficial discussion and decision-making.
(2) User–IT specialist gap and adversarial client–vendor relationship in request for procurement environment.	Vendor–client partnering.	The basis of the relationship is an economic one. The vendor realizes that he must deliver value in order to be paid. The client, on the other hand, has a huge investment in solving its business problem. Both parties have a fairly balanced risk–reward relationship. In short, both parties have strong incentives to partner.
(3) Protracted contract disputes and bickering over request for procurement contract details.	Placing a premium on contracted services.	The benefits-funded project creates a focus which keeps the project on track.
(4) Bickering over request for procurement contract details.	Controlling project scope.	As a result of the mutually beneficial decision-making environment, both parties are very critical of any 'feature' that does not add directly to the 'best value' of the technical solution.
(5) Discontinuous project measurement in request for procurement approach.	Defining lifecycle benefits and the on-going measurement thereof.	The refined benefit streams resulting from the performance-based procurement process provide a set of measurements which encompass the life of the project. Additionally, the client is left with a measurement and management approach which enables the implementation of an on-going continuous improvement program.
(6) Technology-driven nature of a request for procurement solution.	Aligning IT strategy with business strategy.	As the performance-based procurement process starts with the search for a solution to a business problem rather than the dictation of a specific technical solution, the ultimate use of technology to solve the business problem is readily aligned with the business strategy.
(7) Inflexible request for procurement contract.	Creating a flexible contract.	The contract resulting from the performance-based procurement process did not contain extremely detailed technical specifications; instead, it contained an agreed solution to a business problem with the flexibility to adopt the solution to changing circumstances.
(8) Restricted technical solution in request for procurement. .	Introducing innovation.	The performance-based procurement project balances leading-edge solutions with risk by leveraging the strategic investments in resources and products which the vendor community has made. This allows the partnership to build best value solutions.
(9) Low-cost request for procurement solutions that do not provide competitive advantage.	Creating competitive advantage for the customer.	The performance-based procurement/benefits funding process allows the vendor to pursue 'competitive' projects (versus low-cost ones); consequently, the client can take advantage of the competitiveness introduced.
10) Outdated, restricted solutions in request for procurement process do not align with strategy.	Achieving strategic goals.	The vendor community is induced to identify the best-value solution that aligns with the strategic goals of the client.

Figure 4.2 Emerging results from performance-based procurement/benefits funding process

that result, and had longer-term inducements to make the partnership productive.

– A second critical success factor was the *contract*, which clearly defined the expected benefits from the project, providing a value-based target for both parties, as well as providing the setting for the two parties to actively engage in problem-solving on an as-needed basis. Additionally, in the particular instance of these two contracts, the client and vendor were induced to produce a top-notch solution because of the strategic importance of the solution to their position in the marketplace, based on the contract specification of a royalty to be paid to the agency in the case of future sales of the product by AMS to other parties.

– Related critical success factors were:

(1) the establishment of an effective vendor – client relationship;

(2) the 'deep' understanding of business processes by both client and vendor;

(3) quantifiable results in the form of benefit streams;

(4) executive support for the solutions pursued;

(5) commitment from key staff;

(6) high-end, high-risk projects; and

(7) the implementation of a pervasive measurement system.

– Finally, for AMS and the FTB, IT measurement was a by-product of the larger-scale management process which dictates how the business solution is solved and, ultimately, how the vendor is paid. Consequently, measurement in this instance is truly measurement for the sake of management and decision-making rather than isolated, un-aligned measurement of IT processes.

4.7 Key learning points

- To attain benefits from IT investments identified during feasibility assessment, the evaluation process must continue through project development and into the post-implementation phase. In other words, lifecycle evaluation is a precursor to understanding and recognizing technology investment benefits.

- Generally, fewer organizations practise project management measurement than investment feasibility, and even fewer practice post-implementation evaluation, indicating that a significant number of organizations are not necessarily attaining all available benefits from IT investments.

- Project management measurement must continually address the project risk variables identified in Chapter 3, including degree of user involvement, management/user commitment, flexibility, strategic alignment of IT undertaking, time constraints, project size, project scope, contingency planning, and the existence and use of feedback from the measurement process.

- Organizations should seek to implement project management and post-implementation measurement practises that suit organizational culture, rather than merely adopting those labelled as 'best practice'.

4.8 Practical action guidelines

- Implement project management and post-implementation evaluation processes, based on cultural fit with the organization.

- Ensure that all parties involved in the evaluation shoulder an appropriate level of risk.

- Ensure on-going user involvement in the evaluation process.

- Make the evaluation discussion a 'value' discussion as opposed to merely a financial discussion – answer the question 'how does this technology investment add value to the organization?'

- Attain organizational commitment to the evaluation process.

5 | Developing a balanced business scorecard for IT

5.1 Introduction

> Information age organizations are built on a new set of operating assumptions.
>
> Robert Kaplan and David Norton[1]

> Industrial-age control ratios persist as a way of thinking about IT costs ... (but) the effects of computers are systemic.
>
> Paul Strassmann[2]

> My overall conclusion is that our scorecard experience was highly successful in terms of engendering a strong performance culture, and in significantly improving the performance of the IT Division in a way which could not have been achieved without the use of a highly structured scorecard program.
>
> Senior IT Manager, GenBank

The attraction of the balanced business scorecard approach promoted by Kaplan and Norton[1] has been its claimed ability to provide an holistic and integrated set of measurements linking disparate organizational activities with key corporate goals. Many organizations have now taken up this approach or their own specific variants. Consider the following examples from our research base.

– The Unipart Information Technology (UIT) group pursued the implementation of a scorecard by trying to follow a generic scorecard format. After a year invested in the process, UIT management recognized that the scorecard effort was not providing the desired results. Instead the process had become mechanistic and not that useful. Consequently, UIT management focused its subsequent efforts on identifying measurements to address the primary UIT issue: that of removing cost from the business. The resulting CAPRI program encompassed three programmes: (1) delivering more value to the customer; (2) increasing internal productivity; and (3) becoming a preferred employer. Upper management was now happy with the direction of the tailored measurement program, which generated support and focus in the organization for the pursuit of identified goals.

– The BP Exploration IT group introduced a balanced business scorecard. This initial scorecard was based on the Kaplan and Norton version. Over the next few years, the scorecard was continually refined to reflect measures appropriate to the organization. The mid-1990s version proposed some 40 measures per site, triggering a concern over the amount of data that would be required to evaluate 40 measures and the effort that would be required to collect the data. IT management returned to the drawing board and developed a simplified scorecard with fewer measures. In the late 1990s, the scorecard had metamorphosed once again into a 'performance contract' based on the 1994 quadrants as well as an added measure for health, safety and environment performance. The performance contract provides the basis for a monthly performance management report and for quarterly performance reviews.

– Genstar Container Corp, a subsidiary of GE, spent a lot of time dramatically overhauling its computer applications with the primary focus of 'shortening the distance to the customer'. This overhaul involved moving the entire IT department from mainframe-based systems to Intranet. In the process of this drastic modification, the CIO introduced a scorecard as means to collect historical qualitative data about the status of projects and the productivity of teams and staff members. The scorecard qualitative data was distilled further in order to provide 'dashboard' measures that demonstrate status at a glance on a daily basis. These dashboard indicators provide a current picture of status and assist employees in deciding a course of action.

These cases demonstrate the wide variety of approaches and attempts in developing scorecards, some very successful, some less so. This chapter will look at the scorecard in great depth, finishing with a case study covering the successful implementation of a scorecard in GenBank's IT group.

5.2 The need for a scorecard

Industry specialists and academics alike cite a number of weaknesses in broad-based performance measurement, including:

– the failure of measurement systems to provide strategic direction;

– financially based measures that short-change softer, qualitative benefits;

– the historical, as opposed to predictive, nature of measurements;

– a failure of measurement systems to reinforce appropriate behaviours; and

– measurements that are 'inward-looking' to the exclusion of an organization's customer and competitive environment; in other words, performance evaluation that fails to measure the value-creating factors of quality, service and speed.

Indeed, a number of these weaknesses are illustrated in the cases presented throughout this chapter. For example, as will be explained below, the incoming IT Director at B&Q saw that the measures selected for the IT group did not get at the heart of the performance problem: the difficulty and/or inability to measure benefits delivered, hard and soft, against cost. Genstar, on the other hand (see above), recognized the historical nature of measures and subsequently relied on dashboard indicators to tell the up-to-date measurement story.

Regardless of the mixed bag of success, organizations recognize the need for measurement of various sorts, but, as demonstrated in previous chapters, they tend to rely on traditional, widely used financial measures to answer that need. Unfortunately, these financial measures usually fail to tell a complete story and, although significant to the review of *some* organizational dimensions, when used alone they are not appropriate to today's information age-based businesses. Many organizations have made steps in the right direction with the creation of vision statements and strategic objectives, but those statements and objectives rarely find their way into concrete measurement programs. Additionally, management usually fails to include measurement as an essential part of organizational strategy, not least due to difficulty in conducting measurement and/or the perceived cost of measurement.

Given the difficulties with measuring performance in the organization as a whole, it is not surprising that companies struggle with measuring performance of their IT investments. Previous chapters have examined the variety of difficulties that arise in IT/e-business investment performance. An oft-lodged complaint about decisions made by and about the IT function and its use of technology is a failure to align such decisions with corporate strategy. The balanced business scorecard, as introduced by Kaplan and Norton, seeks to remedy this alignment failure.

As noted repeatedly, amongst the inadequacies listed is the failure of many measurement programmes to reinforce corporate strategy *and* the failure of corporate strategy to encompass measurement as a key enabling mechanism for ensuring implementation. A significant advertised benefit of the scorecard is the alignment with strategy provided by both the scorecard planning process and the subsequent use of scorecard measures. Moreover, the customer-facing content in a scorecard provides an organization with some degree of external focus rather than the use of merely internal measurement. Closer investigation will reveal that the scorecard also responds to other shortcomings typical of measurement programs.

In its ultimate implementation, the scorecard concept encompasses the entire organization. The IT function can be effectively included in this panorama. In particular given that the proliferation of technology in the organization is difficult to control, the scorecard approach can help to harness known benefits as well as those that are less tangible.

Ultimately, what is required of a measurement program is a set of measures that addresses both external and internal processes and outputs for an organization. More specifically, any new class of performance measures should:

- increase the scope of the measurement focus beyond financial reporting to less tangible benefits;

- create value through a focus on quality, service and speed;

- instigate organizational learning and innovation; and

– motivate appropriate long-term behaviour at all levels of the organization.

The scorecard concept can address these requirements.

5.3 What is a 'balanced business scorecard'?

A balanced business scorecard is ultimately a translation of a company's strategic objectives into a set of performance measures. As the ultimate source of the measures, the company strategy is the driving force behind the claim that a scorecard assists in focusing the organization on strategic vision. The use of the word 'balanced' in the description of the approach implies a set of measurements that spans the significant processes and focuses of an organization. It also implies a balance between short- and long-term focus; between strategic and operational measures; between hard and soft measures; and between identified cause and effect factors. 'Scorecard' implies measurement against a goal or target.

In the words of Kaplan and Norton: 'the balanced scorecard provides executives with a comprehensive framework that translates a company's vision and strategy into a coherent set of performance measures'. An organization must start with a statement defining its strategy and mission. The organization can then use the scorecard to translate strategy and mission into objectives and measures, generally organized into four per-spectives: financial focus, customer focus, internal business processes, and learning and growth focus. Note that, although a 'typical' scorecard contains these four quadrants, many organi-zations have implemented scorecards with varying numbers of 'quadrants' based on the need to account for 'cultural' differences.

Executives are most familiar with the financial aspect of the scorecard. The customer-facing, internal process, and learning and growth quadrants and their respective measures are used in a complementary fashion and can be thought of as operational measures that are drivers of future financial performance. Overall, the integrated financial and non-financial scorecard measures can contribute to both current and future success.

Given that a good balanced scorecard then tells the story of an organization's strategy, the scorecard can be viewed as a language and benchmark against which new projects and businesses can be evaluated. There follows detailed description of the generic scorecard quadrants.

Financial quadrant

Despite claims that financial measures alone do not tell the whole story about any investment or process, technological or otherwise, financial measures will always be required to tell part of the story. Organizations must be able to measure costs and profits in order to manage direction of the organization and provide shareholders with a financial estimation of their investment. Simply put, if an organization is not profitable within a reasonably short period of time, it will not stay in business.

Regardless, organizations can develop financial measures that align more clearly with their strategic, long-term goals. Such financial measures may have both short-term and long-term horizons, as well as a variety of focuses, including competitive pressures, shareholder perspective and internal profitability. In the case of competitive pressure, for instance, an organization may focus on a reduction in the financial value of 'sales backlog'. Shareholders, on the other hand, will have short-term requirements for profitability as well as a desire for organizational stability over the long-haul. Return on capital employed provides one short-term shareholder measure, while profit forecast reliability is a longer-term measure. Finally, the company will want some means of reviewing financials internal to company processes, such as project cost versus profitability.

Customer quadrant

Many organizations have only recently begun to act upon, as opposed to merely understand, the importance of the customer. This move toward a focus on the customer follows a long and increasingly ineffective focus on product development and delivery. Generally, the customer focus helps the organization develop an externally focused strategy. Customers' concerns tend to fall into four categories: (1) time, (2) quality, (3) performance and (4) service. The scorecard allows managers to translate general mission statements about customer service, in relation to these types of concerns, into specific measures that reflect what really matters to the customer. For example, an organization may choose to measure 'time to market for product', and/or a desire 'to become customers' supplier of choice'. Regularly administered customer surveys are one means of obtaining such feedback.

Internal process quadrant

While customer focus is certainly important, organizations cannot neglect the focus on the internal processes that will assist in meeting customer focus goals and measures. Popular theories of re-engineering can illustrate the need for this quadrant: internal processes are a fundamental source of sustainable organizational advantage and people provide the coordination required to harmonize processes with enabling technology. Measures developed for internal processes should relate to the business processes deemed critical to customer-focused goals. Our scorecard research reflects the regular inclusion of quality and productivity measures to capture internal process information.

Learning and growth quadrant

The fourth quadrant is, in effect, the measure of an organization's ability to respond to and learn from its experiences in the market. In today's world, most markets are changing rapidly, and an individual organization's strategy of today may require adjustments for continual success in the market. For example, consider the rapid development of e-business initiatives and the corresponding organizational adjustments required to support such initiatives. Consequently, this fourth quadrant should include measures of the organizational ability to improve and innovate. Measures in this quadrant should ultimately provide efficiencies to the organization that ultimately translate into shareholder value as the organization improves from learning.

In their article 'Using the Balanced Scorecard as a Strategic Management System' (1996), Kaplan and Norton[3] suggest that:

> Once the strategy is defined and the drivers are identified, the scorecard influences managers to concentrate on improving or re-engineering those processes most critical to the organization's strategic success. That is how the scorecard most clearly links and aligns actions with strategy.

Our research indicates that the learning and growth segment tends to be the most neglected, and least understood, quadrant. In fact, however, all measures on a scorecard exist to achieve learning and improvement, a fundamental purpose of measurement. Consequently, executives need to think through the specific, distinctive and fundamental ways in which their organization needs to learn and grow, and how these processes can be measured.

5.4 How to develop a scorecard

The scorecard's ability to align organizational action with strategy has been noted repeatedly. The first step in scorecard development is the identification and agreement on vision – the

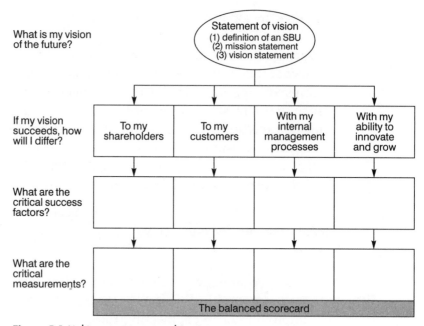

Figure 5.1 Linking measures to objectives

linking of measurement to strategy. Refer here to Figure 5.1, which shows how to begin the scorecard development process.

Working through the figure, it is possible to discern the high-level steps in the creation of the scorecard. After agreement on vision, the organization must determine the critical participants/processes that will make a difference to the success of the vision. In this respect, the example identifies:

(1) shareholders,

(2) customers,

(3) internal processes, and

(4) organizational ability to innovate and grow.

These participants/processes roughly translate into the quadrants discussed earlier. In order to pave the way for specific measurement identification, the organization must identify the critical success factors for each quadrant and translate those factors into critical measures. It is important to note that each organization is unique; consequently, the outline provided here for scorecard development must be tailored to organizational needs. A purely generic application of the scorecard will most likely *not* breed the desired results. Any given organization may differ in a number of scorecard aspects.

- From which level in the organization will the top-level scorecard generate?

- Will individual incentives be tied to scorecard measures?

- How many different scorecards will the organization have? (Note that all scorecards should be related.)

- How many quadrants does an organization want in order to describe satisfactorily its strategy and related measurements?

Once the quadrants are agreed and characterized by *objectives* statements (e.g. 'reduce time to deliver'), the organization can identify specific *measures* that provide valuable feedback about the objective. See Figure 5.2 for an outline of this process. For instance, the objective 'reduce time to deliver' could be measured by 'the number of projects delivered within 12 months'. To set bounds around the measurements, the organization will then establish *target measurement results*. In keeping with our example, the target measurement for 'number of projects delivered within 12 months' might be 'deliver 80% of all projects within 12 months'.

Scorecard development introduces a management process around its development and links long-term strategic objectives

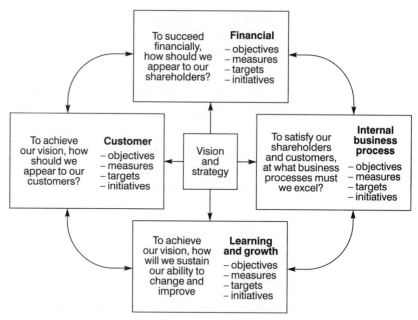

Figure 5.2 The balanced scorecard provides a framework to translate strategy into operational terms

with short-term actions. The key pieces of the scorecard management process include the following.

– Translating the vision – management must seek to provide an integrated set of objectives and measurements that allow employees to act on the words of the vision and strategy statements. The scorecard, when implemented effectively across and down an organization, translates the organizational strategy into concrete measurements that can be understood by all employees.

– Communicating and linking – management must provide an educational program to explain the scorecard and its use to its employees. Ultimately, the organization as a whole must be driving toward a long-term strategy rather than just to short-term financial goals. The scorecard provides the ability to create finite measurements at all levels of the organization upon which even individual reward and compensation can be based. In this way, the scorecard ties personnel performance to strategy.

– Business planning – management must seek to integrate business and financial plans. Unfortunately, in many organizations, we find a separation of the budgeting process from the strategic planning which a budget ultimately needs to support. The scorecard creation offsets this separation and sometimes even eliminates it. In addition, process design within an organization focuses on short-term payback to the exclusion of longer-term strategic goals. As in the discussion of scorecard development, the scorecard provides a format whereby appropriate members of management must agree both on long-term strategic goals and shorter-term measurements.

– Feedback and learning – management must be willing to make the scorecard process a 360° one. As such, short-term monitoring of all scorecard quadrants provides a double learning loop to allow management to adjust scorecard measures that do not provide useful information. As the scorecard measurements are ultimately a translation of an agreed strategy into related measures, the focus moves from purely operational control to strategic management. It is in this manner that the scorecard can be used as a comprehensive management tool rather than a mere measurement program.

Finally, it is necessary to refocus on the 'balance' in the balanced scorecard. Balance in this context should be taken to mean effectiveness and efficiency achieved in concert. It does *not* mean that success in some areas of the scorecard cancels out failure(s) in other areas. Instead, an effective approach to words achieving the balance would be for an organization to establish minimum threshold levels for a critical subset of measures. In other words, if all minimum thresholds are not met, then goals proscribed by the measures have not been attained. Additionally, because the scorecard is a radically redesigned approach to measurement in an organization, it is a good idea for management to establish short-term interim targets for balanced scorecard measures, in order to encourage stepwise successes throughout the organization.

5.5 The IT scope of the scorecard

Just as the scorecard can align the organization as a whole with its vision and strategy, the use of a scorecard within an IT department can:

(1) align the IT department with the overall organizational strategy, thereby combating one of the frequent complaints about IT organizations, namely their failure to incorporate organizational strategy; and

(2) allow the IT department to measure its own strategies according to the multifaceted dimensions of the scorecard (the integrated use of scorecards throughout the organization, including within the IT department, can focus on the measurement of *integrated* key business processes rather than merely focusing on individual functional departments).

The *financial quadrant* measurements can be used to measure the more traditional financial aspects of IT investments and projects. Perhaps the crucial difference offered by the scorecard is the ability to be more effective in associating financial measures with strategically based goals.

The *customer quadrant* introduces an important facet of measurement into the IT organization to date and in general. IT has been considerably lacking in its ability to focus on customer needs. However, if the IT scorecard derives from the corporate level scorecard, IT's ability to focus on specific customer needs will be enhanced.

The *internal processes* quadrant supports IT's ability to focus on customer-facing measures. Most organizations studied saw this quadrant as critical to the desire to transform themselves into more effective, performance-oriented organizations.

The *learning and growth* quadrant provides an IT organization with the ability to assimilate measurement results and experiences to attain process improvement and finetuned management of the organization.

The case study that illustrates these key scorecard points most fully is that of the GenBank IT organization. This will be examined in detail at the end of the chapter. Here, simply note that the GenBank IT organization saw the scorecard programme as a powerful transformer; it was the scorecard that allowed GenBank IT to become a performance-focused organization.

5.6 Scorecard risks

Before looking at the benefits, and the ways in which a balanced scorecard can minimize the weaknesses of less holistic IT assessment approaches, it is important to note several risks in scorecard creation. While it is true that 'what gets measured gets managed', the reverse is also true, namely 'what is not measured is not managed'! It is possible that important aspects of organizational performance are left out of the scorecard and consequently are not managed effectively under this umbrella. If careful attention is not paid to the effect of scorecard measurements on the organization, inappropriate behaviours might be enforced by the scorecard.

It is clear that initiating and sustaining a balanced business scorecard programme is not easy in complex modern organizations. One UK retailer struggled to get the business to buy in to the scorecard, as the business viewed the scorecard as 'a techie thing'.

Many other organizations are still finding difficulties in quantifying performance and soft benefits, and this could inhibit full application of a scorecard approach. Thus, in light of the implementation of a new balanced scorecard approach across the company, one major European retailer considered the establishment of scorecard performance measures for IT. The measures chosen focused on 'IT expenditure as a percent of sales' and 'IT customer satisfaction' as the IT contribution to the scorecard. The IT Director acknowledged that these were poor substitutes for what he saw as the key performance measures: delivery of IT benefits compared to IT investment. Unfortunately, he found this measure a great deal more difficult to describe with firm numbers in a scenario where the majority of IT benefits are soft, that is not readily quantifiable.

Organizations must be very careful to tailor the scorecard to their own needs. A scorecard developed according to a generic map without a supporting belief system would probably result in a complex measurement system that loses sight of strategic vision and long-term goals. A major UK manufacturer provides an example whereby the generic application of a scorecard program did not provide the desired results, but a more tailored version did. This experience suggests that adopting uncritically Kaplan and Norton's balanced scorecard as presented may not be the wisest approach, and that detailed analysis and tailoring will be necessary if the balanced scorecard concept is to be operationalized effectively.

One other risk emerging from the researched organizations was an excessive focus on IT evaluation and assessment. While it is encouraging to see IT departments take measurement initiatives, sometimes they attempted to implement a scorecard in isolation. Such an independent approach may not deliver desired results given the potential lack of connection to the strategy of the organization as a whole.

Additionally, and notoriously, measurement systems do erode quickly. While much effort in this chapter has been focused on illustrating the strategic alignment concept provided by the scorecard, it is a strong probability that a once-aligned scorecard will fall out of date with changing corporate strategy. This possibility reinforces the need to revisit continually and question critically scorecard objectives and measures.

Finally, and most importantly, the use of the scorecard does not guarantee a 'correct' strategy. The scorecard can only translate the company's strategy into measurable objectives – failure to convert improved operational performance into improved financial performance should send executives back to the drawing board.

5.7 Scorecard benefits

Once again, the development of the scorecard requires:

(1) agreement on strategic aims of the organization;

(2) the distillation of the strategy into a set of measurements; and

(3) continual review of measurement data and resulting on-going improvement.

In the course of these steps, additional scorecard benefits can be identified:

– scorecard development clarifies business strategy;

– the organization develops a shared understanding and commitment to the scorecard programme;

- measures reflect the clarified business strategy;

- measures are comprehensive and well-rounded – not just 'the easily measured';

- the act of distilling measures for the scorecard results in a set of agreed priorities and trade-offs as the organization seeks to identify only those measures which truly contribute to strategy/vision attainment

- as a management tool, the scorecard measurement data collected provides focused management information for the organization;

- accountability for measurement and performance is spread across functions;

- measurement processes are transformed into a management process; and

- the organization becomes focused on customer service and delivery.

Perhaps the most significant contribution of the balanced scorecard to both organizational and IT measurement is the alignment with strategy and vision engendered by the effective creation of a scorecard. The scorecard, implemented across the organization, assists in conveying strategic goals to all levels of the organization and ties longer-term strategic goals to shorter-term actions via the measurements involved. In addition, the creation of the scorecard links two activities which are generally separate, resource planning and strategic planning, to the detriment of the organization. This separation generally makes for difficulty in linking change programmes to long-term priorities as change programs are usually a product of resource allocation and long-term priorities are usually a result of strategic planning.

Perhaps another way to look at the scorecard with respect to IT organizational alignment with business strategy is to consider the scorecard effect on the business – IT gap which is identified as a major issue by IT practitioners and businessmen alike. The Logistics Controller of a major UK high street retailer described the scorecard process as that 'which examines it (IT investments) from a technical perspective and from the user perspective and tries to get some agreement'.

5.8 Summary

In light of an understanding of scorecard measurements, we now consider how the scorecard addresses the weaknesses in other broad-based measurements identified at the beginning of the chapter.

(1) The scorecard drives the organization to agree upon organizational vision and strategic goals, offsetting the failure of other measurement systems to provide strategic direction. Taking this step as the basis for the development of all further scorecard measures ensures that a common understanding of strategy and vision underlies such measures, thereby providing the elusive strategic alignment.

(2) The comprehensive scorecard contains a number of non-financial reasons for the sake of capturing those less tangible, qualitative benefits, offsetting the likelihood that financially based measures will short-change softer, qualitative benefits.

(3) The continual measurement process that should be undertaken with scorecard development should assist management in more readily identifying problem areas and taking action to correct such problems. Naturally, the rigour with which scorecard measurements are pursued affects the timely response to measurement trends. In other words, the pro-active scorecard approach addresses the need for predictive, rather than historical measures.

(4) The ideal scorecard measurements are cascaded throughout the entire organization and, in some cases, even tied to individual plans/goals with the hope of encouraging individuals to pursue activities that contribute to the attainment of strategic goals. The cascade of the scorecard throughout the organization reinforces desired behaviours.

(5) The non-financial scorecard quadrants provide the 'outward-looking' perspective. Other measurement systems tend to be 'inward-looking' to the exclusion of the customer and competitive environment; in other words, performance evaluation that fails to measure the value-creating factors of quality, service and speed.

5.9 In-depth case study: the balanced scorecard at GenBank

Background

GenBank Group (the name of the bank has been anonymized) is an international organization, with banking facilities in several countries and a large retail operation in the UK. This case study looks at the development of the scorecard at GenBank from the 1990s to 2000. Based on increased competition, deregulation and globalization of the financial industry in the late 1980s, GenBank needed to modify its approach to business in general and to IT in particular in order to maintain its customer and profit base. In the early 1990s, GenBank agreed to pursue a 'first choice in our chosen markets' approach to business. This had significant ramifications for the future of the centralized IT department supplying services to the retail banking arm. One IT focus throughout the financial industry became efficiency. IT had to focus on efficiency not only in pure cost terms, but also in terms of the services provided to the bank branches.

At this time, the central IT group of 3,000 was a traditional IT organization. It supported large mainframe systems working separately from the business community it served. IT projects at the time had both an IT manager and a business manager, yet the business took little responsibility for IT success and/or failure. The IT organization and the divisions for which it provided services could not agree on a common perception of the performance of the IT organization.

Perceived need for a scorecard

In 1991–1992, the management turned to the GenBank internal consultancy to establish a rangé of key performance indicators which IT management could use to help run the business. Until that time, IT measures were few and far between – the primary control on IT had been 'did IT comply with its cost budget?' Given that the IT organization continually made demands for more money, its control of a budget was questioned by other parts of the organization. As a result of the 1991–1992 initiative, IT's focus become the development of efficiency, productivity and a set of measures which would give the IT management a much better sense of what they were controlling and how they should control it. Ultimately, the IT group decided on the balanced scorecard as the vehicle for carrying out a new measurement and management program.

The need for a scorecard approach can be summarized in terms of the goals sought by GenBank:

– a more efficient IT department;

– to provide management focus on the achievement of its corporate vision;

– to move from a management focus dominated by short-term financials to a longer-term, more balanced focus;

– to support transformation of the IT Division (new performance management discipline, a link between financial and non-financial and a link between business and IT disciplines); and

– to transform the management focus of IT into a genuine business partnership with the business units it supported.

GenBank management and IT management already envisioned that long-term decentralization of the IT organization would be necessary in order to drive IT decisions off of business needs more effectively. Despite this long-term plan, it was agreed that the implementation of a scorecard should not be delayed – the scorecard could provide the measurement framework required for IT to be successful on a long-term basis.

Initially, during the early 1990s, phased organizational changes would be implemented into the retail banking business side to provide a clearer sense of segmentation and accountability. Then a similar set of changes would be made to the existing central IT organization, in terms of efficiency, service, reliability and improved applications for branch use in dealing with customers.

The scorecard was to be implemented all the way through the IT organization, from a top-level group scorecard to individual goals and bonus plans. The new management team brought into place in 1994 wanted IT staff to envision the scorecard and related plans as a *performance contract*, with a focus on results. The objective was dramatic improvement by putting in place a structured set of principles to incentivize people by telling them very clearly what they would get on delivering results.

Developing the GenBank IT scorecard

GenBank viewed the scorecard as 'an accepted profile of the strategy'. The scorecard was about 'genuine balance not just between finance and customer, but also between short-term and long-term balance and an understanding of priorities'.

GenBank IT used a series of workshops, discussions and off-site meetings to agree upon the key measures for the business. Twice a year, the top 12 people in the IT Division went off-site for two days largely to debate the plans for the organization in scorecard terms. GenBank wanted the top IT management team to collectively own the scorecard.

The resulting GenBank IT scorecard had five quadrants (see Figure 5.3). Three were the traditional ones set out by Kaplan and Norton: finance, customer/client and the organizational/ human resource development quadrant. But GenBank split Kaplan and Norton's fourth internal process quadrant between productivity and quality. The productivity quadrant was aimed at continuously improving value for money and included objectives related to increased manpower productivity, reduction in the time taken to deliver projects and the reduction of unit costs. The quality quadrant specified the delivery of IT projects/services to specification and included objectives for service level improvement and internal performance improvement.

Looking at the other quadrants, the human resources quadrant was directed at improving the management of and satisfaction of GenBank IT's human assets. The *client* quadrant specified the delivery of first-class services as measured by a variety of satisfaction surveys. Finally, the *financial* quadrant was aimed at the effective management of finances through budgetary review and increased cost flexibility.

Each of the 15 departments in the centralized GenBank IT was required to create a scorecard. The scorecards were linked downwards to individual reward and upwards to the divisional scorecard. Non-managerial staff were ultimately eligible to receive bonuses related to a combination of their personal objectives and departmental performance.

The resulting scorecard represented a very complex, interrelated set of measures which the management team wanted to distil

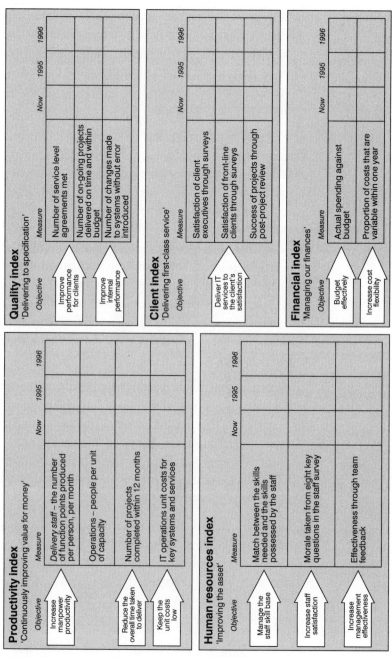

Figure 5.3 The GenBank IT scorecard in the mid-1990s

down to an aggregate level. Each measure had a scale and a weighting or prioritization. The measures were structured in such a way that they could be aggregated to provide one bottom line number.

GenBank IT experienced a number of patterns in the attainment of the scorecard measures. In some instances, measures declined before improvement; in others, measures accelerated rapidly then plateaued and so on. To account for the vagaries of the measurement process and to provide a well-rounded platform for on-going measurement, GenBank built into its scorecard plan a pattern for improvement. The pattern aimed to:

(1) achieve greater realism in planning by recognizing the inherent trade-offs and tensions between different dimensions of the scorecard; and

(2) generate future plans which were quantified, measurable and explicitly prioritized.

Communicating the scorecard organization-wide

GenBank IT intended for the scorecard to be a comprehensive measurement and management system. To that end, the scorecard had to be explained to the 3,000 IT staff. A number of managers communicate the messages of the scorecards while two wall charts were used to explain the scorecard and the related reward system. The consistent messages to staff focused on transformation of the IT support to the business by creating a new performance culture.

Regular scorecard reporting was distributed to a wide variety of individuals both in and out of IT; the reporting process was intended to made the scorecard and related measurements well understood and out in the open within the organization. The main driver for generating scorecard understanding was the monthly meeting of the executive management team of the IT

Division. It concentrated on areas of actual performance falling below target. Each measure had an executive IT manager nominated to be its owner, particularly in terms of taking a view of future performance. The entire IT staff was informed of the scorecard progress via a monthly staff newsletter and through the efforts of top management staff.

Using the scorecard: objectives and benefits

The scorecard was used to drive the following objectives.

(1) The scorecard attempted to focus management on issues critical to the delivery of services to the rest of the business. The scorecard also drove the managers to understand what the organization wanted to accomplish in its transformation of the IT Division. A number of specific measurements reflected this desire to focus management on delivery issues. The change performance index (see Figure 5.3) for instance, created management focus on reliability problems when system changes were made. Likewise, the productivity index's objective of reducing the overall time taken to deliver stemmed from major IT developments taking on average three years and six months. The result was the measurement of 'projects completed within 12 months'.

(2) GenBank saw the scorecard as a management tool, not just a measurement tool. The IT General Manager spent a great deal of time driving the measurement process and then making management decisions as a result of it.

(3) The scorecard was designed to drive the organization in a consistent direction. These marching orders were the result of the aggregation of measurements upwards from departmental scorecards and the checks and balances provided by the senior group overseeing the creation of departmental scorecards. Some divisional measures, such as compliance

with budget and staff morale, could clearly be aggregated or disaggregated down the organization and were applied to all departments. Other measures were unique, but these were fewer in number.

(4) The scorecard was intended to assist GenBank IT in understanding the business better so that undertakings such as the upcoming decentralization and occasional outsourcing were made easier. A senior IT manager claimed:

> I think the scorecard helps you – I think you understand the business much better and therefore whether you decide to stay as you are, decentralize, outsource, whatever, you do it from a position of much greater strength than if you don't have the resulting measurement, disciplines and controls in place.

Ultimately, this version of the GenBank scorecard contributed to several benefits and successes. The implementation of the scorecard ultimately eased the decentralization process, and it:

- 'paid for itself';

- was successfully used as a management tool;

- improved service levels; and

- was used to drive IT organizational transformation.

In fact, the IT organization decided to undertake significant effort to roll out a scorecard despite the longer-term GenBank plan to decentralize. The IT organization believed that:

> ... during the two years or so that we used this system prior to decentralization, we improved very substantially the innate performance of IT, the engine of IT, and we also substantially improved its relationship with the business and mutual understanding. We didn't achieve everything

we wanted to, but it was much easier to decentralize, to integrate the business, as a result of this discipline than if we'd done it two years earlier.

In practice, the scorecard did not entirely align to the enablement of the business, but it was successful in *focusing attention on the appropriateness of service level agreements*, which are an indication of service required by and provided to the business. The initial focus of scorecard service level agreement measurements was to achieve a higher service level performance. However, the IT Division recognized that the more focus it placed on performance of service level agreements, the more it became apparent that the service levels themselves didn't necessarily reflect what the business really wanted. Consequently, the business updated and clarified the service levels it desired, while the IT Division prioritized service level agreements and witnessed dramatically improved performance of those agreements as a result.

Post-decentralization: evolution of the scorecard 1995–2000

In early 1996, application developers were decentralized from Group IT into their respective business units. Only a much smaller 'IT Operational Services' group remained as centralized.

Although IT Operational Services, a group of 1,200, organizationally reported into the UK Retail Group, it provided services to all of the GenBank business units (Insurance, Mortgages, Cards, Corporate Accounts and Retail). With the advent of decentralization, changes to the scorecard and its usage were bound to occur. Most obvious was the streamlining of the scorecard from five quadrants into four (financial, customer, internal quality and organizational development) and the addition of an element of risk assessment, subsumed within the internal quality quadrant (see Figure 5.4).

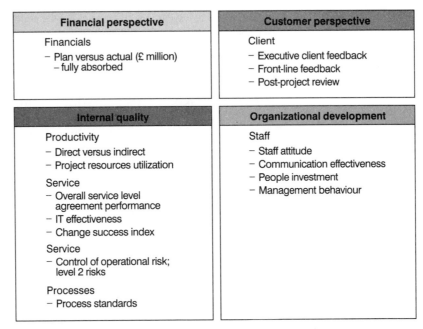

Financial perspective	Customer perspective
Financials – Plan versus actual (£ million) – fully absorbed	Client – Executive client feedback – Front-line feedback – Post-project review

Internal quality	Organizational development

Productivity
– Direct versus indirect
– Project resources utilization
 	
Service
– Overall service level
  agreement performance
– IT effectiveness
– Change success index
 	
Service
– Control of operational risk;
  level 2 risks
 	
Processes
– Process standards
	Staff
	– Staff attitude
	– Communication effectiveness
	– People investment
	– Management behaviour

Figure 5.4 The post-decentralization IT scorecard at GenBank

The Scorecard measurements

Figure 5.4 outlines the measurements in the revised scorecard. They are explained in more detail as follows.

(1) Financial perspective quadrant

– Planned versus actual: a straight comparison of current YTD actual expenditure and yearly forecast versus a planned budget.

(2) Internal quality quadrant

Productivity measures

– Direct versus indirect head count: monthly measure comparing resources engaged in activities directly sponsored by the client in project and service provision against resources used in managing and supporting IT operations/departments/units/teams as a business unit.

- Project resources utilization: a monthly measure expressed as a percentage of billable days utilized in service introduction and technical operations departments of IT Operations.

Service measures

- Performance of service level agreements: a monthly measure reviewing the percentage of 'failed' service level agreements. A 'failed' agreement is characterized as one that does not meet the designated target(s) for the month.

- IT effectiveness: a new measure which reviews the scores from the post-project review to determine the success of IT solutions delivery and how well IT has worked with the business to deliver business needs.

- Change success index: a monthly measure reflecting the percentage of implemented changes that were successful.

Risk measures

- Control of operational risk: under development.

Processes measures

- Key performance standards arrived at through analysis.

(3) Customer perspective quadrant

- Executive client feedback: a twice yearly survey of central and regional business unit policy/decision-makers about their satisfaction with quality of service provided by IT

Operations. Average scores for questions are calculated and used to target where improvement is needed.

– Front-line feedback: a monthly survey of front-line staff about IT services and systems provided by IT Operations.

– Post-project Review: a monthly survey of clients about the quality of project management and delivery by IT Operations.

(4) Organizational development quadrant

– Staff attitude: a point-in-time measure assessing staff satisfaction with the terms and conditions of their work and work environment.

–   Communication effectiveness: a point-in-time measure assessing the effectiveness strategy and policy communications from bank executives to the rest of the employees.

–   People investment: a measure assessing the knowledge of and communication to staff about availability of development and career opportunities within the bank.

– Management behaviour: a point-in-time measure assessing staff views of the IT Operations management team.

Now that GenBank IT was spread across all business units, how did it handle the post-decentralization planning and measurement processes? In practice, by 1998 all of the business units used scorecards and provided input into a corporate level IT plan. The keys to putting the plan together were the scorecards and action programs. These programs all had milestones against them which reflected key deliverables. Each month a management information pack was produced. This enabled executive management to focus their review on areas requiring attention.

Below the top level of key deliverables for IT operational services there were performance contracts for each head of department. Progress against the key deliverables was reviewed quarterly. In a dynamic business environment, new priorities emerged regularly and these were factored in at the appropriate time.

One result of the use of scorecards across the business units and within the IT Operational Services Group, was that, post-decentralization, IT across the organization had in fact been more effectively aligned with the businesses. Now each business had a scorecard that reflected its contribution to the overall Group and that measured its particular priorities. Moreover IT Operations in a particular business unit, for example Retail, had its own scorecard supporting the relevant elements of Retail's objectives and also focused on Retail's key responsibilities.

In practice, decentralization and the drive for operational excellence served to increase the focus on IT measurement. One result, for example, was that, by 1998, in a typical internal quality quadrant there would be a mixture of IT effectiveness and efficiency measures. In the 1998–1999 planning process there was widespread insistence that business unit scorecards be even more closely integrated with those of IT Operational Services. Moreover, out of recognition of the critical role IT played in underpinning customer service, IT managers were contributing new specific measures on this to make IT performance more visible.

Overall, the decentralization process was about creating a much greater focus on the customer and increasing levels of accountability across the organization. Formerly, even with the scorecard, the picture of who was responsible for delivering a target could occasionally become blurred. By 2000, GenBank was also experimenting with using the scorecard process for agreeing and assessing objectives with their IT suppliers.

IT scorecard risks and challenges

From GenBank's experience with the scorecard, we can identify a number of risks and challenges.

A senior IT manager identified the failure to align effectively IT scorecard measures with the business which IT was to enable. He explains:

> I think if there was one lesson that . . . was learned during the 1994–1996 period when the concept was developed at GenBank it was that it was not harnessed sufficiently to the business that IT was supporting. We communicated to them and tried to have our measures relate as far as possible to the business. But with hindsight it's clear that we didn't get the balance sufficiently right; in other words there was too much emphasis on the engine of IT, on the innate ability of IT, rather than on its capability of enabling the business.

Scorecard measuring schemes run a risk of becoming too complicated to be manageable. In GenBank's case, a senior IT manager identifed a key lesson: 'We did on occasion let the scorecard measurement system become too complicated. For instance, how should we prioritize the 50 plus service levels?' Specifically, he explained that, while attempting to prioritize the numerous service level agreements, the management team were sucked into an overly complicated weighting process, to the detriment of focusing on business needs.

Respondents repeatedly identified the need to develop measures that are truly important to the business. Given the radical change in measurement and management introduced by the scorecard, however, difficulties can arise, for example the inappropriate use of measures (i.e. not obtaining an end result that is significant to the business).

Given the general tendency in IT investment and usage evaluation to rely on tangible, financial factors, the scorecard runs the risk of being implemented merely for the 'sake of appearances' – to implement the other three non-financial quadrants for good press, but to continue with heavy reliance on the financial factors. A senior IT manager explained this risk: 'There is a potential problem with the scorecard in terms of "are you driving for a genuine balanced scorecard with the traditional four quadrants, or are you actually driving for three non-financial quadrants and taking the finances separately?".' In other words, a scorecard runs the risk of becoming too mechanistic in its application.

Perhaps the most significant complaint about the early scorecard was its failure to take into account any sort of risk assessment. The generic Kaplan and Norton scorecard does not contain a risk dimension, nor did the pre-decentralization GenBank implementation. More specifically, one can apply a scorecard discipline very effectively in an organization, but that will not guarantee its success. All sorts of things can derail the implementation and use of the scorecard – risk management and security management are two very important ones.

GenBank conquered some of these challenges by cascading the scorecard throughout the IT organization and by regularly reinforcing the 'transformation of IT' business message. Subsequently, the balanced business scorecard became more widely applied throughout the business units of GenBank, and this greatly facilitated the further aligning of IT activity with goals and measures related to business value.

5.10 Key learning points

- When implemented with commitment and care, the balanced scorecard can address many of the measurement shortcomings noted in earlier chapters.

- Financial measures are included in the scorecard, but they are not the sole basis for scorecard measurement.

- The use of a scorecard can align IT usage with organizational strategy.

- The use of a balanced scorecard provides a comprehensive measurement system that is ultimately usable as a management tool.

- The word 'balanced' in balanced scorecard implies that all measurements are significant and the attainment of some measurement goals does not cancel out the failure of other measurement goals.

- Research and survey results reveal that organizations are increasingly turning to the scorecard as a measurement/ management tool.

- The development and use of a scorecard provides the organization with the opportunity to agree on and disseminate a clear organizational strategy, deliver this in detail and improve on the delivery on a continuous basis.

- The implementation of a scorecard requires the commitment to implement and pursue in a tailored fashion to suit the given organization.

- The scorecard can be used throughout the lifecycle of a specific IT undertaking/investment.

5.11 Practical action guidelines

- Implement a scorecard as a comprehensive measurement system with attention to cultural issues in the organization.

- Consult heavily with future users at all levels; get them to be part owners of the scorecard and related process.

- Pursue a scorecard only if upper management is truly committed; encourage upper management's commitment and support.

- Pursue a scorecard only if the organization is willing to put in the time and effort.

- Make sure scorecard measures are not just ancillary; define measures precisely.

- Make sure measures can be measured – who is accountable, timing/frequency, drill down data, etc.

- Make measurement part of the organizational strategy.

6 Sink or swim: evaluation as the key to IT outsourcing

6.1 Introduction

> The one clear thing to me was that business people that I dealt with through this contract had very little awareness of the costs of the services provided over many years. Somebody said we were being taken to the cleaners by this vendor. The reality was that they had been taken to the cleaners by the internal people for years ... in fact they were getting a better deal from the outsourcing company.
>
> Contract Manager, US retail company

> A lot of the disciplines and processes we've put in should be utilized in the normal business world, and applied to internal sourcing too – it just so happens, with outsourcing, you are forced to do it.
>
> IT Director, European manufacturing organization

In outsourcing, stop measuring the givens, for example 98% availability, and measure something that actually matters, for example the business impact for the 2% when the system is not available. Too often we find people measuring what's easy, not what they actually need ... ultimately the vendor's information achievement and technology achievement have to be linked and partly rewarded against the business's value propositions. If these propositions are not clear, and subject to a measurement system, it is unrealistic to expect the vendor to add business value.

Robert White, Lucidus Management Technologies

From our research base, we have identified five main occasions when organizations are pushed into improving their IT evaluation practice. The first is when a new senior executive feels the need to get to grips with what is going on in the organization, and institutes new management and evaluation practices. The second is when senior executives are exposed to a new evaluation tool that seems to address their concerns, such as the balanced business scorecard described in Chapter 5, and decide to adopt the approach across the organization, or at least in several sub-units. The third is when the organization is experiencing a crisis and it is not clear what is wrong and why. The fourth is when the IT function comes under strong pressure to justify its, invariably, rising expenditure. The fifth and more enduring influence tends to be where an organization is considering, then enters an outsourcing agreement of any size, consuming say 15% or more of the IT budget. Very often, however, organizations do not anticipate this, and are dragged into many of the evaluation improvements needed for outsourcing, with experience being a hard learning route.

This is a particularly important finding because IT outsourcing – the handing over of IT assets, services and activities to third-party management – has been a fast-growing phenomenon. On Yankee Group estimates the global market revenues were US$50 billion in 1994. According to IDC reports, this was predicted to rise to US$121 billion in 2000. Lacity and Willcocks see the global market exceeding US$150 billion by 2004[1]. From the mid–1990s, the UK has seen a 15–20% revenue growth rate, with 2000 revenues probably exceeding £6 billion. By 2004 most large organizations will be outsourcing on average at least 30% of their IT budgets.

If IT outsourcing is to be a central plank in an organization's business and IT/e-business strategy, how can business value from outsourcing be assessed, managed and captured? Referring back to the cost/contribution framework shown in Chapter 2, it is clear that IT outsourcing, in theory, and often according to vendor claims, can contribute to all five value drivers. Historically, the most obvious contribution has been to the 'cost efficiency' area, particularly where organizations have outsourced IT infrastructure and operations. This also has been one of the easier areas to monitor. IT vendors can also make contributions as a 'service to the business', although many organizations realize only late in the game that there is usually a cost-service trade-off in an outsourcing arrangement. Moreover, often 'service' is measured against technical criteria rather than impact on the business, and so the value of the service is not leveraged as much as it could be. The years 1998–2001 have seen a rising trend towards vendors claiming they can also add value by leveraging business improvement, direct profit generation and making a competitive edge contribution. All three contributions require much closer partnering between client and vendor than has traditionally been the case.

The levels of success being achieved from these arrangements is regularly under scrutiny, and Lacity and Willcocks in their most recent work on global IT outsourcing sound many notes of caution[2]. However, it is clear that these different sorts of outsourcing arrangements require different but connected evaluation regimes if there is to be any chance of exploiting their potential business value.

Before looking at the establishment of an evaluation system for an outsourcing arrangement, we will review organizational patterns and contract economics that contribute to and influence the evaluation system.

6.2 Outsourcing: patterns of assessment

In practice, the pre-existing pattern of IT evaluation has a large part to play in the effort required to assess a vendor bid. Several patterns of pre-outsourcing performance measurement dominate. We will call these 'traditionalist', 'service to business' and 'trading agency'.

(1) **Traditionalist** – these organizations tend to focus their evaluation around the feasibility, development and routine operations stages of IT investment. For feasibility, the traditionalists use predominantly financed-based cost-benefit criteria. For IT development the major criteria can be summarized as 'within time and budget to acceptable technical quality'. For routine operations the technical efficiency of IT performance combined with some end-user service measures dominated.

In the move to outsource, traditionalists tend to either spend a long period of time thrashing out detailed parameters of service requirements from the vendor *or* they established a general rule that service will not deteriorate from pre-outsourcing levels.

(2) **Service to business** – prior to outsourcing, these organizations have moved the evaluation focus from IT efficiency towards the IT function's level of user service and business contribution. Such objectives are sought through chargeback systems, IT as a profit centre and/or the introduction of service level agreements with or without penalty clauses. These organizations find it a less difficult transition to evaluate a vendor's performance.

(3) **Trading agency** – here organizations allow the IT function to market its services internally as well as to the external

marketplace. In these trading agency arrangements, the business divisions frequently also have the right to buy IT services either internally or externally (or both), although the internal IT provider is regarded as the 'preferred supplier'. In some examples, the in-house IT department is made a part-owned separate company.

From these assessment patterns, there are several evaluation routes into outsourcing. Organizations jumping straight from a pre-existing 'traditionalist' approach to outsourcing evaluation find the most difficulty in assessing vendor bids, drawing up contracts and assessing subsequent vendor performance. If such organizations attempt to stick to pre-outsourcing levels of service, they will invariably experience unanticipated costs, conflicts over service quality and disaffected business users. Organizations closer to the 'service to business' type evaluation still find a number of problem areas when carrying out an in-house versus out-of-house assessment, and when setting up performance measures for an outsourced aspect of IT. 'Trading agencies' offer the clearest comparisons between bids by the in-house team and those by external vendors. The experience of setting up a trading agency can also feed into developing measures to assess performance of an alternative vendor.

The move from a 'traditionalist', through a 'service to business' to a 'trading agency' assessment pattern suggests a maturing of the ability to assess in-house IT costs and performance against a vendor bid. As always, it is difficult to jump from the earliest state to the most advanced state overnight – most organizations need to evolve through the stages. Evaluation problems will always exist relative to the outsourcing contract, regardless of the pre-outsourcing assessment pattern. The 'service to business' or 'trading agency' patterns, however, are much better suited to the assessment of a vendor bid and ease the transition to outsourcing.

6.3 The centrality of the contract

If an organization outsources IT, the outsourcing contract is the only certain way to ensure that expectations are realized. In practice, weak contracting, based on inadequate assessment of a vendor bid and backed up by poor monitoring systems, results not only in unanticipated, higher costs but also in creation of major problems for client organizations. It is easy for all parties involved in the contract to agree broadly on what is required from a vendor. Those same parties often rely on notions of 'partnership' to offset any difficulties arising from loose contracting. These assumptions rarely proved a sufficient base from which to run effective outsourcing arrangements.

When it comes to drawing up effective outsourcing contracts, we found that the devil is indeed in the detail. Kevin Tomlinson, a vendor manager, stated: 'Outsourcing contracts are agreed in concept and delivered in detail, and that's why they break down.' Figures 6.1 and 6.2 provide summaries of the typical benefits that organizations look for and vendors promise.

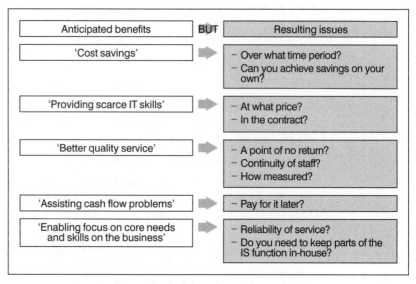

Figure 6.1 Assessing the vendor bid: benefits and issues – 1

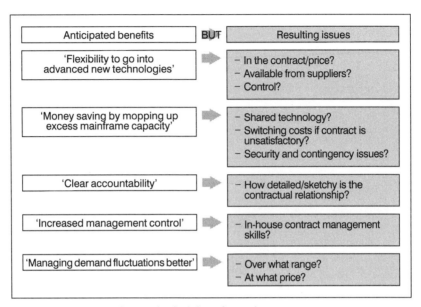

Figure 6.2 Assessing the vendor bid: benefits and issues – 2

It becomes clear that unless, as a minimum, the questions listed here are addressed before IT outsourcing contracts are signed, then unanticipated costs and some significant problems tend to fall upon client organizations.

Bid economics: ten lessons

By way of summary, a number of cautionary points can be raised for those assessing the economics of vendor bids.

(1) You may be able to achieve similar savings internally as those offered by a vendor.

(2) Some savings may be less real than others (and arise from creative accounting).

(3) Your IT costs may already be falling.

(4) You may be comparing total in-house costs against a vendor's selective bid.

(5) Vendors do not necessarily get better deals on hardware and software.

(6) Examine carefully the assumptions behind the vendor bid.

(7) The economics can change quickly even during three-year contracts.

(8) Establish if and where the vendor makes a profit (to avoid opportunistic behaviour).

(9) Outsourcing can carry hidden costs (e.g. through incomplete contracting, post-contract management time and effort, and ambiguities in the contract exploited by the supplier).

(10) The vendor bid can reveal ways of improving in-house performance.

6.4 Setting up a measurement system

Once an organization has decided to outsource any aspect of its IT function, it will need to monitor vendor performance. In this section we extend the discussion on the importance of the contract as the fundamental building block for a measurement system, and look at different types of outsourcing contracts. We then focus on issues relating to measurement systems and service level agreements, and provide guidelines on these topics.

Tight and loose contracting

Where organizations are setting up and running measurement systems for vendor performance, the most common potential 'bad practices' observed are:

(1) over-reliance on the pre-existing standards and measurement systems; and

(2) failure to define comprehensively in the initial contract the detailed expectations of both sides on standards and how measurement will proceed.

These usually occur as a result of either time pressures or a belief in the 'good offices' espoused by the vendor. Much depends on the quality of the relationship between vendor and client. Many organizations are still actually refining measures during the first six months of the contract. This works reasonably well where, in the early stages of a contract, the vendor is anxious to demonstrate flexibility and good partnering.

However, in other contracts, vendors are more concerned about maintaining the letter of the original contract. This creates contract management issues that become exacerbated where the contract is vague or does not cover issues that are arising. The problem arises from different perceptions by the vendor and client of the meaning and role of the contract. The client may believe in the rhetoric of partnership much more than the vendor. The emerging lesson is that participants need to be clear as to what the relationship amounts to and how both sides understand it.

Moreover, while clients have a tendency to believe that the quality of the vendor–client relationship will see them through the limitations of performance measurement arrangements in the contract, in fact the latter can affect the former adversely. In one contract at the high street retailer WH Smith it took 18 months of vigorous contract management finally to get the performance measures right and end disputes on service. The contract manager described the situation as follows:

> There was a contract, a legal one with our signatures on it, with various sections in it, but really it did not define what

the service was going to be. And worse still when we invoked penalty clauses, the section in the contract that talked about the penalty clauses was so ambiguously written that we had a bun fight for nearly six months over it ... I think that all of that proved to me at that stage anyway, that we needed to get out of this partnership issue and back into a proper business contractual relationship and that is what really set us off, I think, down the right road.

The learning point is to ensure that in the period just before signing the contract what is actually said is written into the contract, and be prepared to spend time chronicling the agreement in monotonous detail. One reason that a vendor might want to adhere rigidly to the contract deal is because of very slim profit margins.

More recently, as Lacity and Willcocks note, there have been creative attempts to improve on contracting practice. These have included:

– longer evaluations, for example Ameritech studied outsourcing for 15 months before awarding a contract to IBM;

– customer written detailed contract included with the request for proposal/ITT (invitation to tender);

– provision for competitive bidding for services beyond the contract, as in the British Army's Logistics Information Systems Agency-EDS five-year deal signed in 1996 and extended beyond 2001;

– flexible pricing, for example a share in the vendor's savings, 'open book' accounting and reduced fees based on the vendor's other customers; and

– beginning a long-term contract with a short-term one.

Measurement: systems and service levels

We have seen that it is possible to operate on a more flexible partnership basis and also that some areas to be outsourced may be difficult to specify precisely in terms of service and performance required. However, in outsourcing, discretion may be the better part of valour. In reviewing 18 organizations contemplating or undertaking outsourcing, Lacity and Hirschheim[3] suggested the following 'safety first' guidelines on creating a measurement system.

(1) Measure *everything* during the baseline period.

(2) Develop service level measures.

(3) Develop service level reports.

(4) Specify escalation procedures.

(5) Include cash penalties for non-performance.

(6) Determine growth rates.

(7) Adjust charges to changes in business, technology and volumes.

Our own research base reflects the finding that it is advisable not to start a contract until current information systems services have been measured in a *baseline period*. There are a number of points here. Some organizations leave the contract incomplete with a view to carrying out measurement in a baseline period *after* the contract has started, or trusting in a good relationship with the vendor to deal with problems as they arise. Both approaches are hardly low risk and can leave an organization as a hostage to fortune. See the following case study of a UK retail and distribution company for an example.

– A contract between this company and a vendor of telecommunications services was producing major cost savings, but the measurement system still needed tidying up during the course of the contract because of lack of specific targets when it was drawn up. The Contract Manager stated:

> (The vendor) largely wrote it and we signed it. All we were looking for was escalation procedures, what the nap connection charges were, and there was some discussion as to how they would respond and that they wouldn't do this that and the other. Even those comments were ambiguous in the way that they had been written. In undertaking the service level agreement procedure and the definition of our service level agreements I think two things were sorted out. First of all, we then developed a service level agreement that was ours . . . Once we'd done that, we then realized that we had no telecommunications targets and strategy relative to the vendor, so we developed them. It was from that point onwards that we rested control from . . . (the vendor) . . . of our telecommunications strategy, back to where it should have been, which was here all along.

There may be time pressure to get a contract started. This may cut down on the time in which the baseline period for measurement is allowed to run. Lacity and Willcocks recommend a six-month period to allow for fluctuations in service levels due to factors such as tax season, seasonal business oscillations and end-of-year data processing. If service levels are measured monthly and compared, this allows the setting up of a target variance for each service performance within which to fluctuate before 'excess' charges to the vendor will become payable, or underperformance by the vendor can be penalized.

Refining the measurement system after the contract has started can work, provided this was part of the contractual agreement in the first place. Thus, a major US-based bank signed an outsourcing contract for running its mainframe service. A notable point here is that the pre-existing measurement system was already fairly rigorous.

> Broad inferences were given based upon the service agreements that . . . (the bank's) . . . data centre already had on its businesses. They were not really formal service level agreements. They were merely statements of what the on-line day would be from when to when by service, of all the many different services we have across all the different hardware platforms . . . All that was made available to . . . (the vendor) . . ., and established as the initial service level agreement guidelines. The bank then tasked itself with the vendor's agreement to getting much more crisp service level agreements and we spent a lot of time with piloting and doing various other things to try to come up with standard, across-the-region support agreements and service level agreements which everyone could sign up to. We are on to reiteration three and close to signing off what will be the final service level agreements.
>
> Contract Manager

A further stipulation about the baseline period is to measure everything, not just what is easiest to measure. The problem is less prevalent where what is being outsourced is an area that was heavily measured before and is on the more traditional 'factory' or production side of IT operations. However, there can be a learning curve even here. Thus, WH Smith outsourced telecommunications to DEC, and from the experience was able to formulate much tighter measurement for a contract between Our Price Records, a company in the group, and the vendor Racal.

A more difficult area to measure, whether outsourced or not, is systems development. Our own view is that these areas are probably best managed on an 'insourcing' (hiring resources from the market to operate under in-house management) rather than on a strict 'outsourcing' basis. The problem is that the end goal for systems' development, and how to get there, can rarely be well-defined. Some organizations, Pilkington for example in their on-going deal with EDS, handled this by stipulating that the vendor will make defined resources available for a defined period. Measures of vendor staff productivity must also be in place. However, these measures should not be based merely on the speed with which development proceeds through a defined methodology and timetable. The outputs of development also need to be measured in terms of business impact, for example improvements in cost, quality and service, systems reliability, ease of use and ease of user learning. The elapsed time to business use is also a useful measure, with financial penalties built in for under-performance.

These are difficult types of measures to formulate unless there are in-house systems people on the team, who already have key targets and measures in place before outsourcing. (See the following case study of a UK manufacturing company for an example).

– The company outsourced software development of warehouse and carousel control systems in the factory. There was a lack of in-house expertise in this area. It emerged that there were complex interfaces with the company's mainframe systems and the mainframe development work was outsourced to a further vendor. According to the IT manager, the company had no complaints about the work of these vendors:

> It was lack of appreciation of the complexity of the interface early on because of not high enough calibre staff internally to recognize that. Also nearly every department was affected in some way by these systems. Yet despite the fact that at the outset it was recognized as

a business objective to enhance the capability of the site to deal with orders, we found ourselves in a situation where as software was developed and then went to user acceptance testing it was only then that users realized what the system was doing and then raised very real problems . . . it has enabled us to rationalize production in Europe but it was longer than it should have been and cost more and it took us longer to become self-sufficient. We were too dependent on a third party for a core, essential business application.

In later development projects this company successfully operated an 'insourcing' approach, bringing external expertise to in-house teams to ensure that transfer of learning took place. They have also operated with clearer objectives and measures on development performance, not merely on hours worked and effort expended.

In addition to the above areas, there may be a series of services commonly provided by the IT department, but not documented. Before outsourcing, it is important that these are analysed and included in the service agreement with the vendor along with measures of their delivery. What is not included in baseline period measurement will not be covered by the fixed price offered by the vendor and subsequently may be open to 'excess charges'. Examples of such services may be consultancy, PC support, installation and training services.

Clearly, specifying service level measures is critical. While this is regularly prepared, a common mistake is to then not stipulate 100% service accountability from the vendor. At one help desk support contract we researched in a major oil company, 80% of service requests had to be responded to within 20 seconds and 90% within 30 seconds. Financial penalties were attached to failure to meet these criteria over a specified period of time. However, the vendor was also made responsible for reporting in detail on this performance and providing explanations when 100% was not achieved. Essentially, a measure was also needed to ensure that the service requests not handled within the stipulated criteria were subsequently dealt with in an agreed reasonable time. Note the importance of detailed service level reports in this example, as well as the importance of agreeing in advance what happens when problems require escalation. This must lead to financial penalties for non-performance as shown in this statement of an IT manager of a major bank:

> It was agreed at contract time there would be financial penalties ... for failure to perform of two kinds. One, if a direct operational loss is caused because of negligence on (the vendor's) part in any one instance and the bank has to pay its clients money in terms of interest charges or penalties, then (the vendor) will indemnify ... (the company) ... up to certain limits, and that's on a one time basis ... Secondly, if on an overall average service evaluation, taking its ability to provide a service over the course of a month, it fell below a specified level. So we have two specific financial implications of failure to deliver the service, one over time and one for a particular occasion, and that's well in place.

It is important to look to the future when negotiating service levels and their price. In particular, the rate at which service needs will grow is often underestimated. Organizations need to include realistic growth rates in the contract agreement's fixed price. Specific clauses may also be needed to cover large service volume fluctuations due to merger, acquisitions or sale of parts of the business.

Overall, client organizations need to make measurement work for rather than against their interests. Thus, in one US manufacturing company, the contract specified a two-second response time for key applications such as order entry and customer service. It also specified vendor support for up to 20 users at a given time using a 4GL. However, during the first week the 11 4GL users were taking up more than 30% of the machine cycles and making response times for critical applications unachievable. The vendor could have been forced to upgrade the technology provided, but the client, in this case, felt the demand would have been unreasonable. A tight contract reasonably handled by both sides was felt to improve the vendor–client relationship and levels of satisfaction all round.

6.5 Outsourced: anticipating evaluation issues

In this section we signpost some further problem areas encountered. Some of the following issues are quite widely known, and yet are still experienced by organizations undertaking outsourcing. Other problem areas identified below are more difficult to predict. All are very real possibilities which any organization contemplating outsourcing should consider.

Significant effort may be required to develop adequate measuring systems

This was stressed earlier in the context of assessing vendor bids. Here we look at the issue for organizations that have already outsourced. As an example, a UK County Council signed a five-year contract with a major vendor. The contract involved mainframe operations and applications service. This was the first of three major contracts for the council. Even though the IT department had been operating largely as an internal trading agency, there was still an immense amount of work needed to get the measurement system in place. The IT Director stated:

There was a lot of information available to the outsourcing companies about the current equipment, current costs of running equipment and staffing costs. A lot of information from us to them. But although we had been operating as a trading organization, there weren't any service level agreements in place to build up a business relationship between the departments buying the service and the operations area itself. That was why it took five months to get from preferred supplier to contract stage. We actually wanted to have the whole of the contract underpinned by agreed and signed service level agreements before we entered into the contract.

It is interesting to note here the desire to get the detailed service level agreements in place before the contract is entered into. From a review of our research base, it emerged that user involvement in the establishment of service level agreements was particularly important if user needs were going to be identified properly and if there was to be user buy-in to the measurement activity. However, more detailed service measures and costing procedures can have unanticipated effects on user behaviour, as will be discussed below. The sheer detail of the service level agreements may also create a monitoring problem. Reflecting on their experiences, outsourcing organizations stressed the importance of focusing on the key measures in any service level agreement. As Robert White of outsourcing consultants Lucidus stressed:

> You can actually reduce the number of measures if you focus on what is valuable. One US manufacturer we advised had over 150 measures and a unit of 50 collecting the stuff ... no one there acted on the results, the information was reported up. Now they are working with 17 measures and the unit of 50 people has been dispersed to do something more useful.

Outsourcing can require a culture change in measurement

It is all too easy to underestimate the gap between the pre- and post-outsourcing approaches to measurement and control. Many organizations do not, at least in their early contracts, move that far away from their existing measures and standards for IT performance. This can leave latent problems and conflicts that will emerge across the life of the outsourcing contract, as one IT director of a UK public sector organization explains:

> The performance measures were not strong enough. This was because of the culture we operated in. I think they took us and I don't blame them, we weren't very professional. I think there have been some very good attempts at tightening up performance measurement. But once you've got a contract you've got a contract and if you are dealing with sharp guys like them, then it's very difficult.

The fact that this IT director is getting a better deal on service towards the end of the contract suggests one reason why many organizations might choose to go for contracts of five years or less in length. The prospect of contract renewal reinvigorates vendor motivation to deliver service.

The possibility of vendor opportunism

This issue was hinted at in the previous point. A number of organizations operate a multivendor strategy explicitly to limit vendor opportunism. Other organizations learn over time about vendor opportunism and how to deal with it. As one example, a manufacturing company outsourced IT to a major bureau in order to cut costs. A year into the contract it still had no real in-house expertise to manage the contract and no real IT strategy, despite the fact that IT was beginning to impact adversely the conduct of business. The vendor was providing trainee contractors for systems' development, but charging top rates.

Moreover, the company was having to train vendor staff about the company and the industry in which it was operating. Subsequently, the company gained contract expertise, built up an in-house technical staff base and renegotiated the vendor role to a much smaller one.

One cautionary case presented by Lacity and Hirschheim[4] reveals another facet of vendor opportunism. One ten-year contract was the product of senior management looking at ways to contain or reduce rising IT costs. A six-month baseline period was measured with the vendor contractually bound to deliver the average service level of this period. However, the contract was signed before the baseline measurement was completed. Therefore, the services covered in the contract were not completely defined. In data centre operations the contract specified a fixed number of resources, for example tape mounts, CPU minutes and print lines for a fixed price. On applications' development and maintenance, the company received a fixed number of man-hours of service. Other utility services were ill-defined in the contract. While the promised 20% reduction of projected in-house IT budgets may be delivered by the vendor on the fixed price, in fact the 'excess' charges as a result of an incomplete contract may well cancel out any benefits.

In fact, responses from the operating companies suggest that the vendor reduced its own costs by degradation of service, lack of responsiveness, 'excess' charges and transferring skilled staff from the client to other contracts. Additionally, despite promises, the vendor failed to develop service levels and performance measures after the contract went into effect. The vendor also took a strict view of the contract's 'change of character' clause, continually interpreting it in its own favour. In a second case there was again failure to negotiate a sound detailed contract: 'The threat of opportunism was readily apparent in the excess charges, degradation of services, loss of IS expertise, antiquated technology and overworked (vendor) staff.'

Internal charging systems may create problems

Even in a well-managed outsourcing contract, there can be latent problems between users in business units, the IT people managing the contract and the vendor. In many examples, the problems built around the charging system as it affected users. In this respect, the experience of a major brewing company in the first year of the contract is quite a common one, as a senior manager explained:

> Complexity of recharging is what's causing those communications challenges . . . They (the business users) are very wary of it because they now realize that it's an outsider who's charging them and maybe there is a risk they will get charged more and people are going to get more commercial.

However, the recharging issue can actually become such a bone of contention that it undermines the whole basis of the contract. For example, consider the five-year contract between a major vendor and a multinational manufacturing company. The strategic thrust in this multinational was to get rid of national data centres and devolve IT to business units. The company also wished to rationalize head office computing and save on IT costs. The vendor took over all existing IT work for head office and European companies in the multinational. However, the inadequate initial analysis of IT costs, together with incomplete specification of performance measures and insufficient detail on what services were required fed into creating large-scale problems in recharging users for services. The IT director stated:

> They came to us and said what do you spend on computing at the moment and I'll tell you it was difficult to actually arrive at that figure. There were bits of computing going on all over the place, so that was a stab in the dark. The best

educated guess we could make, we think all of that costs us that, and they said right we will give you 15% more.

The initial difficulties were unbundling exactly what the client was paying for, and then determining when excess charges became payable. There were also problems over 'change of character', where the hardware base was changing along with the services required:

> Immediately problems began to occur. How much computing power were we entitled to before we paid any excess charges? . . . Of course, there was a billing cost mismatch because they said we will do it for in total about £8 million. So we were going to give them £8 million and they were going to provide services. That then gave us the problem of actually charging out the £8 million, so we had to create an arbitrary invoicing system to recover the £8 million . . . We wondered well the £8 million has got to come down hasn't it. They were saying 'But we are having to take a beating on this, it's all swings and roundabouts.' Well that's all right, but when you're the guy in the department with a PC, you are thinking its madness. They want to cross-charge me £10,000 for a PC, I can go out and buy it for less.

Clearly these problems could have been less contentious if the vendor was making more than a slim margin on the original deal. Here the lack of clarity in measurement at the contract stage led to opportunities for a pressured vendor to argue legitimately that many of the services were in addition to those covered by the fixed price agreement. This also brought additional cost pressure on the hastily erected recharging system. At the end of three years the vendor cancelled the contract and each user negotiated separately directly with it. Most of those companies stayed with the vendor, initially, but some drifted away.

Users may become more wary of the IT service

In the cases of charging systems described above, users clearly became much more anxious about the service they were getting for the money they were being charged. In some respects, this is often a healthy development, and may lead to users focusing on necessary rather than 'nice-to-have' services. It may also induce a much greater commercial awareness about computer use in their department. On the other hand, as one systems' developments manager of a manufacturing company said, there can be some less attractive outcomes in outsourcing situations:

> I think when you talk about service level agreements and the sorts of terminology you start surrounding a lot of the services with then they tend to get in the way of true fast response, and a question of how much does it cost tends to be an issue. We are already finding that by charging internally for services then the idea that you have to locate a customer who has a budget that can pay, gets in the way of getting a fast response. It shouldn't do, but it still does. It's magnified beyond reasonable proportions with an external agency.

IT costs may become too transparent

This would seem to be a contradiction, in the sense that the transparency of costs as a result of outsourcing is usually proclaimed as a desirable outcome. However where there is still a large in-house IT capability, there may arise inflexibilities in the ways in which funds can be utilized and additional IT work achieved. This statement of the IT manager of a US bank confirms this:

> One of the things that some of us were concerned about as part of the deal, but which was overlooked by senior management who signed up to the deal, was the fact that

we know the way we operated here in IT. We could always fudge costs ... There's always a little bit of fat in any budget that allows us to take on something unexpected. I am talking about the ability to bring on a new software package which might enhance processing in an area, a systems software package, a new tool, which might cost you a license fee plus £5000 a year in maintenance costs. We could always do these simple things in-house.

The irony here is that the in-house IT staff felt that the vendor had done too good a job of analysing costs and establishing what the price for different services would be. The problems are very much for operational IT staff rather than more senior management who in fact, as this contract manager of a financial services company explains, continue to see the non-degradation of contracted service plus large cost savings as very much a good deal:

> When we transferred across it was on the basis of our (existing IT) budget ... They (the vendor staff) had up front clearly what we were using at the time of the out-sourcing deal. They were very thorough and did their homework. But it's a loss of advantage to us really. We no longer have the ability to demand flexibility of the data centre in the way it manages its cost. We can't force the vendor to find ways to do things on the cheap which is something we would have sat down and found a way of doing, and they feel under no obligation to do this.

6.6 Staffing: a vital resource

For sound evaluation practice it is vital to have the capabilities and skills in place to monitor and manage vendor performance. In their work on this subject, Feeny and Willcocks[5] show that four core capabilities are needed in-house to set up and run an effective IT market sourcing strategy. Here we will illustrate these capabilities with examples from our research base. The first two capabilities are more directly about evaluation practice, while the latter two have evaluation tasks imbedded in the roles assigned:

Informed buying: 'Managing the IT sourcing strategy which meets the interests of the business'

This involves analysis of the external market for IT services; selection of a sourcing strategy to meet business needs and technology issues; leadership of the tendering, contracting and service management processes. One informed buyer describes the role:

> If you are a senior manager in the company and you want something done, you come to me and I will go outside, select the vendor and draw up the contract with the outsourcer, and if anything goes wrong it's my butt that gets kicked by you.

Informed buying means:

(1) monitoring available services of external suppliers;

(2) analysing the nature of the service requirement for the short and long term;

(3) structuring the tendering process; and

(4) overseeing contact negotiations.

Contract monitoring: 'protecting the business's contractual position, current and future'

A major consequence of IT outsourcing complexity and the commercialization of the IT operation is the need for contract monitoring. The contract monitor ensures that the business position is protected at all times. The role involves holding suppliers to account against both existing service contracts and the developing performance standards of the services market. The capabilities and number of people needed can be considerable. Thus, in the on-going UK Inland Revenue-EDS total outsourcing contract, according to 2001 IT Director John Yard, the contract management team covered 14 disciplines and ran highly detailed monitoring mechanisms. In the on-going BAe-CSC deal in the defence industry, an IT manager in the company commented:

> We need a significant number of people in-house to monitor vendor service performance. In one business unit alone we have 16 people working on contracts, six exclusively on the monitoring side.

The main tasks of contract monitoring are:

(1) monitoring results against goals;

(2) benchmarking existing contracts against developing market capability;

(3) negotiating detailed amendments; and

(4) identifying and protecting against potential precedents.

Contract facilitation: 'ensuring the success of existing contracts for IT services'

Most IT outsourcing situations involve considerable complexity. Typically a large population of users within the business are receiving a variety of services from multiple suppliers (or supply points) under a set of detailed and lengthy contracts. The contract facilitator ensures that problems and conflicts are resolved fairly within what are usually long-term relationships.

In our experience, both users and vendors place high value on effective contract facilitators. The role arises for a variety of reasons:

(1) to provide one stop shopping for the business user;

(2) the vendor or user demands it;

(3) multiple vendors need coordinating;

(4) enables easier monitoring of usage and service; or

(5) users may demand too much and incur excessive charges.

One contract facilitator noted: 'They (users) have been bitten a few times when they have dealt directly with suppliers, and it's a service we can provide, so now we do.'

Vendor development: 'identifying the potential added value of IT service suppliers'

The single most threatening aspect of IT outsourcing is the presence of substantial switching costs. To outsource successfully in the first place requires considerable organizational effort over an extended period of time. Subsequently to change suppliers may well require an equivalent effort. Hence, it is in the business interest to maximize the contribution of existing suppliers. The vendor developer is concerned with the long-term potential for suppliers to add value, creating the 'win-win' situations in which the supplier increases its revenues by providing services which increase business benefits. A major retail multinational has a number of ways of achieving this, including an annual formal meeting:

It's in both our interests to keep these things going and we formally, with our biggest suppliers, have a meeting once a year and these are done at very senior levels in both organizations, and that works very well.

Human resource challenges

In practice, the development of these capabilities presents a number of strong challenges for contemporary organizations. Often in our research these capabilities were found to be missing. A common tendency when outsourcing is initially to appoint a contract manager, whose responsibilities are conceived as some mix of the informed buying and contract monitoring roles. In one major bank, however:

> I am not physically managing anyone in the data centre environment . . . but a lot of my time is being taken up as being not contract management but service relationship management . . . dealing with senior managers in the bank who are coming to me to explain service issues on a day-to-day basis. We are having to do lots of work we thought we had outsourced.

In fact the contract manager was being stretched across many needed capabilities, and the vendor development capability did not exist.

In these situations we found organizations developing and staffing the capabilities outlined above, but over the contract span in response to problems *as they arose*, rather than proactively. In many cases this was a response to the difficulties inherent in developing what in fact needs to be an in-house, high-performance vendor management group. According to Feeny and Willcocks, the people required to staff such a group need to be high performers with strong business orientation, interpersonal skills, as well as different degrees and types of technical know-how. These are not easy to find in the current skills market. Moreover, organizational human resource policies are often not set up to pay such people the (volatile) going rate, offer them the challenges they need and provide suitable career paths. However, these challenges cannot be shirked, because sound evaluation practice will depend on the staff, the processes they put in place and the staff's capability to improve continuously evaluation practices and, therefore, vendor performance.

6.7 Summary

The economics of IT outsourcing uncovered by our research suggests that organizations need to pursue in-house improvements first, identify full IT costs and establish performance benchmarks, pursue further in-house improvements, and only then make in-house versus outsourcing comparisons. If the outsourcing option is rejected initially, it needs to be revisited at regular intervals, not least because the reassessment can act as an external benchmark on in-house IT performance. However, in practice, we found a number of other objectives and interests often impacting this economic logic.

Organizations found it difficult to assess vendor against in-house bids on a comparable basis, especially where prior evaluation practice exhibited the kinds of weaknesses discussed in this and earlier chapters. However, research base experiences suggested that the time and effort spent on fully assessing in-house performance, and revamping measurement systems proved vital in feeding into more effective contracting. All too often outsourcing deals can be based on varying degrees of 'voodoo economics'. Another finding was that in order to enable comparison with and assessment of vendor bids, this evaluation work is best done before any contracts are signed, even where a specific vendor has been chosen. Organizations cannot assume safely that vendor opportunism will not occur. From this perspective, we found the contract to have the central role in determining whether outsourcing expectations would be realized. Hidden costs in outsourcing arrangements were identified, and these were found to be most frequently the outcome of weak contracting.

It also became clear that even good contracting, based on detailed IT evaluation and supported by comprehensive service measures and reporting systems, did not stop problems arising during the course of the contract. This stresses again what emerged strongly from our research: the importance of active monitoring and management of the vendor. As one IT director remarked ruefully about a particularly difficult outsourcing experience, 'the one definite thing I have learned is that it's not like ringing for room service'.

6.8 Key learning points

- IT outsourcing offers a major opportunity to improve evaluation practices. Organizations not accepting the opportunity will be forced into making the changes or will have significantly disappointing outsourcing experiences.

- Prior patterns of IT evaluation greatly influence the degree of difficulty experienced in entering and running an outsourcing arrangement. A number of significant concerns emerged, namely evaluating total IT contribution, identifying full costs, benchmarking and external comparisons, the role of charging systems, and the adoption of service levels agreements by the in-house operation.

- Assessing the economics of a vendor bid is fraught with difficulty. A client organization needs to understand the likely sources of hidden costs and the centrality of the contract in monitoring and conditioning vendor performance. The ten lessons in bid economics need to be understood.

- Measurement systems need to be carefully designed and staffed, ideally before the contract is finally signed.

- Once outsourced, certain evaluation issues can be anticipated. Much effort will be needed to set up a measurement system. A cultural change in measurement will usually be required.

Guard against the possibility of vendor opportunism. Internal charging systems may create problems. Users may become more wary of the IT service. IT costs may become too transparent.

– Staffing for improved evaluation practice provides often unanticipated challenges. In-house informed buying, contract monitoring, contract facilitation and vendor development capabilities are required. Attracting and retaining the high performers with the necessary distinctive skills, attitudes and behaviours presents traditional human resource policies with considerable problems in a fast-moving labour market.

6.9 Practical action guidelines

– Understand where your organization is on the scale of assessment patterns in order to best prepare for a transition to outsourcing evaluation.

– Follow the ten lessons of bid economics.

– Ensure that your outsourcing contract is specific enough to document what was said in negotiations and flexible enough to deal with arising situations.

– Limit the length of the contract (3–5 years is most typical).

– Measure *everything* during the baseline period.

– Commit the resources required to develop an adequate measuring system.

– Develop service level measures.

– Develop service level reports.

– Specify escalation procedures.

– Include cash penalties for non-performance.

– Determine growth rates.

– Adjust charges to changes in business, technology and volumes.

– Ensure that the staff/roles required to support the contract exist, including in informed buying, contract monitoring, contract facilitation and vendor development.

7 | E-valuation (1) : not business as usual?

7.1 Introduction

> There are many, many companies on the Internet, but very few businesses.
>
> Analyst Mary Meaker, Morgan Stanley (2000)

> E can stand for electric or electronic, but at some point it will have to stand for earnings.
>
> Chairman of the New York Stock Exchange, May 2000.

During the last few years we have witnessed rapid expansion in the use of the Internet and the World Wide Web. The e-business opportunity in the individual company is typically seen as dividing into internets, extranets and intranets, covering business-to-consumer (B2C), business-to-business (B2B) and internal use of web-based technology. On conservative figures, B2C will be worth US$184 billion by 2003, and B2B US$1,300 billion. We have also seen the rise of C2C and C2B uses, and E2E (everywhere-to-everywhere) connectivity is the next step to be contemplated. However, the rising expectations of payoff from these investments, fuelled by high stock valuations of Internet-based companies, dived from spring 2000. Subsequently, it has become obvious that the new technology's ability to break the old economic and business rules, and to operate on 'new rules' in a 'new economy', is constrained by the effectiveness of the business model it underpins and of business and technology management. Of course, this is a familiar story, which is also true of previous rounds of technology.

At the same time, the use of Internet-based technologies, in terms of speed, access, connectivity, and its ability to free up and extend business thinking and vision represents an enormous opportunity to create e-business, if it can only be grasped. This chapter, and Chapter 8, will focus on laying a framework for identifying e-business value, with the following observations as guidelines.

(1) As argued in Chapter 3, for any IT investment the contribution of Web-based technologies to business has to be defined before the allocation of resources.

(2) The changing economics of e-business breed discontinuities and uncertainties which need to be explored thoroughly in order to understand the implications of e-business investment decisions and related strategic decisions.

(3) Use of e-technologies does not contribute value in the same way to every business; thus, different types of e-business investment cannot be justified using the same approach. The various forms of e-business that evolve and the way they apply in different organizations and industries need to be explored.

In this chapter we establish the context of the evaluation challenges that businesses now face. We then look at the emerging possibilities for a new economics of information and technology as a result of the latest technologies. Finally, we illustrate some of these with an in-depth case study (see Chapter 8).

7.2 IT eras: a further complication to the evaluation problem

Reference has been made to the rapid evolution of information-based technologies, and the pervasiveness of their use in organizations. In his book *Waves of Power*, David Moschella[1]

	Systems-centric 1964–1981	PC-centric 1981–1994	Network-centric 1994–2005	Content-centric 2005–2015
Key audience	Corporate	Professional	Consumer	Individual
Key technology	Transistor	Microprocessor	Communications bandwidth	Software
Governing principle	Grosch's Law	Moore's Law	Metcalfe's Law	Law of Transformation
Vendor offerings	Proprietary systems	Standard products	Value-added services	Custom services
Channel	Direct	Indirect	Online	Customer pull
Network focus	Data centre	Internal LANs	Public networks	Transparency
User focus	Efficiency	Productivity	Customer service	Virtualization
Supplier structure	Vertical integration	Horizontal computer value chain	Unified computers and communications chain	Embedded
Supplier leadership	US systems	US components	National carriers	Content providers
Number of users at end of period	10 million	100 milllion	1 billion	Universal
End of period market size	US$20 billion	US$460 billion	£3 trillion	Too embedded to be measurable

Figure 7.1 The resolution of the IT industry (adapted from Moschella, 1997)

frames this evolution as a series of technology eras and describes the dimensions of each era. The significance of this theory to IT evaluation is that most organizations do not transition cleanly and completely from one era to the next, but seek to apply a variety of technologies. However, invariably, they use a limited number of well-tried evaluation methods that, in fact, can rarely capture the full costs, benefits, risks and value of different technologies, embodying different economic laws.

Figure 7.1 charts various aspects across the eras. Up to 2001 and the present 'network-centric era', each has seen roughly six- to seven-year cycles of investment in specific technologies. Although technology innovation cycles have shortened, computer adoption times have stayed at about seven years because it takes at least that long to institutionalize related managerial, social and organizational changes. Let us look at each era in more detail.

The systems-centric era (1964–1981)

It is generally accepted that this era began with the IBM S/360 series – the computer industry's first broad group of steadily upgradable compatible systems. The dominating principle throughout most of this period was that of Grosch's Law. Arrived at in the 1940s, this law stated that computer power increases as the square of the cost, in other words a computer that is twice as expensive delivers four times the computing power. This law favoured large systems. Investment decisions were fairly simple initially and involved centralized data centres. IBM dominated supply and protected its prices. In response to dissatisfaction with centralized control of computing by finance functions, there followed centralized time-sharing arrangements with non-finance functions, some outsourcing by scientific, engineering and production departments to independent service suppliers, and subsequently moves towards small-scale computers to achieve local independence. This led to stealth growth in equipment costs outside official central IT budgets, but also a dawning understanding of the high lifecycle support costs of systems acquired and run locally in a de facto decentralized manner.

From about 1975 the shift from centralized to business unit spending accelerated, aided by the availability of minicomputers. Also, in a competitive market, prices of software and peripherals fell rapidly and continuously, enabling local affordability, often outside IT budgets and embedded in other expenditures. *Without centralized control, it became difficult to monitor IT costs.*

The PC-centric era 1981–1994

This era began with the arrival of the IBM PC in 1981. The sale of PCs went from US$2 billion in 1980 to US$160 billion in 1995. This period saw Grosch's Law inverted; by the mid-1980s the best price/performance was coming from PCs and other microprocessor-based systems. The underlying economics are summarized in Moore's Law, named after one of the founders of Intel. This law stated that semiconductor price/performance would double every two years for the foreseeable future. This law remained fairly accurate into the mid-1990s, aided by constantly improved designs and processing volumes of market-provided rather than in-house developed microprocessor-based systems. Additionally, the PC-centric era saw shifts from proprietary corporate to individual commodity computing. The costs of switching from one PC vendor to another were low, while many peripherals and PC software took on commodity-like characteristics. A further shift in the late 1980s seemed to be toward open systems, with the promise of common standards and high compatibility. However, it became apparent that the move was not really from proprietary to open, but from IBM to Microsoft, Intel and Novell.

These technical advances provided ready access to cheap processing for business unit users. IT demand and expenditure were now coming from multiple points in organizations. *One frequent tendency was a loosening of financial justification on the cost side, together with difficulties in, or lack of concern for, verifying rigorously the claimed benefits from computer spending.* From 1988 onwards, technical developments in distributed computing architecture, together with organizational reactions against local, costly, frequently inefficient microcomputer-based initiatives, led to a client-server investment cycle. The economics of client-server have been much debated. The claim was that increased consolidation and control of local networks through client-server architectures would lower the costs of computing significantly.

Although the PC-centric era is marked by inexpensive equipment and software relative to price/performance calculation, the era did not usher in a period of low-cost computing. Constant upgrades, rising user expectations, and the knock-on costs over systems' lifecycles saw to that. By the mid-1990s the cost per PC seat was becoming a worrying issue in corporate computing, especially as no consistent cost benchmarks emerged. Published cost of ownership estimates range from US$3,000 to US$18,000 per seat per year, probably because of differences in technology, applications, users, workloads and network management practices. One response to these rising costs is outsourcing, examined in more detail in Chapter 6.

The network-centric era (1994–2005)

Although the Internet has existed for nearly 20 years, it was the arrival of the Mosaic graphical interface in 1993 that made possible mass markets based on the Internet and the Web. This era is being defined by the integration of worldwide communications infrastructure and general purpose computing. Communications bandwidth begins to replace microprocessing power as the key commodity. Attention shifts from local area networks to wide area networks, particularly intranets. There is already evidence of strong shifts of emphasis over time from graphical user interfaces to Internet browsers, indirect to on-line channels, client–server to electronic commerce, stand-alone PCs to bundled services, and from individual productivity to virtual communities.

Economically, the pre-eminence of Moore's Law is being replaced by Metcalfe's Law, named after Bob Metcalfe (inventor of the Ethernet). Metcalfe's Law states that the cost of a network rises linearly as additional nodes are added, but that the value can increase exponentially. Software economics have a similar pattern. Once software is designed, the marginal cost of producing additional copies is very low, potentially offering huge economies of scale for the supplier. Combining network and software economics produces vast opportunities for value creation. At the same time, the exponential growth of Internet user numbers since 1995 suggests that innovations which reduce usage costs whilst improving ease of use will shape future developments, rather than the initial cost of IT equipment – as was previously the case.

By 1999, fundamental network-centric applications included e-mail and the Web – the great majority of traffic on the latter being information access and retrieval. By 2001, transaction processing in the forms of, for example, e-commerce for businesses, shopping and banking for consumers, and voting and tax collection for governments was also emerging. The need to reduce transaction costs through technology may well result in a further wave of computer spending, as we have already seen with many B2B applications. Internet usage is challenged in terms of reliability, response times and data integrity when compared to traditional on-line transaction processing expectations. Dealing with these challenges has significant financial implications.

Many of these developments and challenges depend on the number of people connected to the Internet. Significant national differences exist. However, as more people join, the general incentive to use the Internet increases, technical limitations notwithstanding. One possibility is that IT investment will lead to productivity. In turn, this will drive growth and further IT investments. The breakthrough, if it comes, may well be with corporations learning to focus computing priorities externally (e.g. on reaching customers, investors and suppliers), rather than the historical inclination primarily towards internal auto-mation, partly driven by inherited evaluation criteria and practices. Even so, as Moschella notes:

> . . . much of the intranet emphasis so far has been placed upon internal efficiencies, productivity and cost savings . . .

(and) ... has sounded like a replay of the client–server promises of the early 1990s, or even the paperless office claims of the mid-1980s.

A content-centric era (2005–2015)

It is notoriously difficult to predict the future development and use of information technologies. One plausible view has been put forward by Moschella. The shifts would be from e-commerce to virtual businesses, from the wired consumer to individualized services, from communications bandwidth to software, information and services, from on-line channels to customer pull, and from a converged computer/communications/consumer electronics industry value chain to one of embedded systems. A content-centric era of virtual businesses and individualized services would depend on the previous era delivering an inexpensive, ubiquitous and easy-to-use high bandwidth infrastructure.

For the first time, demand for an application would define the range of technology usage rather than, as previously, also having to factor in what is technologically and economically possible. The IT industry focus would shift from specific technological capabilities to software, content and services. These are much less likely to be subject to diminishing investment returns. The industry driver would truly be 'information economics', combining the nearly infinite scale economies of software with the nearly infinite variety of content.

Metcalfe's Law would be superceded by the Law of Transformation. A fundamental consideration is the extent to which an industry/business is *bit* (information) based as opposed to *atom* (physical product) based. In the content-centric era, the extent of an industry's subsequent transformation would be equal to the square of the percentage of that industry's value-added accounted for by bit- as opposed to atom-processing activity. The effect of the squared relationship would be to widen industry differentials. In all industries, but especially in the more 'bit-based' ones, describing and quantifying the full IT value chain would become as difficult an exercise as assessing the full 1990s value chain for electricity.

Let us underline the implications of these developments, because they help to explain why IT/e-business evaluation presents such formidable challenges. As at 2001, organizations have investments in systems from the systems- and PC-centric eras, will be assessing their own potential and actual use of technologies of the network-centric era, while also contemplating how to become 'content-centric'. We find that too many organizations tend to utilize across-the-board legacy evaluation methods, which in fact are more suitable for the economics and technologies of previous eras. What is needed is a much keener understanding of the economics of the network-centric era now upon us, so that better decisions can be made about choice of evaluation approaches.

7.3 The changing economics of e-business

Is a new economics developing? Consider some of the following emerging possibilities.

(1) Metcalfe's Law will become increasingly applicable from 2001 as information networks and e-commerce continues to expand globally, as a result of more users transacting via the Web.

(2) Digitalizing transactions can greatly reduce transaction costs both intra-organizationally and between businesses. Dell and Cisco Systems, for example, report massive savings from operating virtually. A senior manager at Dell explained that he saw inventory as the physical embodiment of the poor use of information. Lower transaction costs are a strong incentive to perform more business functions on the

Internet. According to the established pricing schemes for the Internet, the price of some services is disproportional to their real value, that is the price consumers are prepared to pay. For commercial uses it is usually very low, thus giving more incentives to firms to migrate to Internet electronic transactions.

- In 1997, Morgan Stanley (the major investment bank based in New York) was reported to have achieved over US$1 million in annual savings after introducing a Web-based information server for firm-wide use. The 10,000 employees used the company's network on a daily basis to access information that used to be published and circulated internally on paper. By eliminating paper, the company reduced costs, whilst improving service and productivity. Information was up to date and it could be searched electronically. The user could find what he or she needed in much less time.

(3) On competitive advantage, it is true that wider availability of information can eliminate power asymmetry between corporations to a certain extent. However, new sources of information asymmetries are likely to appear. Furthermore, while low capital asset specificity of virtual business allows more firms to enter the market, talented, knowledgeable and innovative individuals will become an expensive and difficult-to-acquire asset of virtual corporations and a source of competitive advantage (see the case study of Virtual Vineyard in Chapter 8). Taking a resource-based view of how to compete would seem to be as important in the Internet era as in previous ones.

(4) Digital assets are often re-usable and can redefine economies of scope and scale. Production costs may be minimal. Digital goods comprise information that has been digitized and the medium on which the information resides, such as an application software disk.

Virtual goods, on the other hand, are the subset of goods that exist only in the virtual world. In the virtual value chain information as a by-product can become a marketable asset, cheap to create, store, customize and produce quickly on demand. Virtual goods are indestructible, in the sense that they do not tear off with use or consumption. However virtual goods may still be perishable or devalue over time; for example, people pay a premium to have early access to information about the stock market which is available for free just a few minutes later. As a result of the slippery nature of information value, business strategy must be defined very precisely and carefully through information value.

It is easy, fast and relatively cheap to reproduce digital goods, and it is even faster and cheaper to reproduce virtual goods. Production costs are almost zero, or are at least minimal. Therefore, it is the willingness of the consumer to pay rather than the marginal production cost that will determine the price of virtual goods. Inexpensive reproduction on demand also implies that there is no need for factories, production lines or warehouses. In the case of a virtual company selling a virtual good, there is not even need for physical presence. The logic is that low asset specificity will probably lead to new corporate and organizational forms. Size, hierarchy and assets management will be affected. Lower asset specificity also implies lower entry barriers to the market. This will result in a major shift of the balance of power in certain markets.

(5) In the traditional economics of information there is a trade-off between richness and reach. According to Evans and Wurster[2], this law is being challenged by the use of electronic communication networks. Richness refers to the quality of information, while reach refers to the number of people who have access to it. This pervasive trade-off has determined the way companies communicate, collaborate and contact transactions with customers, suppliers, dis-

tributors or internally. If this trade-off were eliminated or minimized, the established relations would be challenged and redefined.

(6) The significant disintermediation effects of applying Web-based technologies have been remarked upon for some time in a range of industries, including entertainment, travel, retail goods, computer sales and financial services. Even more interesting has been more recent developments in re-intermediation, as value-added services has sprung up to facilitate B2B and B2C in a variety of industries. As an example, there are now a range of meta-agents available to help view the best price and terms for buying books and CDs and many other items over the Web.

(7) As we shall see, the arrival of Web-based technologies creates an even wider range of possibilities than this, including:

- permitting a global presence in a virtual marketspace;

- the development of multimedia convergence enabling bundling of sounds, images and words in digital form, thus opening up new products and new market channels – which could be the prelude to a content-centric era;

- the development of virtual communities and their attendant economic value; and

- the further establishment of service- and information-based differentiation on-line.

7.4 The e-business case: need for an evolutionary perspective

In light of these changing economics and the ever-developing power of Web-based and complementary technologies, the e-business case for investment is not always clear. Reporting in

2001, Willcocks and Plant[3] found that many that had already gone forward with Web-enabled transactions perceived financial payback and time savings coming much later. One reason for caution would be the ability of Internet usage to magnify mistakes and make them intensely public. Thus, Machlis[4] reports a major US credit-reporting agency sending 200 credit reports to the wrong customers, after 2,000 requests to the Web site over an 11-hour period triggered a software error, which misdirected the credit data. US firms have shown less caution with intranets, with 85% having installed them or planning to install them by mid-1997. By comparison, by 2001, the figure in the UK has been lower – the fear of being left behind often being counteracted by difficulties in identifying 'killer applications' for an intranet.

What then are the real benefit opportunities emerging? Considering the Web and the Internet, there can be several types of Web site. According to Quelch and Klein[5], the primary drivers of the business model adopted are types of customer and preferred business impact (see Figure 7.2).

Existing companies, for example Motorola, UPS, Federal Express and 3M, have tended to evolve from using a site for image and product information purposes, to using it for information collection/market research, customer support/ service and internal support/service and then for transactions/ sales. On the other hand, simple economics require Internet start-ups, for example Amazon.com and Software.net, to begin with transactions, then build customer support/service, provide a brand image and product information, then carry out information collection and market research to win repeat purchases. These two different evolutionary models involve plotting different routes through the four quadrants shown in Figure 7.2. Whatever the positioning, it is clear that a Web site business case needs to show how revenue can be generated, costs reduced, customers satisfied and/or business strategies underpinned.

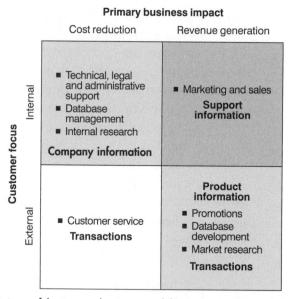

Figure 7.2 Drivers of the Internet business model (source: Quelch and Klein 1996)[5]

In fact, significant cost reductions are possible. In the first 18 months of Web usage Morgan Stanley, the US investment bank, documented nearly US$1 million in savings on internal access to routine information and electronic routing of key reports. By moving external customer support functions on to the Web, Cisco Connection Online saved US$250 million in one year. One immediate advantage and (following Metcalfe's Law) exponential add-on value of a Web site is that it can reach a global audience, although this may not be its initial focus. This global product reach can offer multiple business opportunities, including faster new product diffusion, easier local adaptation and customization, overcoming import restrictions, reducing the competitive advantage of scale economies in many industries, and the effective marketing and selling of niche/speciality products to a critical mass of customers available worldwide.

Clearly, the technology enables new business models, but these are a product of new business thinking and business cases that can recognize at least some of the longer-term benefits, although evidence suggests that many will also grow from use and learning. At the same time, on the cost side, Web sites, like other IT investments, are not one-off costs. Annual costs just for site maintenance (regardless of upgrades and content changes) may well be two to four times the initial launch cost.

Exploiting the virtual value chain

Benefits may also arise from exploiting the information generated in the virtual value chain of a business. Rayport and Sviokla[6] have pointed out that if companies integrate the information they capture during stages of the physical value chain – from inbound logistics and production through sales and marketing – they can construct an information underlay for the business. One internal example is how Ford moved one key element of its physical value chain – product development of its 'global car' – to much faster virtual team working. Externally, companies can also extract value by establishing space-based relationships with customers. Essentially, each extract from the flow of information along the virtual value chain could also constitute a new product or service. By creating value with digital assets, outlays on information technologies such as intranets/internets can be reharvested in an infinite number of combinations and transactions.

Exploitation of digital assets can have immense economic significance in a network-centric era. However, organizations would need to rethink their previous ways of assessing benefits from IT investments. Rayport and Sviokla summarize the five economic implications. Digital assets are not used up in their consumption, but can be reharvested. Virtual value chains redefine economies of scale allowing small firms to achieve low unit costs in markets dominated by big players. Businesses can also redefine economies of scope by utilizing the same digital assets across different and disparate markets. Digital transaction costs are low and continue to decline sharply. Finally, in combination these factors, together with digital assets, allow a shift from supply side to demand side, more customer-focused thinking and strategies.

Further benefits and challenges

To add to this picture, Kambil[7] shows how the Internet can be used in e-commerce to lower the costs and radically transform basic trade processes of search, valuation, logistics, payment and settlement, and authentication. Technical solutions to these basic trade processes have progressed rapidly. At the same time, the adoption of trade context processes to the new infostructure – processes that reduce the risks of trading (e.g. dispute resolution and legitimizing agreements in the 'marketspace') – has been substantially slower. This has also been one of the major barriers to wider adoption of electronic cash, along with the need for a critical mass of consumer acceptance, despite compelling arguments for e-cash's potential for improved service.

Some further insights into the new economics and the power to create value in on-line markets are provided by Hagel and Armstrong[8]. They too endorse the need for an understanding of the dynamics of increasing returns in e-commerce. E-business displays three forms of increasing returns. Firstly, an initial outlay to develop e-business is required, but thereafter the incremental cost of each additional unit of the product/service is minimal. Secondly, significant learning and cost-reduction effects are likely to be realized, with e-based businesses driving down the experience curve more quickly than mature businesses. Thirdly, as has been pointed out above, Metcalfe's Law applies – network effects accrue exponential returns as membership increases and more units of product/service are deployed. As Microsoft showed spectacularly in software, harnessing the power of increasing returns means 'the more you sell, the more you sell'.

The new economics of electronic communities

Hagel and Armstrong focus particularly on the commercial possibilities inherent in building electronic communities. Here networks give customers/members the ability to interact with each other as well as with vendors. In exchange for organizing the electronic community and developing its potential for increasing value for participants, a network organizer (a prime example being that of Open Market Inc.) would extract revenues. These could be in the form of subscription, usage, content delivery or service fees charged to customers and advertising and transaction commission from vendors. Customers would be attracted by a distinctive focus, for example consumer travel, the capacity to integrate content such as advertising with communication (e.g. through bulletin boards) both of which aggregate over time, access to competing publishers and vendors, and opportunities for commercial transactions. Vendors gain reduced search cost, increased propensity for customers to buy, enhanced ability to target, greater ability to tailor and add value to existing products and services. They also benefit from elements more broadly applicable to networked environments: lower capital investment in buildings, broader geographic reach and opportunities to remove intermediaries.

Hagel and Armstrong point out that the dynamics of increasing returns drive revenue growth in virtual communities, but these are easily missed by conventional techniques of financial analysis. Using static revenue models and assumptions of straight-line growth, these conventional techniques can underestimate greatly the potential of virtual community investment. As a result, organizations may forego investment altogether or under-invest, thereby increasing the risks of pre-emption by competitors and business failure.

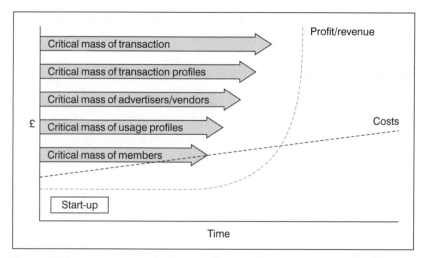

Figure 7.3 Revenue, cost and milestones for virtual communities (modified from Hagel and Armstrong[8])

Increasing returns depend on the achievement of four dynamic loops. The first is a content attractiveness loop, whereby member-based content attracts more members, who contribute more content. The second is a member loyalty loop. Thus, more member-to-member interaction will build more member loyalty and reduce membership 'churn'. The third is a member profile loop, which sees information gathered about members assisting in targeting advertising and customizing products/services. The fourth is a transaction offerings loop, which sees more vendors drawn into the community, more products/services being offered, thus attracting more members and creating more commercial transactions. According to Hagel and Armstrong, it is the aggregate effect of these dynamic loops in combination that could create the exponential revenue growth pattern shown in Figure 7.3.

To achieve these four dynamic loops the first step is to develop a critical mass of members. The other four growth assets are shown in Figure 7.3. These may reach critical mass in a sequential manner, but community organizers may well seek to develop them much more in parallel as shown in Figure 7.3. The important point is that as each growth asset reaches critical mass and their effects combine, the revenue dynamic is exponentially influenced. However, despite Hagel and Armstrong's optimism, it should be emphasized that there is no inevitability about the scenario depicted in Figure 7.3. This has already been demonstrated throughout 2000 and early 2001 by the high-profile failures, such as Boo.com, Levi Strauss, Click-Mango, Boxman and Value America, which have attempted this route. Business and competitive risks do not disappear, but are fundamental to the development and running of electronic communities.

In all this, as in more conventional businesses, the key economic asset is the member/customer, and critical activities revolve around his/her acquisition and retention. This can be costly on the Web, where 'surfing' is much more typical than member loyalty. Up to 1999 even an experienced on-line service such as America Online was losing up to 40% of its members a year and spending up to US$90 to acquire each new member. Other cost aspects need to be borne in mind. Start-up costs for an Internet site are commonly cited as low – typically between US$1 million and US$3 million depending on size and ambition, although this is a figure regularly being re-estimated upwards. On one model, technology-related costs in an electronic community may start as a small (say 35%) and decline as a proportion of total costs over a five-year period, being overwhelmed by member and advertiser acquisition and content-related costs – as many Internet-based companies have found already.

However, those making investment decisions do face a number of challenges. A look at Figure 7.3 would suggest that fast returns on investment are unlikely, while short-term cost pressures are certain. Moreover, evidence from the Internet has been that early revenue sources such as membership subscription and usage fees, and advertising charges, act as dissuaders and can slow long-term growth substantially. Moreover, even by 2001, the Internet was still not a wholly commerce-friendly environment, with key robust technologies on payment, authentication, security and information usage capture still to be put in place, and with already a history of security breaks, virus attacks and organizations with inadequate e-business infrastructure.

7.5 Summary

With the network-based era now upon us, we usher in for ourselves many new technological and economic realities. These have to be understood if IT evaluation practices are to be properly informed and are to perform meaningful asessments of the IT investments made by organizations. This chapter, together with Chapter 2, has attempted to make clear that the difficulties experienced consistently with IT evaluation over the years are now being compounded by the many layers of types of technology and their often differing purposes found in most reasonably complex organizations in the developed economies. Moreover, there is always tomorrow's technology, the uncertainty about its necessity and the question of whether it will be the 'killer application' or just another expensive addition to the corporate budget. In increasingly competitive markets there are also rising concerns about being left behind, by-passed or locked out, for example when a start-up company or an existing competitor moves from the marketplace to the 'marketspace'. In such circumstances, properly informed IT assessment practices are as vital as ever. The technology shifts and their underlying economics detailed in this chapter imply that for IT evaluation practices, in several important ways, it can no longer be business as usual.

7.6 Key learning points

- The rapid expansion and massive potential of the Internet sets significant challenges for businesses and their IT investment procedures.

- The contribution of e-business has to be defined before the allocation of resources. As with other IT-based applications, the business drivers behind the investment must be totally clear. Otherwise, the project must be treated as R&D and an investment in learning.

- Significant discontinuities stem from the fluid, underlying economics of e-business. It is necessary to explore these thoroughly in order to understand the context and economics underpinning stategic and investment options.

- Internet-based applications offer a multitude of business-to-consumer, business-to-business and intra-business options. It also offers new opportunities to intermediation and electronic communities, for example. However, these options need to be examined on a case-by-case basis, and different e-business investments cannot be properly examined using the same evaluation criteria.

- The economics of e-business are increasingly marked by Metcalfe's Law. Characteristics of virtual goods, information and the marketspace can drive costs down substantially. At the same time, costs of maintaining and developing sites into profitable operations have frequently been underestimated or not tolerated for a sustainable enough period.

- At the same time, information as a by-product of transactions can become a customer offering in itself. Information can be cheap to accumulate and highly profitable to exploit. It is sophisticated understanding of the complex and dynamic economics of such factors that determine the level of success achieved in e-business.

7.7 Practical action guidelines

– Identify where your different investments lie on the diagram depicting the eras in the IT industry revolution (Figure 7.1). Analyse the degree to which the evaluation regimes for these investments, and for future investments, appropriately capture the likely costs and benefits.

– Ensure that e-business investments, in particular, are not being limited because of unsuitable assessment procedures. Check against the suggestions for evaluation made in Chapter 8.

– Sensitize yourself to the changing economics that e-business applications can bring. Consider how these different opportunities can be identified and how your business could take advantage of them.

– Become aware of the risks and down-sides also inherent in moves to e-business. Learn to check these aspects, especially where commentators fail to raise these issues themselves.

8 E-valuation (2): four approaches

8.1 Introduction

> The large US Internet companies are overvalued by just over 30% assuming revenue grows at 65% compound, and overvalued by 55% using a 50% revenue growth projection.
>
> Research finding by Perkins and Perkins,
> *The Internet Bubble* (Harper and Collins, 1999)

> E-business is such a wide-ranging phenomenon that there is something in it for everybody. The trouble is that it is not always obvious what's right for which company.
>
> Willcocks and Sauer,
> *Moving to E-business* (Random House, 2000)

In Chapter 7 we spelled out the e-opportunities and the underlying economics, while also sounding notes of caution where appropriate. In this section we put forward some ways in which the e-opportunities can be evaluated and grasped, including sustainable competitive advantage, differentiation analysis, real options and scorecard approaches. Before doing this, one issue we can deal with quickly is how to evaluate the Internet business itself.

The period 1998–2000 saw much 'irrational exuberance'[1] on Internet company stock valuations. One famous example saw Priceline.com, an auction-based travel agency, with a market value of US\$7.5 billion in February 2000, while making losses of over US\$150 million a year. Its value was presented as higher than that of United Airlines (yearly profit US\$400 million) and Continental Airlines (yearly profit US\$300 million) combined. The only real way to judge such valuations is to ask whether they represent reasonable expectations about the future growth and profitability of Internet businesses. Even on optimistic estimates of performance, Perkins and Perkins[2] concluded that in 1999 the big US Internet companies were overvalued by 30%.

Higson and Briginshaw are correct in suggesting that we need to apply free cash flow valuation to Internet businesses in their start-up phases – a function of sales and the profitability of those sales[3]. Price/earnings and price/revenue multiples are not very revealing for early stage businesses. A company's free cash is its operating profit less taxes, less the cash it must re-invest in assets to grow. A company creates value when free cash flows imply a rate of return greater than the investor's required return, and that only happens when they can sustain competitive advantage in the markets they serve.

To model the cash flow of an Internet business, one needs to:

(1) forecast the future market size and sales;

(2) project the company's costs; and

(3) forecast the investment in the balance sheet (the company's asset needs) as it grows.

What matters, of course, are the assumptions behind these estimates. Higson and Briginshaw make the point that often the implicit assumptions have been that the competitive environment will be benign and that Internet companies will earn old-economy margins or better. They posit a much more strenuously competitive environment where 'companies will need to be lean, nimble and constantly innovative ... in such a world, the market keeps companies on survival rations, no better'.

Having looked at Internet stock valuation, let us now consider four approaches to evaluating businesses: analysis for opportunity and sustainability; real options, a scorecard approach and Web metrics. These are designed to complement and build on the ideas and approaches in previous chapters, all of which still apply in the e-world.

8.2 Analysis for opportunity and sustainability

Given the changing economics of e-business and accompanying high levels of uncertainty, it becomes even more important when evaluating it to focus on the big strategic business picture, as well as on issues such as Web site metrics and technical/operational evaluation. In Chapter 3 we met the business-led approach and the five IT domains navigational tool. In our work we have found both approaches immediately applicable to the e-business world. More recently, David Feeny has extended his work into providing a set of matrices for evaluating the e-operations, e-marketing, e-vision and e-sustainability opportunities[4]. Here we will sketch the first three and focus more attention on the issue of e-sustainability.

E-operations – uses of web technologies to achieve strategic change in the way a business manages itself and its supply chain. The main opportunities here are in:

(1) automating administration;

(2) changing the 'primary infrastructure', that is the core business processes of the business, and achieving synergies across the company (e.g. sharing back-office operations or intranets);

(3) moving to electronic procurement; and

(4) achieving supply chain integration.

Feeny suggests that if the information content of the product is high, then the e-investments should be in primary infrastructure. Where there is high information intensity in the supply chain, then electronic procurement and integrated supply chain are the most obvious targets for investment. Where value chain activities are highly dispersed, then e-investments may be able to achieve high payoffs from introducing much needed synergies.

E-marketing – use of the technology to enable more effective ways of achieving sales to new and existing customers. The opportunities here are to enhance:

(1) the sales process (e.g. by better market/product targeting);

(2) the customer buying process (e.g. by making it easier to buy); and

(3) the customer operating process, enabling the customer to achieve more benefits while the product is in use.

Of course, one could take action on all three fronts, but much will depend on how firms are competing in the specific market, how differentiated the product/service is and could be, and how regularly customers purchase. The key here is to diagnose these factors and discover where an e-investment will achieve maximum leverage.

E-vision – using Web-based technologies to provide a set of services which covers the breadth and lifespan of customer needs within a specific marketspace. This means analysing where e-improvements can be made and where competitors may be weak in servicing the customer at all stages of the purchase process and beyond, in other words in all dealings the customer is likely to have with the business. The major iterative components of the analysis are:

(1) diagnose customer needs;

(2) identify relevant providers;

(3) construct options for customer choice;

(4) negotiate customer requirement; and

(5) provide customer service.

Feeny points out that this vision of the perfect agent may seem too good to be true, but that firms are already moving in this direction. Thus, Ford's CEO is seeking to transform Ford into 'the world's leading consumer company for automative service', and this is already influencing the firm's acquisition policy and the levels of IT literacy for which it is striving.

Beyond all these concerns, organizations also need to carry out a fundamental analysis of where sustainable competitive advantage comes from when utilizing Web-based technologies. Feeny's analysis suggests that there are three main sources of sustainable competitive advantage (see Figure 8.1).

The first component of sustainable competitive advantage is generic lead time. Being first into e-initiatives can offer a time advantage, but this has to be continually renewed and taken advantage of. Thus, generic lead time is widely considered to be the most fragile of the three sustainable competitive advantage components. However, although Web applications can be rolled out in weeks by followers, some aspects may not be replicated as quickly, for example IT infrastructure, and a business may also stay ahead by continuous technical enhancements that have business value.

The second component, asymmetry barriers, may come from competitive scope which a competitor cannot replicate, for example geographic spread or market segments serviced. They may be from the organizational base, reflecting non-replicable advantages in structure, culture and/or physical

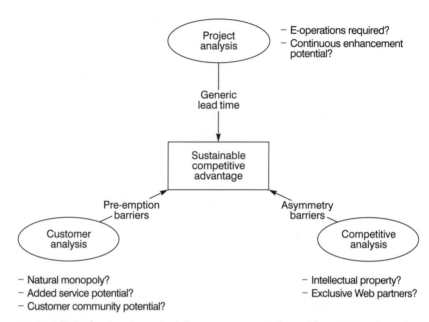

Figure 8.1 Evaluating e-sustainability components (adapted from Willcocks and Sauer, 2000)

assets, or from non-replicable information resources, in terms of technology, applications, databases and/or knowledge bases.

The third component of sustainable competitive advantage is pre-emption barriers. In being first, a business needs to find an exploitable link in terms of customers, distribution channels and/or suppliers. It needs to capture the pole position through its value chain activity, creating user benefits and offering a single source incentive to customers. It also needs to keep the gate closed, for example by its application interface design, its use of a user database or by developing a specific community of users.

We will see these sustainability issues being played out in the in-depth case study of Virtual Vineyards at the end of this chapter.

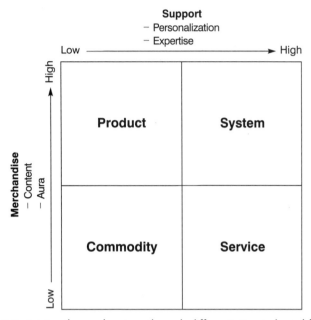

Figure 8.2 Sustaining the e-advantage through differentiation (adapted from Mathur and Kenyon, 1997)[6]

In moving to e-business, the practice of differentiation emerges as key to success. Our own findings suggest that in most sectors commodity-based, price-sensitive competition on the Web will not be an ultimately sustainable business model[5]. Mathur and Kenyon's work is particularly pertinent here, and its prescriptions have been seen in many of the leading B2C companies found in our research. What competes in the marketplace is what a customer sees as alternatives or close substitutes, in other words what the customer can choose instead[6]. A business enters the competitive arena with a customer offering – the inseparable bundle of product, service, information and relationship. The challenge over time is to continually differentiate and make this offering less price-sensitive in ways that remain attractive to the targeted market segment. The options are captured in simplified form in Figure 8.2.

The support dimension of an offering represents those differentiating features which customers perceive in the way the seller helps them in choosing, obtaining then using the offering. All other differentiating features belong to what is called the merchandise dimension. The merchandise features of a car sold over the Web would include its colour, shape, size, performance characteristics and in-car entertainment. Its support features would include availability of information, ease of purchase, the test-drive, promptness of delivery and service arrangements. The merchandise component can be further differentiated by augmenting content (what the offering will do for the customer) or aura (what the offering will say about the customer). Amazon can make available a wider range of books and products, whereas Merit Nordbanken can provide WAP phone access to a customer's account – both companies' brands will augment the aura of the offering. The support dimension can be augmented by personalization (the personal attention and distinctive familiarity offered to each customer's needs) and expertise (the superiority displayed by the seller in the brainpower, skill or experience in delivering and implementing the offering). Federal Express facilitates personal Internet tracking of your parcel, whereas Virtual Vineyards offers on-line access to information on wine and to the expertise of a sommelier (see the in-depth case study, below). In our own work, we found leading organizations striving to leverage both collective sources of differentiation, not least leveraging information bases to get closer to and 'lock-in' customers.

What matters is achieving differentiation in a particular changing competitive context so that the dynamic customer value proposition (simplified in Figure 8.2 as commodity, product, service or systems alternatives) is invariably superior to what else is available to the customer. This may sound simple, but it is deceptive. It requires a knowledge of and relationship with customers, and a speed and flexibility of anticipation and response that many organizations have found difficult to develop, let alone sustain. Moreover, as many commentators observe, it has to be achieved in specific Internet environments where power has moved further, often decisively, in favour of the customer.

8.3 Real options evaluation of e-business initiatives

In finance, options are contracts that give one party the right to buy or sell shares, financial instruments or commodities from another party within a given time and at a given price. The option holder will buy, sell or hold depending on market conditions. 'Real options' thinking applies a similar logic to strategic investments that can give a company the option to capture benefits from future market conditions. Real option thinking applies particularly in situations where contracts are vague and implicit, where valuation models are much less precise, and where a real options investment can open out a variety of possible actions and ways forward.

As such, real options thinking might be appropriate when considering e-business/technology investments. The objective here would be to invest an entry stake, for example a pilot or a prototype, so as to retain the ability to play in potential markets and to change strategy by switching out of a product, technology or market. Clearly, real options thinking and analysis is most appropriate in conditions of high uncertainty, where much flexibility in future decisions is required – a good definition of the prevailing circumstances with regard to moves to e-business in the new decade.

The arrival of the Internet has increased the complexity of issues to consider when we invest in the technologies. Return on investment approaches can lead to under-investment and not adopting a long-term horizon. The most sensible, risk-averse route might be to build more options into the strategy, that is to invest in e-technologies in ways which create a variety of options for the future.

Kulatilaka and Venkatraman[7] suggest three principles for pursuing real options analysis for e-business.

(1) **Pursue possible rather than predictable opportunities**. Opportunities in the virtual marketspace are anything but predictable. Using predictable, sector-bound models will miss out on many opportunities that are not obvious in their initial stages, and which may close, especially if competitors apply their learning from the sustainable competitive advantage analysis detailed above. Consider Microsoft, which in 1999 invested US$5 billion in AT&T, the largest US cable provider. At the same time, it invested US$600 million in Nextel, the US mobile services group, and collaborated with NBC to produce an on-line news site and television channel. These investments create many possible options for Microsoft's competitive future.

It is important to create at least three types of options. The first is to enable a company to be flexible about its scale of operations, for example allowing migration or scaling up of operations and business processes on the Web. The second is to create scope options enabling changes in the mix of products and services offered. Thus, Amazon has moved from books to videos and CDs and, because of its business model and investments, is able to incorporate other products. The third is timing options, allowing the company to be flexible about when to commit to particular opportunities.

(2) **Explore multiple avenues to acquire your options**. For example, real options can come from alliances and partnerships. The challenge is to move away from just adding business lines and those things that are easy to assess, towards the acquisition of capability options. Kulatilaka and Venkatraman suggest four different avenues for acquiring real options:

- entry stakes: options inside a company that allow it, but do not oblige it, to act (e.g. on-line brochureware and registration of a Web address);

- risk pooling: arrangements with external players through various forms of contract;

- big bets: major commitments, for example Toys R Us created a separate unit to expand on-line aggressively and Charles Schwab made major commitments from 1995 and is now the on-line market leader in its sector; and

- alliance leverage: establishing a portfolio of alliances in many areas, for example the Microsoft cited above.

(3) **Structure the organization to unleash the potential of the digital business**. Traditional organization structures may limit fast execution and continuous adaptation. What will need looking at, typically, is the provision of appropriate incentives for creating and developing digital businesses; the reorganization of information flows to respond in Internet time; and the ability to develop and contract dynamically for external relationships.

In summary, in many ways e-business investments are like R&D investments. In both cases the application of real options analysis may well produce much more value than for example the traditional net present value analysis (see Chapter 3). There are several effects in a detailed analysis that favour investments in supposedly more risky e-business projects, when valued using real option pricing methods.

(1) Net present value techniques are heavily dependent on the applied discount rate. In the case of risky e-business projects, these would be heavily discounted. In real options pricing, the use of risk adjusted rates is avoided.

(2) This effect is further strengthened by the long-time horizons that would need to be applied to R&D and many e-business investment decisions.

(3) Long-time horizons leave more time to react to changing conditions. The possibility of changing direction is taken into account in real options valuation, but not net present value calculations.

(4) The high volatility of the value of e-business or R&D outputs positively influences the option value because high returns can be generated, but very low returns can be avoided by reacting to the changing conditions. In net present value evaluations, high volatility leads to a risk premium on the discount rate and so to a lower net present value.

8.4 E-business: a scorecard approach

Work carried out by Willcocks and Plant[8] and developed further by Plant[9] has led to the development of a proposed scorecard approach for assessing an e-business on an on-going basis. The principles that apply are very similar to those detailed in Chapter 5. However, the content of the scorecard has been refined as a result of our own research work into leading and lagging e-business practices over the 1998–2001 period. In particular, our work uncovered four types of strategy that leading e-businesses went through in their evolution. The four are 'technology' (superior technology application and management), 'brand' (the business use of marketing and branding), 'service' (the use of information for superior customer service) and 'market' (the integration of technology, marketing and service to achieve disproportionate profitability and growth). In terms of business value, there turned out to be good, and less effective, ways of conducting each strategy.

With this in mind, we can build a scorecard approach using the following procedure, adapted from Plant (2000)[9].

(1) Assess performance according to seven factors:

- financial impact;

- competitive leadership;

- 'technology' achievement;

- 'brand' achievement;

- 'service' achievement;

- 'market' achievement; and

- Internet site metrics.

(2) Develop an effectiveness rating scale, for example 1–10.

(3) Develop the detailed metrics.

(4) Establish goals, results, 'industry standard' and effectiveness rating.

(5) Make individuals responsible for results and incentivize them to deliver.

(6) Decompose criteria to ownership, process and transaction levels.

(7) Automate the evaluation system for real-time accurate management information.

By way of illustration only, Figures 8.3, 8.4 and 8.5 show what such a scorecard could look like at the fourth stage of development. In the effectiveness rating column we show, again as an illustration only, that effectiveness on each dimension may also include a weighting element.

Factors	Metric	Forecast initial goal	Actual results	'Industry best practice'	Effectiveness rating
(1) Financial impact, for example: − cost reduction − revenue generation − transfer of revenues to low-cost channel					ER/8
(2) Competitive leadership − generic lead time − competitive asymmetry − customer lock-in					ER/10
(3) Brand − brand re-inforcement − brand repositioning − global branding achievement					ER/6

Figure 8.3 A scorecard approach − 1

Finally, as a way of summarizing the findings on a regular basis, Plant suggests the use of an effectiveness rating polar graph. An illustration of what such a graph would look like is provided in Figure 8.6.

Factors	Metric	Forecast initial goal	Actual results	'Industry best practice'	Effectiveness rating
(4) Service, for example: information improves service building of affinity relationships, effective e-mail, call centre					ER/6
(5) Market, for example: market share, niche profitability, effective mass customization strategy					ER/10
(6) Technology, for example: flexible infrastructure, responsive technology partners, mean time to upgrade a server					ER/8

Figure 8.4 A scorecard approach − 2

Internet site metrics	Metric	Forecast initial goal	Actual results	'Industry best practice'	Effectiveness rating
The number of hits per month (as a measure of customers' interests and site potential value)?					
The number of purchases per registered customer per month?					
The average purchase size per transaction?					
The length of time a registered customer spends (as a measure of site information value)?					
The repeat visit rate by registered users (as a measure of site value)?					
The purchase/hit rate (as an indicator of interest converted to revenue)?					
Other (any other metrics you use for measuring the effectiveness of your site) with description					

ER7

Figure 8.5 A scorecard approach – 3

This section has indicated that the balanced business scorecard concept and its underlying principles as detailed in Chapter 5, have considerable applicability in the e-business world, but that detailed tailoring, and the development of new quadrants and specific metrics, are necessary – something we also highlighted for other IT-based applications of the scorecard.

8.5 Web metrics and the one that matters

In the previous section we detailed a scorecard approach which included a separate evaluation area for Internet site metrics. At the operational level, there has been much interest in Web metrics, that is how the performance of a Web site can be

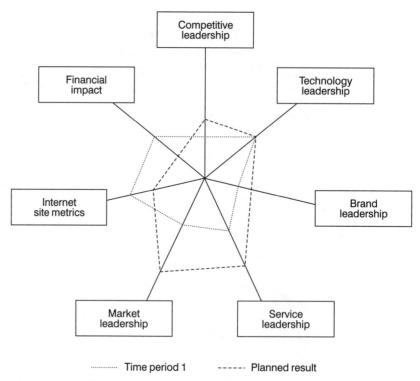

Figure 8.6 An effectiveness rating polar graph

evaluated. From the earliest days of transactions on the Web through to 2001, there has been an evolution towards metrics that are more meaningful in business terms. There have been perhaps six stages in this evolution:

(1) 'hit rate' – requests for data from a server;

(2) 'page view' – number of HTML pages served to users;

(3) 'click-through' – percentage of people responding to an on-line advert;

(4) 'unique visitors' – total number of individuals visiting;

(5) 'percentage reach' – percentage of sampled users visiting a site page each month; and

(6) 'new breed' – in the light of the inadequacies identified above, evaluations have taken on measures such as length of stay, number of registered users, number of repeat visits, site behaviour and return on investment.

All these measures generate information, although the usefulness of that information depends on what business purpose it can serve. In all too many cases information has been generated with no great evaluation payoff; in fact, worse still, it has probably contributed to an information overload and lack of clarity. In all this, one abidingly useful measure is the conversion rate, which can be defined as that percentage of visitors who take the desired action, for example purchase the item at a price that generates profit. Such a measure contributes to understanding the real business value of the Web site.

Using the conversion rate as a major control parameter is important for a number of reasons. Firstly, small changes in the conversion rate can produce large gains (or losses) in business value. Average conversion rates on the Web still come in at between 3 and 5%. However, consider the maths. For one company that failed in 2000 it was costing US$13 million to get 100,000 customers (US$130 per customer). Average sales were US$80 a time. The conversion rate was a very poor 1.5%. Instigating policies to push the conversion rate up just another 1.5% would probably have seen the company in profit.

Secondly, the conversion rate reflects important qualitative aspects that are not otherwise easily captured. Thus, easy-to-use interfaces have high conversion rates. Sites that are slow or dragged down by site errors or time-outs have low conversion rates. Frequent users value convenient sites, for example Amazon's one-click service, and this drives up conversion rates. Low conversion rates may also indicate that clever advertising and high click-though rates are not converting into effective advertising. High conversion rates may also indicate the extent of word-of-mouth, which is the most powerful and cheapest form of advertising. Sites with good user interfaces, that are fast and convenient, with great service, attract this form of advertising and high conversion rates.

Having stressed the importance of adopting the conversion rate as a method of evaluating Web site performance, it would be remiss not to spell out some of the issues that need to be dealt with when using conversion rate as a metric. Firstly, conversion rates will be low for new customers and higher for returning customers. Watch them both and the blended rate. Secondly, be aware that seasonality affects the conversion rate. Thirdly, always also keep an eye on profitability. Do not rent customers by cutting prices too long to drive up conversion rates. Into 2001, Egg, the UK-based on-line bank, has many customers and a strong conversion rate. Even so, its pricing strategy has been described as 'giving away £10 in order to gain £5', and it was still making losses.

8.6 In-depth case study: Virtual Vineyards (subsequently Wine.com)

Virtual Vineyards (V-V) is a prime example of a company that created a new kind of offering for an old product, by enhancing the information and the relationship dimension of selling wine. V-V was established in California in January 1995 by Peter Granoff (a master sommelier) and Robert Olson (a computer professional). Olson believed that there was a market on the Internet for high-value, non-commodity products. The product was chosen according to three criteria:

(1) the information on point of sale should influence buyers' decisions;

(2) the product should be customizable; and

(3) expert knowledge should offer added value if bundled with the product.

Clearly, he wanted to find a product rich in information content, so as to be able to take advantage of IS capabilities. Eventually, he decided to market and sell Californian wine from small producers. The structure of the distribution channel had left small producers isolated and Olson saw an opportunity there. Granoff, an expert in wine, liked the idea and the two formed Net Content Inc. Virtual Vineyards (V-V) was the company's first Web site, but it soon became synonymous with the company.

Californian wine dominated the US market, accounting for three-quarters of the total volume of wine sold. The US market had been shrinking over the previous ten years, but there were signs of recovery. V-V targeted the higher end of the market, which consisted of people who appreciated good wine, were interested to learn more about it, were willing to pay a premium for a bottle of fine wine, but who were not connoisseurs, and therefore could benefit from the knowledge of an expert. Along with a wide selection of wines from small producers, V-V offered information about wine and its history, ratings and descriptions of all the wines it sold, and personalized answers to individual questions and requests. The site was a quick success on the Internet attracting thousands of users and increasing revenues at a fast pace.

As a virtual company, Virtual Vineyards' business idea has been fundamentally tied to the Internet. The case provides an excellent opportunity to demonstrate how competitive positioning frameworks can be used to evaluate e-business investments at both the feasibility and post-implementation stages. Here the company's strategic positioning will be assessed relative to its use of the Internet. Although the business idea is the most important characteristic of every venture, a strong business idea may fail, if not properly supported by IT. This is especially true in the case of Internet companies, where IT is pervasive to the organizational structure and daily operations.

Assessing V-V: using five forces analysis

Michael Porter has suggested that an organization needs to analyse its positioning relative to five industry forces in order to establish its competitive position. These are its buyers, suppliers, competitors, the threat of new entrants, and the threat of substitutes.

Buyers

The targeted market was defined as 'people interested in a good glass of wine, but not wine connoisseurs'. Clearly, V-V adds value to the consumer by providing guidance through suggestions and ratings. Once the buyer has accepted the authority of V-V, he/she has surrendered bargaining power. The endless variation of wine and the specialized information associated with that make it practically impossible for the buyer to make comparisons among the various wine catalogues/ratings, etc. Even though the buyer has many choices, he/she has not the necessary knowledge and information to make the choices. Therefore, the key issue is reputation.

Once established, it gives a decisive competitive advantage to the virtual intermediary. The relationship with the customer is strengthened by repeating orders that lock in the consumer and reduce even more his/her bargaining power; as long as the customer is satisfied with the offering (i.e. gets good wine at a decent price and enough information to satisfy his/her need for knowledge), there will be no real incentives to switch. Price, although always important, is not a decisive parameter of the offering. The buyers who are prepared to pay the premium to ultra-premium price perceive the product as highly differentiated, and therefore are less sensitive to price and more concerned about value. The offering is not easily comparable to alternative ones, and therefore V-V has found a source of information asymmetry which protects it against the price competition that electronic markets introduce.

Suppliers

In the USA there are hundreds of small vineyards, mostly in California. The distribution channel is dominated by few large wine distributors, leaving the small producers without proper access to the consumer, either directly or through retail outlets and restaurants. The costs of direct marketing or establishing relationships with retail outlets is rather high for a small producer and an intermediary may be more efficient, as it can achieve economies of scale. The intermediary represents a number of small producers to the retailers and can establish better relationships through volume and variety. At the same time, the client can enjoy one-stop shopping for a variety of wine. Most of the producers, with the exception perhaps of a few established brands, have little bargaining power.

The market targeted is people who appreciate good wine, but they are not connoisseurs with specific needs; therefore, a bottle of wine from one producer can easily be substituted for another with similar characteristics and quality. A powerful intermediary, with an established reputation among customers, has more bargaining power than the numerous small suppliers, as the case of the large wine distributors has demonstrated. That does not mean that the various vineyards are desperate for distribution channels. Many vineyards that produce a small number of bottles annually have established the necessary relationships with bars, restaurants and speciality shops, and distribute their production through those channels. At the same time, in an industry were the product has high aura, reputation is important for producers as well. Reputation for wine is developed and maintained mainly through ratings, positioning in shelves and pricing. It takes a long time for a producer to establish reputation and, therefore, vineyards are cautious as to whom they sell their wines, for fear of harming their reputation. However, if an intermediary is regarded as knowledgeable and impartial, then it can build relationships based on trust with enough suppliers so that they have little bargaining power on an individual basis.

Large producers dominate the market, and are more attractive to distributors, as their nationally established reputation allows a higher profit margin. Small producers are selling either directly to consumers (direct mail or the Internet) or to restaurants and speciality shops. Distributors sell to restaurants, speciality shops and supermarkets. Off-premises sales account for 80% of the wine volume sold to consumers. Supermarkets account for 70–80% of that volume. As mentioned before, most of that wine comes from the large producers through the distributors.

Competitors

In order to identify V-V's competitors, we will examine what consumers see as alternatives. V-V sells directly to consumers for home consumption and therefore compete with other off-premises points of sale. V-V does not compete with supermarkets as they address a different kind of consumers and price range. Nevertheless, it may attract a small portion of the upper end of supermarket clients who would like to know a little bit more about the wine they buy, but do not have the time or the desire to go to speciality shops.

Compared to any direct mail catalogue, V-V is more up-to-date and interactive, and it delivers more and faster (although not in all cases), information, which is better presented and may be customized. All these are the inherent potential characteristics provided by the Internet. In addition, it offers a larger variety than mail order catalogues compiled by specific producers. The market addressed is more likely to have Internet access and appreciate expert advise to help (guide) their choice. V-V has a clear advantage over direct mail.

V-V competes with other Internet sites, mainly maintained by small producers or wine shops. V-V offers more variety than any small producer, and more guidance and information than the wine shops sites. Therefore, it has an advantage over both.

V-V's main competitors are the shops specializing in selling wine. They target the same consumer group and both add value through information and guidance. IT allows V-V to offer more services, such as information and ratings about every wine and a comparative lists of ratings, prices, etc. Some people may prefer the face-to-face contact with the expert sommelier in the shop, whereas others may feel uncomfortable with that and prefer the personalized answer through email at V-V. Until more data is available, it is difficult to predict the outcome. However the revenues from sales from the first few months of operation suggest that V-V has found a robust market niche.

Threat of new entrants

This is a serious potential threat for V-V. New entrants, especially other Web sites, may emerge quickly from nowhere. It will be examined later, using more appropriate tools, whether and how V-V could achieve a sustainable competitive advantage.

Threat of substitutes

The market for wine is a subset of the market for alcoholic and non-alcoholic beverages. Therefore, soft drinks and distilled spirits may be regarded as potential substitutes. Those products have less information content, are perceived as less differentiated than wine, consumers tend to make the decisions themselves and are less willing or have fewer incentives to experiment with alternative products. The market is dominated by few brands which control marketing and distribution channels. The structure of those channels is totally different from the wine market. In any case, customers do not need expert advice to make their buying decisions and therefore those products are not suitable for V-V.

There is a favourable position in the market for wine from a virtual speciality retail outlet. The product is rich in information content and the buyer's decision can be affected at the point of sale. Suppliers have limited power, as well as buyers.

The threat of substitute products is more apparent as the market seems to shrink, but this may even work in favour of V-V for a number of reasons.

(1) V-V has few physical assets and very low-cost operations. Therefore, its competitors may be affected first leaving potentially a larger market share for V-V to capture. A bigger market share suggests a higher reputation for V-V, which in turn would increase its bargaining power.

(2) The bargaining power of suppliers is reduced even more. As demand is smaller than supply, wine retailers and distributors have more choices to buy wine and can achieve better prices. Even if V-V does not want to attack prices, it can achieve better relationships, and therefore a greater variety, better wines or exclusive deals, by allowing producers a bigger profit margin.

(3) Although the V-V site specializes in wine selling, Net Contents (the company that owns the site) specializes in Web technology and marketing. Once the technology is in place, it can be used for a variety of purposes by finding new markets and products. The experience of V-V in Internet marketing will also be valuable. Of course, V-V's success is not based primarily on the technology. Having the right content for the right market and establishing relationships with suppliers and buyers are more important aspects of V-V's success than technology. In any case, those are also the potential sources of sustainable competitive advantage for V-V, as the technology can be copied easily.

(4) Knowing the market for wine is an important asset for the company. While ·the US market was shrinking during

1986–1994 the European market did not seem to be affected. V-V had many options to address other markets, perhaps more options than other retailers. Reaching customers is far easier due to the global reach of the Internet. Moreover, V-V's reputation on the Internet is more international, compared to competing physical distributors, which have local (speciality shops) or national (distributors or chains) reputation. The technology could easily be transferred and even translated into other languages for a small cost. Given that, V-V had various choices for expanding to other markets. For example, it could decide to export Californian Wine, or take advantage of the European Union and establish similar operations in Europe with French (and perhaps Italian, Spanish, Bulgarian or Greek) wine or assess the potential of the Australian market, which has many producers of fine wine. The point is that by building a US business, V-V establishes an international reputation at no extra cost. Moreover, the front store (i.e. the Web site and logistics) operations and the relationships with customers can instantly be transferred anywhere in the world. Export restrictions and laws should be investigated, but V-V can still take advantage of the loose Internet legislation. Indeed, V-V has recently expanded its operation to include wine from more countries and to export to many countries.

Sustainable competitive advantage analysis

The analysis above showed that V-V has achieved a competitive advantage by making successful use of the Internet and Web technology. The case of V-V will now be analysed using the Figure 8.1 framework in order to determine sustainability of the competitive edge it has achieved. The framework addresses three questions.

(1) How long before a competitor can respond to the idea of V-V? Source of advantage: generic lead time.

(2) Which competitors can respond? Source of advantage: competitive asymmetry.

(3) Will a response be effective? Source of advantage: pre-emption potential.

How long before a competitor can respond?

The technology behind an Internet project such as that of V-V is rather easily replicated. As the Internet becomes more popular, software companies build applications that facilitate setting up a virtual shop. As a pioneer, V-V had a technological dis-advantage, as it actually had to create much of the necessary software needed for its operations and solve problems of design and integration. With universities and corporations experiment-ing in similar areas, V-V could not expect its technology to be unique or to protect the firm against competition. On the contrary, the longer a competitor waited, the easier and cheaper it would be to set up a similar virtual operation. Applications were also easy to copy. A great deal of thinking is needed to come up with innovative ideas about service to customers, but it is a matter of few days before a skilled developer can copy them.

It is important here to make the distinction between IT and IS. Although the technology and applications would be easy to replicate, IS consists of more than the technology that enables it. Databases are a key component of IS – mainly the customer and wine databases.

The customer database is a proprietary, key asset that cannot easily be replicated by any potential competitor. Once the V-V site was launched, it was essential to try to capture as much of the targeted customer base as possible. Once customers start to buy from V-V, IT can be used to help lock them in. Locking in customers is the result of IT enabled services to the customers that have visited the site. New entrants have to deliver far more value, offering superior service at a considerably lower price in order to provide incentives for buyers to switch. A follower would have difficulty in offering a superior service, as that would require vision and thinking from scratch. Moreover, differentiation on service is based largely on the number of customers on the database and the individual history of each customer. Based on a customer's history, V-V can develop software to offer a personalized service and, therefore, incur switching costs.

On the other hand, a price war would not necessarily be effective for a series of reasons.

- Prices are not immediately comparable because of the high degree of perceived differentiation of the product.

- The targeted customers are not very price sensitive, as they are prepared to pay premium prices for quality wine. They are more interested in having the necessary information to make their decisions. This requires a database of wine information and ratings. A competitor could certainly create a similar database, but this would take a lot of time and resources.

- V-V could take advantage of the lead time to establish its reputation and authority both to consumers and producers. Building good relationships with producers, could result in exclusive deals with some of them. Moreover, if the producer is offered a good deal, both in profit and promotion terms, a partnership evolves and the producer has little incentive to move to another virtual distributor.

Generic lead time gives V-V the following potential sources of sustainable competitive advantage:

- established reputation;

- customer database;

- wine database;

- lock-in of customers by offering personalized service in conjunction with the databases; and

- building of partnerships.

However, project lifecycle analysis also suggests that V-V should expect its technology and applications to be copied easily by potential competitors.

Which competitors can respond?

A new entrant who tries to imitate V-V's virtual site on the same market would appear to have no means to offer superior value and, therefore, give incentives to customers to switch from V-V, as it cannot match the potential sources of sustainable competitive advantage. However, the potential sources of sustainable competitive advantage for V-V, if examined carefully, reveal that they are specific to the US market. Although virtual as a company, V-V cannot take full advantage of the global reach of the Internet, because its products are tangible and, therefore, they are not as easily accessible outside the US. The geographical scope of V-V's operations present boundaries to the potential sources of competitive advantage. Outside this scope, a new entrant is not very handicapped. This suggests a general Internet strategy – try to lock-out competition by taking advantage of local markets.

An existing competitor may already possess similar sources of sustainable competitive advantage. For the US wine distribution market those may be:

- large producers with established reputation and partnerships;

- mail order catalogues with large customer and wine databases, as well as perhaps an established reputation;

 – speciality shops, known to wine connoisseurs and with established relationships with producers, can expand their operations on a national level; and

 – distributors wishing to integrate forward and access customers directly.

From these potential threats, it is mail order catalogues that appear to have the necessary resources to counterbalance V-V's competitive position, as their function is similar. Speciality shops could also take advantage of their knowledge base, established reputation (even though it is usually local) and relationships with producers. Distributors are not very likely to want to integrate forward, as they would move out of their core business with doubtful results. They might want to take advantage of Internet technology to make their business more efficient, but that does not concern competition with V-V, unless V-V decides to address restaurants and supermarkets, playing the role of distributor. Again this may be outside the core competence of V-V, as professionals tend to experiment less with wine, preferring repeated big orders of few wines.

Another source of competitive advantage comes from V-V organizational base. IT enables a very cost-effective, small and efficient organizational structure. In addition V-V has very few physical assets and none is tied to the business.

Will a response be effective?

Supply chain analysis reveals whether the potential sources of competitive advantage can ensure sustainability for the prime mover. V-V had successfully identified a beneficial point within the supply chain. This would be defined as being the link between the numerous small producers of quality wine and the market group that appreciated good wine, that was keen to learn more about it and was prepared to pay a small premium to get it, but did not have the specialized knowledge required to make the selection.

Although the need for such a link existed, the current structure of the distribution channel inhibited such arrangements. IT and specifically Internet technology could help establish that link in a cost-efficient way. This is in accordance with the second step of the model which consists of seeking the appropriate IT applications that would establish unique and superior relationships. According to the model, once V-V had established the relationships, it was threatened only by clearly superior offerings. Indeed, this is in agreement with the findings of the complete analysis of the case.

The next step suggests the use of IT to incur tangible and intangible switching costs. Associated costs are related to the application interface, the database and the community of users. In the specific case the interface is not of primary importance. An intuitive and easy-to-use interface could be designed by any competitor which allocated the necessary (comparatively few) resources. However, intangible switching costs may result by the sophisticated use of the customer and wine databases. A high quality of personalized service ties in the customer.

Case learning points

- Strategic frameworks, in particular five forces analysis and sustainability analysis have considerable applicability to the e-business world.

- The robust nature of the business model, arrived at through customer lifecycle analysis and the analysis and development of sources of differentiation, helps to explain much of V-V's successful development, in terms of strategic positioning.

- V-V did not take a real options approach, but nevertheless its positioning allows it to go into complementary markets with the same customer base. Subsequently, it entered the on-line gourmet food market segment.

– The sources of sustainable competitive advantage would appear to be information- and people- rather than technology-based – something we have found in parallel research studies. V-V specialized in being very customer-focused, knowing its customers best, and also in securing long-term relationships with suppliers and distributors.

8.7 Summary

Most extant evaluation approaches can be utilized with e-business investments, but invariably they have to be modified, sometimes considerably, to take into account the changing economics of e-business and the high levels of uncertainty in the marketplace. Strategic, business-focussed evaluation approaches provide key steering mechanisms. At the same time, real options analysis is a complementary approach that can build much-needed flexibility into the assessment and mitigate the risk of missing future options made possible by the potential that Web-based technologies offer. Operationally, as ever, it is important not to get bogged down in evaluation metrics that ultimately may not provide useful information for management purposes. Select a few key, strong indicators, one of which is the conversion rate, and analyse carefully what they are telling you.

8.8 Key learning points

– Many of the modes of analysing the alignment of IT investment to strategic positioning (as detailed in Chapter 3) can still be applied in order to develop the e-business case. However, costs and benefits analysis will vary substantially from other types of IT investment. This has considerable implications for existing IT investment procedures and criteria.

- It is important to get behind the optimistic scenarios widely generated about Internet use. The research shows downsides and lack of clarity in important areas in the economics of e-business. Develop the business case thoroughly; make optimistic, realistic and pessimistic scenarios for the costs and benefits. Risk analysis and management as detailed in Chapter 3 must remain central to the evaluation and structure the way development and implementation proceed.

- When assessing the value of an Internet business in its start-up phases, use free cash flow valuation – a function of sales and the profitability of those sales. Price/earnings and price/revenue multiples are not very revealing for early stage businesses.

- One can make business sense of the e-opportunity by analysing the possibilities in terms of operations, marketing and the ability of Web-based technologies to support transformation of the business. Once this has been accomplished, it is necessary to evaluate how sustainable competitive advantage can be achieved – by maintaining generic lead time, by building asymmetry barriers and by exploiting pre-emption potential.

- Consider real options thinking for strategic management of e-business investments. Real options thinking and analysis is most appropriate in conditions of high uncertainty, where much flexibility in future decisions is required – a good definition of the prevailing circumstances with regard to moves to e-business in the new decade.

- A balanced business scorecard approach – suitably tailored and informed by research into leading and lagging e-business practices – can be applied to e-business investments.

- In building Web metrics, focus particularly on the conversion rate – be aware of what it does and does not tell you.

8.9 Practical action guidelines

- Stop using existing IT evaluation approaches merely because they have seemed to work for you in the past. Re-analyse how useful they are when applied to the realities of e-business in the new millennium.

- Use free cash flow as the dominant target for assessing the value of your e-business.

- Look at evaluating e-business opportunities in new ways, using strategic analysis frameworks especially developed for this purpose.

- Look to use a balanced scorecard approach but, as ever, the metrics depend on what you are trying to achieve, and what research highlights as the issues on which to focus.

- Do not allow Web metrics to become over-administrative and ultimately unhelpful. Find the key, credible and most informative metrics for the Web site performance of your particular business.

- Regularly revisit the analysis of your e-business investments, using, for example, the five forces and sustainable competitive advantage frameworks.

9 Perennial issues: from infrastructure and benchmarking to mergers and acquisitions

9.1 Introduction

> Focusing on infrastructures you have to support the efficiency world because that's your life line . . . But on the other side you have to be innovative otherwise you have a grey image and the business people don't want to visit you even for their basics.
>
> Jan Truijens, Senior IT Manager, Rabobank

> I can make you appear as the best ski jumper, it's just a question of who I choose as a comparative base . . . if you tell me you know nothing about ski jumping, we just have to find a comparative base where people know even less.
>
> President of an IT benchmarking service

> It was the challenge of instability (from the merger) that has caused us to actually understand what's important to the

business and put in place some of these measures. I think our focus has increased tremendously.

Mike Parker, Senior IT Manager, Royal & Sun Alliance

This chapter will address a number of key, perennial issues that either derive from technology evaluation or affect an organization's ability to conduct evaluation. All of these issues are highlighted regularly in journals, trade magazines and the news. Without consideration of the following issues, the IT evaluation story would be an incomplete one:

– IT infrastructure measurement issues;

– quality and the European Foundation for Quality Management (EFQM);

– benchmarking;

– cost of ownership;

– the effect of mergers/acquisitions on technology rationalization; and

– the Royal & SunAlliance case study, illustrating these key issues being played out in a specific organizational context.

9.2 IT and e-business infrastructure

The following organizations demonstrate a variety of perspectives on the management of infrastructure investments.

– In Hewlett Packard's Test and Measurement Organization, infrastructure investments are derived from business strategy. A senior IT manager explains that 'looking first at the business strategy would drive solution investments which would then drive a required infrastructure, which would drive the computer centre charges to support it, and so forth'.

Moreover, 'the infrastructure is usually not based on a return to the business in the more traditional sense. Not because we don't want to, but more because nobody really knows how to do it.'

– Unipart made a major investment in its desktop and networked environment in the mid-1990s. This was not cost-justified. This has been perceived as a sound investment, the value of which no one questions. Since then, policies and standards have been established which allow lean upgrades of desktop and network infrastructures without requiring many individual financial justifications. These policies and standards are updated regularly in line with technological developments and changing business needs.

– Safeway, the UK-based retailer, continually opted for the 'simple' infrastructure solution, differentiating it from many other organizations. In addition, the prototyping approach that is often adopted by Safeway to learn about the feasibility of a business idea implemented with technology prevents unnecessary large-scale investments in infrastructure which could, otherwise, go unused. According to former CIO Mike Winch, 'My view has always been that if the business case is good, then even average to bad technology will work well. If the business case is bad, the best technology in the world will not do a thing for you. So let us concentrate on how we can drive the business forward and don't let's spend lots of time looking at the technology.' Ultimately, Safeway has stood by its IBM investments with DB2 as its lone database product:

> It means we've got a lot less technology, a lot less skill required, and it's cheaper. Take the Compass award, for example, which measures the cost effectiveness of service delivery. We have constantly outperformed all our competitors and one year out-performed the whole of Europe and most of North America as well. We didn't set out to be the cheapest, but strangely we are. We did

however set out to be very uncomplicated, you can therefore relate cost performance with simplicity. If proof is needed everyone wanted to declare how much they were going to spend on doing the Millennium. Again, one of our competitors said they were going to spend £40–50 million, we spent £5 million.

Technological infrastructure needs within an organization expose the weaknesses of any evaluation system and test the ability of the organization to take a comprehensive look at investments. Infrastructure is the prime example of an IT investment which has no obvious business benefits, as the benefits are derived from whatever applications are built upon the infrastructure.

All the organizations we studied that addressed infrastructure issues struggled with the same issues:

- the need to justify infrastructure investments in light of the intangible nature of infrastructure benefits;

- the definitive need to invest in infrastructure regardless of the outcome of evaluation;

- the trade-offs inherent in infrastructure investments; and

- the need to invest in infrastructure in ways that rolled all issues – legacy systems, ERP (enterprise resource planning) and moves to e-business – into a common flexible infrastructure that could support the business, even when its needs were uncertain two years hence.

Sauer and Willcocks[1] suggest that IT/e-business infrastructure investments must, in the base case, be dictated by and aligned with business strategy. In other words, IT infrastructure is the metaphorical and physical platform upon which business processes and supporting technology rest. However, different business strategies and long-term goals

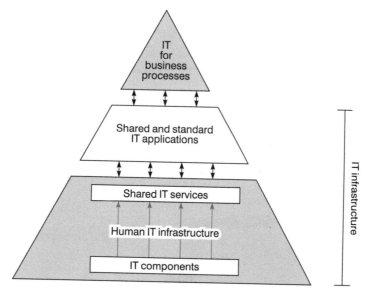

Figure 9.1 Elements of IT infrastructure (adapted from Weill and Broadbent, 1998)[2]

dictate different types and sizes of investment in the IT infrastructure. Figure 9.1 paints the picture of the elements of IT infrastructure derived from research by Weill and Broadbent[2]. At the base are IT components, which are commodities readily available in the marketplace. The second layer above is a set of shared IT services such as mainframe processing, EDI (electronic data interchange) or a full service telecommunications network. The IT components are converted into useful IT services by the human IT infrastructure of knowledge, skills and experience. The shared IT infrastructure services must be defined and provided in a way that allows them to be used in multiple applications. The next building block shown in Figure 9.1 are shared and standard IT applications. Historically, these applications have been general management applications such as general ledger, budgeting, but increasingly strategic positioning drives the adoption of applications for key business processes.

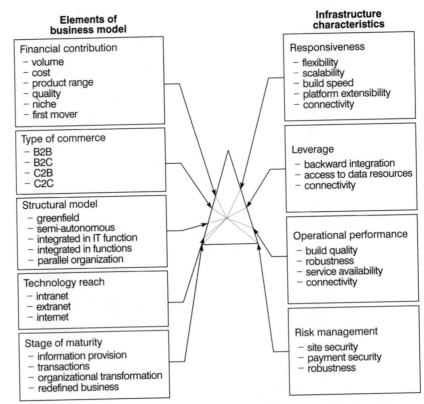

Figure 9.2 Prism model for analysing e-business infrastructure characteristics

Another perspective is provided by Sauer[3], who has developed a prism model for capturing the possibilities that need to be evaluated in designing an e-business infrastructure (Figure 9.2).

Weill and Broadbent suggest that strategic context, or changing business demands, can be articulated through the use of 'business maxims', based on the following categories:

– cost focus;

– value differentiation perceived by customers;

- flexibility and agility;

- growth;

- human resources; and

- management orientation.

From the business maxims are derived IT maxims with regard to:

- expectations for IT investments in the firm;

- data access and use;

- hardware and software resources;

- communications, capabilities and services; and

- architecture and standards approach.

These will ultimately help to clarify the firm's view of infrastructure. In their study of 30 firms, Weill and Broadbent observed the following four different views of IT infrastructure and the likely results.

(1) None – no firm-wide IT infrastructure, independent business units, no synergies. Expected outcome: forgo any economies of scale.

(2) Utility – IT seen as a utility providing necessary, unavoidable services which incur administrative expenses. Expected outcome: cost savings via economies of scale.

(3) Dependent – IT infrastructure a response to particular current business strategy. Derived from business plans and seen as a business expense. Expected outcome: life of strategy business benefits.

(4) Enabling – IT infrastructure investment integrated with strategic context. Enables new strategies and is influenced

by strategies. Seen as a business investment. Expected outcome: current and future flexibility.

A 'dependent' view indicates that infrastructure should respond primarily to specific current strategies; an 'enabling' view means that over-investment in infrastructure should occur for long-term flexibility. The enabling view is that specified by Jan Truijens of Rabobank in his description of the trade-off between efficiency and flexibility, as can be seen in the following case study.

– In the early 1990s, Holland's Rabobank decided it required new, up-to-date client–server architecture. In 1995, after a great deal of human and financial resources were applied to the conversion, Rabobank wrote off the already significant investment in the project. Simply put, the bank had pursued client–server with no serious evaluation performed and no knowledge base within the organization upon which to manage the project. Since that time, Rabobank has paid more attention to the evaluation issues specific to infrastructure investments. Everyone has infrastructure, says Truijens, one of the team of architects of the restructuring, so the issue cannot be ignored. According to him:

> There are various ways of looking at infrastructure: there is the 'efficiency' approach, the search for effectiveness, and there is the enabling concept, putting new infrastructure in place to ease innovations in business. But the way we analyse these type of things isn't the way you can analyse other technology investments. So to look forward you have to do some scenario thinking, otherwise if you are looking at your business plans well there's only one plan.

In other words, Truijens suggests that the way to develop infrastructure is to consider different scenarios, the sorts of options the organization might want to consider as a business in the future and what infrastructure will be flexible enough to support these very different possible options.

Truijens provides insightful observations on the trade-offs inherent in infrastructure investments: a fundamental one is the trade-off between efficiency and flexibility. Increased efficiency in architecture decreases flexibility. Yet flexibility in infrastructure is a requirement for innovation:

> The enabling part is the difficult part. Focusing on infrastructures you have to support the efficiency world because that's your life line, that's a condition you have to address unless you have no constraints financially or no interest in internal customers and prices and such like. So you have to do your basics well. But on the other side, you have to be innovative otherwise you have a grey image and the business people don't want to visit you even for their basics. All these things are projected into your architectures. And also in the organizational part of the infrastructure which is of course complementary to the technical aspect in IT.

Weill and Broadbent pass no judgement on whether any one of these views is 'best practice'. Their case research shows that the important objective is to ensure that the view of IT infrastructure is consistent with the strategic context of the firm/ organization. For instance, consider a firm with limited synergies amongst its divisions and its products. In this situation, no one IT infrastructure is consistent with the highly divisionalized nature of the firm, where the locus of responsibility is as close as possible to each specific product. Lack of centralized IT infrastructure was seen as providing greater freedom to the divisions to develop the specific local infrastructure suited to their business, customers, products and markets – a phenomenon we found in the highly diversified UK-based P&O Group.

On the other hand, Broadbent and Weill researched a chemical company which sought different business value from its IT infrastructure investment, namely cost reduction, support for business improvement programs and maintenance of quality standards. The emerging focus on customer service, where business processes were more IT dependent, was resulting in a shift toward a 'dependent' view of infrastructure.

On average, the 'None' view will have the lowest investment in IT relative to competitors, and will make litttle or no attempt at justification of IT infrastructure investment. The 'Utility' view will base justification primarily on cost savings and economies of scale. The 'Dependent' view is based on balancing cost and flexibility and this will be reflected in the justification criteria. An 'Enabling' view will have the highest IT investment relative to competitors and investment in infrastructure will be well above average. The focus of justifying IT infrastructure investments will be primarily on providing current and future flexibility. The work of Weill and Broadbent provides a highly useful conceptualization of infrastructure investment approaches, when they are appropriate, and the evaluation criteria which will drive their justification.

Sauer and Willcocks have extended this work into looking at investments in e-business infrastructure[4]. They found that infrastructure investments now need to be a boardroom issue if moves to e-business are really going to pay off. They point to the many e-business disappointments recorded up to 2001 due to failure to invest in the re-engineering of skills, technologies and processes needed to underpin e-business. One of the key findings has been that increasingly businesses need to invest in the 'Enabling' form of e-infrastructure, and that the other forms identified by Weill and Broadbent in 1998 may well be too restrictive for moves to e-business.

Another infrastructure evaluation tool has been suggested by Ross et al.[5] They identify a set of trade-offs companies

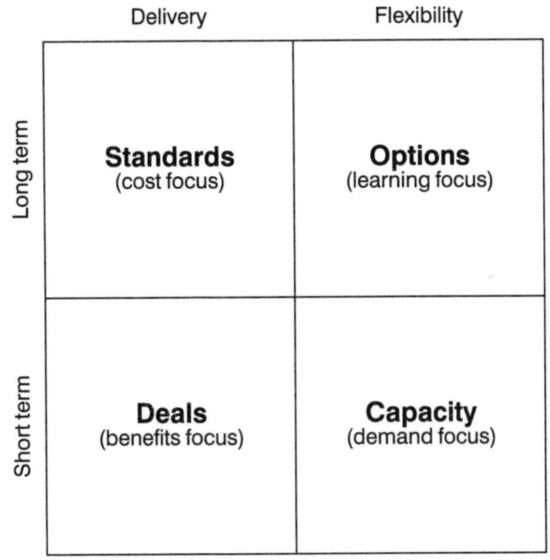

Delivery   Flexibility

	Delivery	Flexibility
Long term	**Standards** (cost focus)	**Options** (learning focus)
Short term	**Deals** (benefits focus)	**Capacity** (demand focus)

Figure 9.3 Infrastructure management trade-offs

typically make in establishing their e-business infrastructure. They posit four approaches based on different emphases (Figure 9.3).

Companies focusing on delivery in the short term will tend to take a 'deals' approach, including for example dealing with a variety of technology providers. This could well be at the expense of tomorrow and flexibility. Companies requiring flexibility in the short term will tend to take a 'capacity' approach, involving the ability to scale to support short-term growth. Companies focusing on long-term delivery tend to take a 'standards' approach, and require a high level of architectural and standards compliance, ensuring infrastructural 'spaghetti' does not develop. Those companies focusing on long-term flexibility take an 'options' approach – experimenting with technologies and new skills to discover how useful these might be if the need were to arise. Their attitude to infrastructure is influenced greatly by the real options thinking described in Chapter 8.

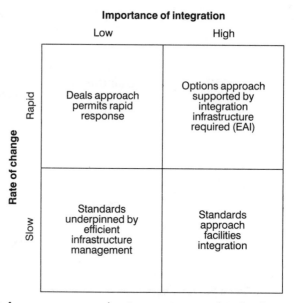

Figure 9.4 Infrastructure approaches (source: Sauer and Willcocks, 2001)

As so much of the benefit of e-business is to be gained from integration and so much of the pressure arises from the rate of business and organizational change, Sauer suggests an alternative matrix for deciding which approach to take to manage the infrastructure and technology platform[6].

In Figure 9.4 Sauer points out that a 'standards' approach offers cost efficiencies through, for example, common deployment of technologies, potential for coordinated purchasing, reduced technology learning costs and less dependence on infrastructure-specific technical knowledge. However, standards are typically constraining, and the approach may well be more suitable where business change is slower and where the most that is demanded from infrastructure is efficiency. However, as Figure 9.4 shows, standards can also facilitate integration by providing common technologies and connections, although this may come with in-built inflexibility in the face of any rapid business or technology change.

Where change is rapid and integration less important, then a 'deals' approach becomes more appropriate. Resulting complexity in the infrastructure carries cost, but if integration is not required, then the deals approach is unlikely to impede delivery of business benefits. Where change is rapid and integration important, the demands on infrastructure are greatest. The 'options' approach is required to prepare the company for rapid changes involving internal and external integration. This must be underpinned by an integrated infrastructure that permits the rapid deployment of technologies identified by the 'options' approach, integrated with either/both the company's internal enterprise systems and those of its business partners.

Some sense of the new evaluation challenges presented by moves to e-business and the need to move more towards an 'options' approach can be gleaned from Liam Edward's comments as head of the Infrastructure Team at Macquarie Bank:

> Infrastructure development here (in 2001) is about, as each of the businesses jump, looking at how you make infrastructure flexible enough so that you can upgrade parts of it very quickly, because those parts impact on other parts of the infrastructure . . . it has been all about learning on the job within the context of a blueprint, as you gradually go out and implement it and take it forwards, putting in the bits that are required to take you to the next stage, and then learn again. Each time you break it into small enough chunks that are sustainable within the company, from both a cost and a service perspective. You then get the buy-in, move it towards the end-gain, and make sure you have an infrastructure that allows you to scale it, as the business growth occurs.

9.3 European Foundation for Quality Management

The EFQM began in 1988 with a group of 14 organizations banded together with the goal of making European business more competitive by applying a Total Quality Management (TQM) philosophy. The EFQM followed in the footsteps of major Japanese and US competitiveness awards. The EFQM embodies a number of objectives, including:

– the creation of an applicable EFQM model;

– an award program for successful users of the EFQM model;

– practical services to foundation members;

– educational services for foundation members;

– developing relationships among European organizations; and

– financial assistance for quality model applications.

The EFQM model is based on the concept of TQM. The more generic TQM philosophy embraces the determination of product and service performance requirements based on customer needs and the ensuing satisfaction of those needs with limited 'defects'. In other words, TQM is the assessment of customer requirements and the delivery of quality in relation to those requirements.

Consequently, the concepts fundamental to the EFQM model are:

– a non-prescriptive framework;

– a customer focus;

– a supplier partnership;

– people development and involvement;

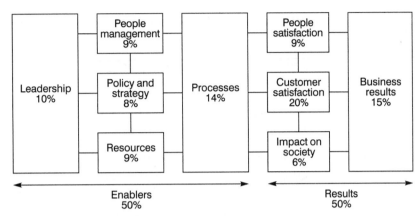

Figure 9.5 IT and quality: the EFQM model

– processes and facts;

– continuous improvement and innovation;

– leadership and consistency of purpose;

– public responsibility; and

– results orientation.

The EFQM model is a *self-assessment evaluation mechanism* based on nine criteria, each of which fall into one of two categories, the *enablers* and the *results*. Figure 9.5 represents the EFQM model, explained by these definitions:

– leadership: the behaviour of all managers in championing business excellence principles;

– people management: releasing the full potential of staff to improve what they do;

– policy and strategy: how the plans are formulated, deployed and reviewed and all activities aligned;

– resources: how assets and resources are managed for effectiveness and efficiency;

- processes: how processes are systematically improved to meet customer requirements and to eliminate non-value activities;

- people satisfaction: what is being achieved in terms of developing trained and motivated staff;

- customer satisfaction: what is being achieved in terms of satisfying external customers;

- impact on society: what is being achieved in terms of satisfying the needs of the community at large and regulators; and

- business results: what is being achieved in terms of planned financial and non-financial performance.

In practical terms, the model is used to identify what the organization has achieved and is achieving, in terms of performance and target setting. Results are reviewed over (ideally) a period of at least three years and are looked at in terms of competitor performance and best in class.

The *self-assessment* approach is defined as a comprehensive, systematic and regular review of an organization's activities and results referenced against the EFQM model for business excellence. The assessment can take place in any number of ways: a workshop, a questionnaire, a peer involvement approach or combinations thereof. Technically there is no one correct way to perform such a self assessment.

In order to examine the process in more detail, however, consider a questionnaire approach. A questionnaire could be developed based on issues relevant to the organization or based on templates that might be available from the EFQM. The questionnaire would then be administered to a group of individuals with each question requiring a 'grade' based on an agreed framework. For example, questionnaire responses could take the form of A, B, C and D grades, where 'A' represents 'fully achieved' and 'D' represents 'not started'. After the questionnaire is administered, consolidated grades can be determined then discussed to reach consensus on the assessment output: an agreed list of strengths, areas for improvement and a scoring profile used for prioritization and subsequent execution of improvement plans.

Potential benefits of self assessment guided by the EFQM include:

- a revitalized and consistent direction for the organization;

- organizational improvement;

- a structured approach to business improvement;

- assistance with business planning;

- a manner of consolidating existing initiatives;

- a way to identify and share 'best practices' with the organization; and/or

- the provision of a common language for business excellence and improvement.

Several organizations have adopted the EFQM model in order to assess quality generically throughout the business, including in the IT function. As such, they have moved to an integrated way of measuring organizational and IT performance. Royal & SunAlliance adopted an EFQM framework as part of their merged evaluation techniques (see below). At the same time, there can be some downsides to the notion of benchmarking against best practice. Such concerns were voiced to us by the IT Managing Director at Unipart:

> Unipart's commitment to provide its customers with constant product and service innovation, and continuous improvements to its processes is at the heart of its success. Therefore, the philosophy of following the lead of best

practices (EFQM) players could, in fact, stifle Unipart's cultural and competitive success.

9.4 IT benchmarking

Consider the following case studies.

– A senior IT manager of Hewlett Packard summarized the organization's use of benchmarking:

> There's a great deal of internal benchmarking. To give an example inside of Test and Measurement, our services are relatively well defined, and clearly priced, and we look very closely at the different cost structures and performance of our different organizations and business throughout the whole company. This allows for easier analysis and learning across the various service departments since we all use comparable data.

> Ultimately, TMO (test and measurement organization) uses comparative benchmarking as a learning tool and to assist with management decision making.

– In 1993, BP Exploration outsourced most of its computer operations to a combination of IT suppliers. In order to get some idea of vendor performance, BPX contractually requested that the vendors benchmark themselves; this approach was initially less than successful. A senior financial manager explained: 'We asked our out-source partners to benchmark themselves, so that became part of the service level agreement. On the whole they failed to provide quality measures for comparable purposes and we expressed displeasure in that area because it is a contractual item.' Moreover:

> It's a competition type thing, I don't think they wanted to give anything away or share. Plus I don't think they

wanted to apply the resources to it. I think they would have liked to see the results, they were not frightened that they were not performing as well as another group. We were asking them to benchmark themselves against others who provided similar services to other parts of BP or to other companies because we wanted to see that they still were one of the best in class. But as I say that's getting nowhere fast.

Although benchmarking has been discussed in Chapter 4 in terms of development and operations evaluation, benchmarking deserves additional discussion because it is widely used by organizations. As illustrated by the cases, benchmarking addresses two challenges faced by IT managers:

(1) delivering cost-effective IT products and services – a rational challenge; and

(2) convincing senior executives that the IT function is cost effective – a political challenge.

According to Lacity and Hirschheim, benchmarking has been directed increasingly toward satisfying these challenges[7]:

> 'From a rational perspective, IT managers can use benchmarks to identify improvements to performance. From a political perspective, IT managers can present benchmarks to senior management as objective evidence that IT is cost effective.'

In addressing these challenges, an organization can view benchmarking as useful for one of the two following purposes.

(1) As a report card, which is politically motivated. This could create a very defensive environment, although many people still think this is a valid benchmarking reason.

(2) For improvement. However, while benchmarking may be appropriate in a number of types of application, there is much debate about whether or not benchmarking is most usefully used for identifying and replicating best practices.

Effective benchmark approaches

IT managers and organizations benchmark in four main ways.

(1) **Informal peer comparisons**. IT managers trust the informal gathering of peer data even if the peers are competitors. However, the problem is that IT performance evidence gathered in such a manner often fails to convince senior business management.

(2) **Informal outsourcing queries**. Outsourcing research indicates that, on an increasing basis, IT managers attempt to get informal 'benchmarking' assessments through potential outsourcing vendors and the bidding process. However, vendors have caught onto the trend and, as a result, no longer take such enquiries seriously. One way forward is for the vendor to charge for a detailed assessment of how its own performance might compare against the in-house IT team.

(3) **Formal outsourcing evaluations**. Such evaluations were dealt with in Chapter 6. An evaluation of this nature can represent one of the most definitive benchmarks available, but can be expensive and disruptive, not just to the company, but also to the vendor, especially if the vendor's bid is turned down in favour of another.

(4) **Benchmarking services**. Formal benchmarking services can provide access to a wealth of data, can be presented to senior management as 'objective', and may overcome political obstacles to internally generated benchmarking. However, customers often fail to clearly articulate their benchmarking

needs to the benchmarking service. IT managers also express concern over who they are actually being benchmarked against in the IT benchmarking services' databases. Furthermore, while many are comfortable with what are termed 'mature' areas for benchmarking (e.g. datacentre operations and customer satisfaction), they may be less sure about applications development and support, cost of ownership benchmarking and benchmarks for the areas of telecommunications and network management. In particular, many organizations are not clear how external benchmarking services could help in the benchmarking of the business value contribution of such operations.

Quality of benchmarks

Based on their research with senior executives and related benchmarking experience, Lacity and Hirschheim identified a number of concerns about the quality of benchmarks. These can be summarized as:

(1) benchmarks are too technical – they don't translate well to user terms, such as customer satisfaction or profitability;

(2) benchmarks do not indicate whether IT has adopted the right architecture – the IT organization can reduce costs endlessly but that reduction does not intimate appropriate results for an organization;

(3) benchmarks sometimes focus on the wrong IT values – for instance, if the organization is focused on service excellence, but benchmarks are focused on cost containment, the means and ends are mismatched;

(4) benchmarks may not be viewed as valid – unless attention is paid to reference group selection, the normalization process, measurement period, data integrity and report design quality.

Benchmarking guidelines

The following guidelines for pursuing effective benchmarking activities arise from the following concerns raised.

– Benchmark what is important to senior management – there is a need to take into account business managers not just IT managers. Are they interested, for example, in cost efficiency or service excellence?

– Ensure that benchmarks are not too technical for senior management. They are not interested in or persuaded by narrow technical benchmarks. They want to monitor items that have salience in business terms.

– Senior management should select the benchmarking service. This avoids suspicion falling on the IT function of selecting a service favourable to it.

– The benchmarking service should select competition that reflects senior management's concerns, for example size, industry and geographic span.

– The perceived objective role of the benchmarking service is crucial. So, for example, its employees should gather the data themselves, hold a validation meeting prior to data analysis and design meaningful reports.

– The benchmarking service should select the reference group which represents the stiffest competition possible. As one data centre manager commented, 'you need to benchmark against the toughest in town'.

– Gather data during a peak period. Avoid a-typical data and data applicable only on a limited basis.

– Keep repeating the benchmarking exercise and regularly update benchmarks.

– Benchmarking must identify concrete, feasible improvements.

9.5 Cost of ownership

The cost of ownership is a means of describing not only the direct, visible costs of technology, but also the indirect, hidden or knock-on costs associated with various types of technology investments – the sort we met in Chapter 1. Specifically, the concept of cost of ownership deals with the idea that, in order to use and support technology through its lifecycle, significant costs are incurred. For instance, the purchase of a desktop system by an organization is not the end of the costs associated with that computer. Instead hardware, software, training costs, network connectivity, support and maintenance, peripherals, end user operations, downtime and upgrade activities all add to the total cost of ownership of that computer. For instance, hardware and software costs account for only 20–25% of the costs of ownership. Gartner suggested in the late 1990s that cost of ownership for maintaining the average PC was about US$9,000 to US$11,000 per year. Compass said it was closer to US$3,000. Mobile users regularly underestimate the cost to own. For example, Gartner has suggested that laptops have been 50% more expensive (in terms of cost of ownership) than desktops and only last 30 months.

Recurring mention in the press of cost of ownership has made both organizations and individuals more aware of these additional costs. It follows that, in order to manage these costs successfully, a measurement regime is required to quantify and establish goals for containing costs. The desktop networks, so insiduous in organizations today, are perhaps the best example of IT investments with related costs of ownership. Given this prevalence, it would make sense that the desktop PC would be the best managed part of IT infrastructure. The reality, however, is that costs are excessive, reliability is poor and compatibility is uncertain. Managed costs and increased integrity depend on increasing the coherence of the infrastructure, based on standards for hardware, software and networks.

According to one experienced practitioner:

> Our goal should not be to minimize costs and downtime, but to maximize the value of IT to the business ... to increase IT's value we should increase our understanding of business needs and apply that understanding creatively ... IT managers should look for ways of increasing the value obtained from existing technology, rather than chasing new technology. And we should encourage line managers to take responsibility for the use of technology in their departments. Desktop systems are a vital part of every organization's systems infrastructure; increasingly they are the infrastructure. Therefore, the future of business will depend more and more on these systems. The future of IT lies in ensuring that they make the maximum contribution to business success.

The cost of ownership can be effectively managed in a number of ways. One way, although certainly not the only or best one, is the possibility of outsourcing the management of technology investments with significant costs of this sort. As demonstrated in Chapter 6, outsourcing should utilize or introduce effective measurement schemes into the process so that an organization can comprehend the size and scope of what it is outsourcing. Expected benefits from outsourcing are clear: improved service, enforced standardization and commercial awareness in users, more resources and stabilized costs. On the flip side, however, users need to understand that suppliers are still going through a learning curve on the desktop and frequently have not yet reached the level of stable, commodity pricing available with mainframe services.

A perennial problem in cost of ownership calculations for the desktop environment is the wide difference in figures arrived at by different benchmarking companies for 'cost per PC seat'. To an extent, this reflects different cost of ownership models, lack of standardization across benchmark services and sometimes immaturity in the benchmark service being offered. What is important is that the model selected offers a structure for understanding what creates the cost of PC ownership. One such model is suggested by Strassmann[8]. Costs are determined by customer characteristics, technology characteristics and application characteristics. In turn, these determine the costs and nature of workload volumes and network management practices. Together workload and network management practices produce the total cost of ownership. Not surprisingly, given the variability in these factors likely from site to site, cost of ownership figures do vary greatly across organizations. Identifying the cost drivers of PC costs in detail and managing these down, creating a consistent technology architecture and insisting on adherence to standards are three of the ways forward for reducing or managing the cost of ownership.

In summary, costs of ownership considerations are additional drivers for the need to measure and manage IT investments. Companies such as Gartner and Compass have developed models to help manage these processes. Gartner Group's updated total cost of ownership model includes direct costs (hardware, software, operations and administrative support), indirect costs (end user operations and downtime), maturity of best practices and complexity in its total cost of ownership calculation. Among other results, this form of evaluation helps organizations evaluate more sophisticated technologies and labour-intensive processes such as peer support.

To manage the cost of ownership more effectively:

(1) don't prioritize line-of-code costs, instead make ease-of-use a top concern when writing in-house code;

(2) remember that hardware and software costs are only a portion of total costs – user satisfaction, technological complexity and best practices maturity also contribute;

(3) if using consultants to advise on cost of ownership, never let them recommend a single solution, instead insist on being given several options;

(4) consider training costs carefully – often staff get only one day a year of technology training and it is poorly targeted; and

(5) ensure your costs of ownership are not being dominated by the 'futz' factor – the time staff use their desktops for personal matters.

9.6 Corporate mergers and acquisitions

Despite the rapidly paced business environment and the related trends in mergers and acquisitions, there is not much literature available on the relationship between mergers/acquisitions and IT usage and/or rationalization. The Royal & SunAlliance case at the end of this chapter provides an example of the effect of a merger situation and the subsequent successful rationalization of information technology usage. In general, however, the scant literature available reports a bleak picture on the successful combination of merged/acquired technology. Jane Linder investigated mergers and acquisitions in the banking industry to discover the effects upon IT applications. Her findings reflect disparity between what managers would describe as the ideal integration among applications in both merger and acquisition arenas and the realities which ensued[9].

Linder conducted a series of interviews in the banking industry to determine the 'ideal' circumstances and results for systems integration in both mergers and acquisitions. Bankers described the ideal integration effort in an acquisition as one that would be implementation-intensive rather than design-intensive, with the smaller partner adjusting its practices to the larger 'parent' organization. Ideally, the acquiring bank's applications would be technically and functionally superior to the acquired partner's. Only unique and innovative applications from the acquired bank would be adopted for the entire enterprise. In mergers, on the other hand, managers described a more collaborative approach as the ideal systems integration process. The equal partners would develop a plan that reflected a resulting operation incorporating the best of both parties.

As mentioned above, the actual results of the systems integration efforts in the mergers and acquisitions monitored by Linder were far less effective than the ideals and usually resulted in:

– slow flow of IT integration savings to the bottom line;

– loss of competitive momentum; and

– adoption of systems not necessarily technologically or functionally superior.

Linder identified that mergers and acquisitions, and consequently their related systems integration efforts, are highly political in nature and are rarely managed effectively. She identifies the critical integration factors as:

– the balance of power between the organizations merging/acquiring;

– a difference in beliefs and cultural values of the involved organizations; and

– deadlines imposed by the merger/acquisition.

Royal & SunAlliance provide an example of a merger situation in which application rationalization worked more effectively than perhaps the picture has been painted by Linder. The Royal & SunAlliance case study provides an effective illustration of the interaction between technology evaluation and a number of the special issues covered in this chapter including corporate mergers, infrastructure rationalization and the EFQM. The case study will describe the business and technology contexts of the merged organization and then examine each of the issues in more detail.

9.7 In-depth case study: Royal & SunAlliance Life and Pensions (1996–2001)

Business context

The SunAlliance Group merged with the Royal Insurance Holdings plc in July 1996 to become the Royal & SunAlliance Insurance Group. The combined organization reported a combined profit of £809 million in 1997 from insurance transactions and related financial services. 1997 represented a year of integration for all of Royal & SunAlliance's (hereafter referred to as RSA) business units, IT included. This merger provided the dominant characteristic of the business environment within which a number of other 'special' issues came to light.

IT context

While the merger of SunAlliance and Royal Insurance obviously provided the most immediate influence over the direction of the combined IT department, RSA Life IT could not afford to ignore a number of other significant issues on the horizon, including infrastructure issues, continuing service delivery and Y2K. Mike Parker, RSA Life IT Manager provides an insightful description of the issues confronted by the IT department going into 1997:

> You can imagine now we have systems that are being used in locations that they were never designed to be, and being used by people new to these systems. This means that we have connected systems together through infrastructure that was never designed to be used in this way. Therefore, we have a real challenge to maintain and upgrade the

infrastructure, the LAN networks particularly, as work has been moved around the country. We've closed some regional offices localizing the servicing in Bristol, Liverpool and Horsham. You can imagine the facilities that have had to be upgraded, etc. So we struggled last year to consistently meet our production service targets. Now it is much more stable.

The combined IT department employed 320 persons in 1998 and maintained three centres with nearly 100 separate applications, of which 30% were designated as 'critical'. The computing service was provided by an IBM-owned datacentre in Horsham, and an in-house datacentre in Liverpool. The IT staff was split 70/30 on development and support activities. Both pre-merger organizations were very traditional about measurement and measuring computing availability; the merger forced the combined organization to consolidate and rationalize systems, thus placing real focus on end-to-end service measurement.

The merger: four issues

The merger alone presented a number of issues requiring examination with respect to the impact on the organization and the organizational response. In part, the impact and response had a direct effect on the subsequent technology evaluation processes undertaken.

(1) Two of everything

As separate organizations, Royal Insurance and SunAlliance had used nearly 100 business applications and in excess of 20 supporting technologies to support their businesses. The merger forced an assessment of applications in light of their 'criticality' to the business and in light of the potential duplication of services that now existed. In addition, because of the size of the combined RSA and the historical depth of available policies, a migration to a consolidated platform was necessary. Mike Parker explained the situation:

> We've gained two of everything at least. We've inherited more technology platforms and more applications than we are ever likely to need in the future, and, of course, where the support is provided from depends on which application is chosen. Therefore, in an integrated systems architecture, you are also faced with having to interface elements of an outsourced computing service to an in-source service.

It is interesting to note, in light of the plethora of systems, that RSA did not consider IT to be on the critical path to product delivery. Instead, RSA chose to look at IT as an 'enabler', which could enhance the product-delivery process. It is perhaps because of this perspective and attitude that the merger presented an opportunity for rationalization rather than a roadblock to continued 'good business'. Client servicing and product availability were seen as dual business drivers.

The organizational response to the duplication of applications and technology was ultimately the rationalization of those systems using a detailed workflow map developed as a guideline. Parker explained:

> . . . both companies had their own strategies to do this kind of integration – they were different but complementary. In fact we had the solution in one company to some of the problems that we had in the other company. For example, we didn't have strategies in SunAlliance for a couple of systems, and Royal had a solution that could (and did) resolve SunAlliance issues.

The result was a strategic systems plan that provided the blueprint for the integration that spanned most of 1997.

(2) Instability

Despite the seemingly successful approach to application integration and rationalization, the complexity of the merging of IT infrastructures introduced a level of instability into the on-going delivery of IT services. Parker described the situation:

> What we did not have initially was a stable environment. Software merger equals instability. Previously, there was not the same requirement from either organization to change what wasn't broken. But immediately you actually have to change systems that you'd rather not touch, you start getting instability ... Overnight things fall over because of transaction volumes processed through the systems being twice as big as they were before, and many weren't designed for that volume (transaction load).

Again, the organizational response to this dimension boiled down to the concept of assessment and evaluation. Parker described the resulting focus of the organization:

> So if you like, it was the challenge of instability that has caused us to actually understand what's important to the business and put in place some of these measures. I think our focus has increased tremendously.

(3) Outsourcing

Events at RSA bring another spin to the outsourcing debate, namely the additional set of complications introduced by a merger process. These generate the need for additional assessment of existing outsourcing contracts. Prior to the merger, SunAlliance outsourced its datacentre to IBM. Royal Insurance, on the other hand, was all in-house. Since the merger, what was once the Royal General business, residing on the Northampton datacentre, moved to the out-sourced contract. By 1999, all that remained of in-house computer operations was the ex-Royal UK Life datacentre in Liverpool. The IT Life plan, mentioned above, provided some level of guidance in terms of identifying strategic development. RSA Life determined, post-merger, not to out-source strategic application development.

(4) Staff retention

The process of the RSA merger created stress on IT staff in two ways: the uncertainty regarding the role to be played going forward and an uncertainty about a go-forward work/living location.

In response to the staff retention issue, Life IT management were determined to make site a 'non-issue'. Consequently, the strategy was to actually challenge everyone to make site a non-issue as far as IT was concerned, regardless of the fact that a lot of the business departments that were previously 'local' had now moved. Whereas all the head office functions and head office systems were originally at Horsham, post-merger head office systems were split between Horsham and Liverpool. In addition, Liverpool moved part of its client servicing to Bristol. Consequently, the majority of systems teams are servicing users not on the same site. The challenge has become to understand what is needed to develop and support systems remote from the user base. This strategy has been very successful.

In addition, RSA Life introduced some measures of self-assessment in the form of the EFQM (see below). Part of that assessment included the consideration of 'people management' as an enabler within the organization.

IT infrastructure: emerging challenges

The combining of RSA Life's IT infrastructure exposed the merged organization to a level of risk. The IT Life plan included a number of infrastructure decisions made as a result of the merger and brought additional focus to bear on future infra-structure issues.

Prior to the merger, both organizations were very traditional in terms of equating CPU availability with the conduct of business, because of a lack of complexity in the infrastructure. After the merger, however, with users dispersed in many different locations, mere CPU availability no longer told the whole story of the users and their ability to conduct business. For instance, often, an application would be running on the mainframe, but a user could not access it. Or an application would be running fine for two locations, but not for a third.

As discussed in this chapter, infrastructure is an issue in and of itself because of the difficulties associated with:

(1) justifying an initial infrastructure investment; and

(2) evaluating the 'performance' of the infrastructure, as bene-fits reaped are usually the result of uses and applications built on top of the infrastructure rather than deriving from the infrastructure itself.

As a result of the merger, RSA Life renewed its interest in rationalizing and evaluating infrastructure investments. The IT department selected a sponsor for infrastructure investments and identified new and more effective means for building the infrastructure business case. Mike Parker was designated as the sponsor for infrastructure investments and commented on the improved business case approach:

> We articulate what would happen if we did not make the investment – in other words, compared with continuing the way we are, quantify the effect on service levels and cost. We've developed some algorithms in conjunction with the client servicing manager and servicing functions to quan-tify the cost of both downtime and deteriorating response

times on the business. So we are building a model of how many people are affected if we lose an hour's worth of processing. Then you can use the model to extrapolate some of your own business infrastructure investments.

The IT Life plan outlined the large infrastructure and platform rationalizations that were in the pipeline; the delivery of the particular aspect of the plan was geared towards Y2K compliance.

The millenium problem

The Y2K compliance issue hosted a number of problems covered above, but the RSA merger could have been considered a potential risk to the organization's ability to attain compliance. Instead, RSA viewed Y2K as a 'godsend' because it provided the management focus which cleared away all the 'nice-to-haves' and hurdles in the way of implementing key aspects of the strategy.

RSA's response to the issues raised by the Y2K focused on the on-going evaluation of resource allocation and compliance. As mentioned above, IT staff felt a degree of strain in relation to the merger. The Y2K project(s) only served to reinforce that strain. To address the staff concern, RSA chose to outsource a part of the Y2K effort and used Y2K compliance to reinforce the migration of a large number of the applications deemed non-critical.

On-going assessment and evaluation of the compliance effort was considered a critical effort. For such critical undertakings, milestones are documented, then each month milestones achieved are checked against milestones planned.

This planning and control process also helped the IT department to address the cross-purpose needs of the business. Some divisions of RSA attempted to bundle non-compliance issues/requests with compliance fixes. Parker explained:

We now have put in place what some might call excess bureaucracy to stop people requesting changes on existing systems. This is in order to ensure that this resource is kept to a minimum. In other words, we only fix it if it fails and we only do things that are essential. Of course, the businessmen could be smart enough to think all they need to do is bundle up their ten requirements inside one legislative requirement and it will get passed as essential. So we have now said sorry we are unbundling everything.

Adopting new measurement models

The EFQM

RSA has experimented with a number of assessment methods, including one on business excellence based on the EFQM model (discussed above). RSA initially used the EFQM, as per Figure 9.5, as a means of self assessment. Although business excellence assessment comprised more parts of the organization than just the IT department, its use in the IT department contributed to the overall evaluation of less tangible benefits. This self-assessment process was conducted within IT by the staff:

> It measures how good we are at all aspects of management. I like that. I've seen a few models in my time now. This one I feel comfortable with in that it measures how good you are at all elements, which are called enablers, and how good the result is. So you should see if you do a lot of improvement work how it does bring results. It is capable of being compared across industry and cross-function within industry as well. There is an absolute score out of the assessment, and you can put yourself into a league table if you so wish.

Monthly reporting models

Post-merger, the RSA IT department also developed a project monthly report process. The process included a number of key performance indicators documented with 'red-amber-green' (RAG) charts. In addition, program boards monitored the key milestones.

In 2001, reporting monthly is continuing up through the IT organization, right from the staff time recording. The project monthly reports capture the effort, the tasks and the key milestones planned and actioned during the period. As it comes up through the organization these are turned into various management graphs of how well IT is doing against its key performance indicators. The RAG chart shows IT its 'health'. The critical projects are also listed. Each project is followed by a trend chart of what has happened over the previous few weeks and months. Production support – in other words, the capability to support RSA production systems – is also monitored, because there are some critical systems there which are also old and less robust. Key performance indicators are also reported, including budget, staff headcount, contractors, movements of staff, attrition rate and absenteeism. Therefore, those things that affect IT's capability to deliver are being controlled independently. The report goes up through the directors to the managing director on a monthly basis.

E-business and future directions: going global

For a conservative industry, it has been necessary to take change in increments. 'Each step is transformational', explained Phil Smith, RSA's Global IT Director. As a result, RSA has taken a softly, softly approach to e-business. Rather than disrupting existing business relationships with intermediaries, it has opted to develop the global infrastructure. Where conventional wisdom insists that the insurance business is different everywhere and, therefore, requires different processes and systems, Smith argues that they are 80% the same worldwide, with 10% regulatory variation and 10% miscellaneous variation. One opportunity being pursued throughout 2000 was the introduction of global communications to underpin global knowledge management within the group.

The idea was to identify, articulate and share current best practices in product development so as to implement them uniformly across the globe and then develop them for the future. Without a budget to underwrite the full global network, country budget-holder support has been crucial. The result of this drive has been that over three years RSA has moved from having a federated platform with few connections to having a global communications network supporting knowledge management processes through Lotus Notes. Smith explains:

> Because we have pieces of wet string between some places and no pieces of wet string between others, Lotus Notes is very suitable for e-mail and intranet because it has a replication capability that can be run over dial-up links such as ISDN . . . it's now pretty much complete throughout the world and we now understand the extent to which a person on a desktop in Thailand can talk to a person on a desktop in Chile.

In addition, a common set of binding technologies has been promoted consisting of e-mail, an intranet, MS Office, Adobe and Internet Explorer. These are technologies that would allow a company to function globally whatever its business. From dismissive comments such as 'Why do we need this?' the responses have changed to 'When can we have more?'.

Planning, evaluation and funding

At present, RSA has set out on its journey but has many more ports of call to visit before the vision is realized. What has it taken to get this far? What change will it take to make further progress?

Planning cycles have been one issue. RSA IT managers are aware from the immediacy of the demands of e-business initiatives that planning has to be reviewed constantly. Linked to this are the issues around evaluation and funding. While some see the need to adjust processes even if it involves taking some losses on investments, others argue that traditional measures such as return on investment have served the company well and should not be abandoned. Phil Smith has adopted a middle way of introducing some new processes, including hot-house incubator environments while retaining some traditional measures. RSA has found infrastructure difficult to justify against the traditional measures. Nobody knows what the savings on their worldwide communications network will be. Even suppliers such as British Telecom have been unable to provide data for similar investments by other companies, so argument by analogy is precluded.

In conclusion, how can you achieve effective global decision-making in a federal organization? The trick, Smith contends, is 'to set up good consultative processes – then sometimes within this you have to be autocratic. Our worldwide e-architecture is going to have to be standard, with buy-in worldwide'.

Case learning points

- A merger combined with Y2K on the horizon provided an opportunity to rationalize technology usage by the combined organization. Rather than becoming the cause of disorientation and distress, the merger was the opportunity for a high level of rationale systems planning and a vision for the combined use of IT.

- A merger should not be thought of as the silver bullet that will clean up decentralized and unorganized technology usage, although in this case RSA chose to view the organizational upheaval as an opportunity for positive change. It is perhaps this positive perspective on the change that allowed RSA Life to succeed under the circumstances, illustrating the significance of psychology in IT evaluation and decision-making.

– However, there are few occasions when an organization will undertake sustained improvement in IT evaluation practices. Clearly, a merger or acquisition requires clarity, change and new ways of working and can act as a catalyst in the IT arena. In such a scenario, evaluation plays a fundamental role and new IT measurement approaches are both likely and sustainable.

– A principal learning point is the difficulty of driving e-business change in a conservative industry from Group IT. The importance of leadership, both business and technological, from the CIO is abundantly clear. When the organization itself is inflexible, it is necessary to step outside the normal boundaries.

– Driving infrastructural change globally is also a challenge in a highly decentralized business which sees itself as differentiated across country boundaries. Evaluation techniques can help the case for infrastructure investment, but there will still be significant political issues to deal with. Group IT needs to be as flexible as possible. The new role of the CIO is to be a global business person with strong IT skills, not just a diehard technology expert. The new CIO role is critical to this model.

9.8 Key learning points

– Since 1996, a number of critical issues have emerged that have caused organizations to revisit and extend evaluation practices. These include the Y2K, EMU challenges, the possibility of utilizing the EFQM model for quality management in IT, IT infrastructure, benchmarking cost of ownership and e-business issues, and the implication of rapid change, in particular mergers/acquisitions, for IT evaluation.

– The Y2K problem was viewed as either a serious difficulty or as an opportunity to review and rationalize large parts of an organization's applications. A minority of organizations took the latter view with the considerable benefits that resulted from it.

– The EFQM model for evaluation is being utilized by several of the organizations researched with benenficial results. At the same time, there can be some downsides to the notion of benchmarking quality against 'best practice' (see Chapter 8).

– IT infrastructure evaluation has emerged as a critical issue in a period of cross-over between technology eras (see Chapter 7). In the base case, infrastructure investments must be dictated by business strategy. From business maxims can be derived IT maxims that inform IT/e-business infrastructure development.

– Benchmarking is a necessary but insufficient evaluation practice for the contemporary organization. It is used both to assist delivery of cost-effective IT products and to convince senior executives that the IT function is cost effective. Both purposes are fundamental – neither can be neglected in the design and operation of the IT benchmarking process.

– Cost of ownership is confused by widely published diverging estimates. Cost of ownership depends on customer, technology and application characteristics which influence work volumes and network management practices. Identifying the PC cost drivers in detail, managing these down, insisting on adherence to standards and creating a consistent technology architecture are three ways forward for reducing costs of ownership.

– Organizational changes, such as mergers and acquisitions, require intense IT rationalization. Previous research paints a bleak picture, but our own research has found examples of effective IT evaluation and management practices being applied.

9.9 Practical action guidelines

– Required, large-scale changes to your technology investments, for example EMU and Y2K, should be considered an opportunity to rationalize IT spend.

– Balance the cost-reducing opportunities with the product-development opportunities in the investment in technology.

– As always, plan the entire lifecycle of the IT investment and evaluate on an on-going basis.

– Remember that no organization can go from 'no best practices' to 'all best practices' overnight. A phased approach is required. For instance, in the adoption of the EFQM, an organization should focus first on those components that are required for the basis of on-going EFQM evaluations that are currently lacking or undermanaged in the organization. Likewise, benchmarking figures are relative and are not necessarily appropriate targets for every organization.

– IT infrastructure investments must be dictated and aligned with business strategy.

– In managing your cost of ownership, take into account not only the obvious 'direct' costs, but also the indirect costs such as user satisfaction, organizational complexity and the maturity of best practices.

References

Chapter 1

1. Bakos, Y. and Jager, P. de 'Are computers boosting productivity?' *Computerworld*, March 27th, 128–130, 1996. See also Quinn, J. and Baily, M. 'Information technology: increasing productivity in services.' *Academy of Management Executive*, **8**, 3: 28–47, 1994.
2. Brynjolfsson, E. 'The productivity paradox of information technology.' *Communications of the ACM*, **36**, 12: 67–77, 1993.
3. Brynjolffson, E. and Hitt, L. 'Paradox Lost? Firm level evidence on the returns to information systems spending.' In Willcocks, L. and Lester, S. (eds) *Beyond The IT Productivity Paradox: Assessment Issues*. McGraw-Hill, Maidenhead, 1998.
4. Cron, W. and Sobol, M. 'The relationship between computerization and performance: a strategy for maximizing the economic benefits of computerization.' *Journal of Information Management*, **6**: 171–181, 1983.
5. Quoted in Willcocks, L. and Lester, S. (eds) *Beyond the IT Productivity Paradox: Assessment Issues*. McGraw-Hill, Maidenhead, 1998.
6. Van Nievelt, G. and Willcocks, L. *Benchmarking Organizational and IT Performance*. Executive Research Briefing, Templeton College, Oxford, 1998.
7. Willcocks, L. and Plant, R. 'Getting to bricks and clicks: B2C e-business leadership strategies.' *Sloan Management Review*, Spring, 2001.

Chapter 2

1. Willcocks, L. and Lester, S. (eds) *Beyond the IT Productivity Paradox: Assessment Issues.* McGraw-Hill, Maidenhead, 1998.
2. Lacity, M. and Willcocks, L. *Global IT Outsourcing: In Search of Business Advantage.* Wiley, Chichester, 2001.
3. Mathur, S. and Kenyon, A. *Creating Value.* Butterworth-Heinemann, London, 1996.

Chapter 3

1. Willcocks, L. (ed.) *Information Management: Evaluation of Information Systems Investments.* Chapman and Hall, London, 1994. Also Willcocks, L. (ed.) *Investing in Information Systems: Evaluation and Management.* Thomson Business Press/Chapman and Hall, London, 1996.
2. McFarlan, F. W. 'Portfolio Approach to Information Systems.' *Harvard Business Review,* September–October, 142–150, 1981.
3. Lyytinen, K. and Hirschheim, R. *Information Systems Failures – a Survey and Classification of the Empirical Literature.* Oxford University Press, Oxford, 1987.
4. Ward, J. and Griffiths, P. *Strategic Planning for Information Systems.* Wiley, Chichester, 1996.
5. Willcocks, L. and Griffiths, C. 'Management and risk in major information technology projects.' In Willcocks, L., Feeny, D. and Islei, G. (eds) *Managing IT as a Strategic Resource.* McGraw-Hill, Maidenhead, 1997.
6. McFarlan, F. W., *op. cit.*
7. Willcocks, L. (ed.). *Investing in Information Systems: Evaluation and Management.* Thomson Business Press/Chapman and Hall, London, 1996.
8. Farbey, B., Land, F. and Targett, D. *How to Assess Your IT Investment: A Study of Methods and Practice.* Butterworth-Heineman, Oxford, 1993.

9. Ward, J. and Griffiths, P., *op. cit.*
10. Feeny, D. 'E-Opportunity – The strategic marketing perspective.' In Willcocks, L. and Sauer, C. (eds) *Moving To E-Business*. Random House, London, 2001.
11. Feeny, D. 'The CEO and the CIO in the Information Age.' In Willcocks, L. and Sauer, C. (eds) *Moving to E-Business*. Random House, London, 2001.
12. Willcocks, L. (ed.) 1996, *op. cit.*
13. Strassman, P. *The Business Value of Computers*. New Canaan, The Information Economics Press, 1990; also *The Squandered Computer*. The Information Economics Press, New Canaan, 1997.
14. Parker, M., Benson, R. and Trainor, H. *Information Economics: Linking Business Performance to Information Technology*. Prentice Hall, Englewood Cliffs, NJ, 1988.
15. Ward, J. and Griffiths, P., *op. cit.*

Chapter 4

1. Lacity, M. and Hirschheim, R. 'Benchmarking as a strategy for managing conflicting stakeholder perceptions of information systems.' *Journal of Strategic Information Systems*, **4**, 165–185, 1995.
2. See Dugmore, J. 'Using service level agreements in maintenance and support functions.' In Willcocks, L. (ed.) *Investing in Information Systems: Evaluation and Management*. Chapman and Hall, London, 1996.
3. Ward, J. and Griffiths, P., *op. cit.*

Chapter 5

1. Kaplan, R. and Norton. D. 'The balanced scorecard: measures that drive performance.' *Harvard Business Review,* January–February, 71–79, 1992.

2. Strassman, P. *The Business Value of Computers*. New Canaan, The Information Economics Press, 1990.
3. Kaplan, R. and Norton, D. 'Using the balanced scorecard as a strategic management system.' *Harvard Business Review*, January–February, 75–85, 1996.

Chapter 6

1. Lacity, M. and Willcocks, L. *Inside IT Outsourcing: A State-of-Art Report*. Templeton College, Oxford, 2000.
2. Lacity, M. and Willcocks, L. *Global IT Outsourcing: In Search of Business Advantage*. Wiley, Chichester, 2001.
3. Lacity, M. and Hirschheim, R. *Information Systems Outsourcing: Myths, Metaphors and Realities*. Wiley, Chichester, 1993.
4. Lacity, M. and Hirschheim, R. *Beyond the Information Systems Outsourcing Bandwagon*. Wiley, Chichester, 1995.
5. Feeny, D. and Willcocks, L. 'Core IS capabilities for exploitating information technology.' *Sloan Management Review*, **39**, 3, 9–21.

Chapter 7

1. Moschella, D. *Waves Of Power: Dynamics of Global Technology Leadership 1964–2010*. Amacom, New York, 1997.
2. Evans, P. and Wurster, T. 'Strategy and the New Economics of Information.' *Harvard Business Review*, September–October, 71–82, 1997. Also *Blown to Bits*, Harvard Business Press, Boston, 2000.
3. Willcocks, L. and Plant, R. 'Getting to bricks and clicks: B2C e-business leadership strategies.' *Sloan Management Review*, Spring, 2001.

4. Machlis, S. 'Internet can magnify mistakes.' *Computerworld*, August 25th, 5, 1997.

5. Quelch, J. A. and Klein, L. R. 'The Internet and international marketing.' *Sloan Management Review*, Spring, 60–75, 1996.

6. Rayport, J. and Sviokla, J. 'Exploiting The virtual value chain.' *Harvard Business Review*, November–December, 75–85, 1995.

7. Kambil, A. 'Doing business in the wired world.' *IEEE Computer*, **30**, 5, 56–61, 1997.

8. Hagel, J. and Armstrong, A. *Net Gain: Expanding Markets Through Virtual Communities*. Harvard Business School Press, Boston, MA, 1997.

Chapter 8

1. Shiller, R. *Irrational Exuberance*. Princeton University Press, Princeton, NJ, 2000.

2. Perkins, M. and Perkins, A. *The Internet Bubble*, HarperCollins, New York, 1999.

3. Higson, C. and Briginshaw, J. 'Valuing Internet businesses.' *Business Strategy Review*, **11**, 1, 2000, 10–20.

4. Feeny, D. 'Making business sense of the e-opportunity.' *Sloan Management Review*, Winter, 2001.

5. Willcocks, L. and Plant, R. 'Business Internet strategy: Moving to the Net.' In Willcocks, L. and Sauer, C. (eds) *Moving To E-Business*. Random House, London, 2000.

6. Mathur, S. and Kenyon, A. *Creating Value: Shaping Tomorrow's Business*. Butterworth-Heinemann, London, 1997.

7. Kulatilaka, N. and Venkatraman, N. 'Using real options to capture e-business opportunities.' *Financial Times Mastering Management Review*, October, 1999.

8. Willcocks, L. and Plant, R., *op. cit.*, 2000.

9. Plant, R. *E-Commerce: Formulation of Strategy*. Prentice Hall, New York, 2000.

Chapter 9

1. Sauer, C. and Willcocks, L. *Building The E-Business Infrastructure*. Business Intelligence, London, 2001.
2. Weill, P. and Broadbent, M. *Leveraging the New IT Infrastructure*. Harvard Business Press, Boston, 1997. Also Broadbent, M. and Weil, P. 'Four views of IT infrastructure: implications for IT investments.' In Willcocks, L. and Lester, S. (eds) 1999, *op. cit.*
3. Sauer, C. 'Managing the infrastructure challenge.' In Willcocks, L. and Sauer, C., 2000, *op. cit.*
4. Sauer, C. and Willcocks, L., 2001, *op. cit.*
5. Ross, J., Beath, C. et al. – personal communication of working paper, July 2000.
6. In Sauer, C. and Willcocks, L., 2001, *op. cit.*
7. Lacity, M. and Hirschheim, R. 'The use of benchmarks in demonstrating IT performance.' In Willcocks, L. *Investing in Information Systems: Evaluation and Management*. Chapman and Hall, London, 1996.
8. Strassmann, P. *The Squandered Computer*. Information Economics Press, New Canaan, 1997.
9. Linder, J. 'Mergers: The role of information technology.' In Earl, M. (ed.) *Information Management – The Organizational Dimension*. Oxford University Press, Oxford, 1998.

Index